"*Two Chefs One Catch: A Culinary Exploration of Seafood* guides you around coastal regions weaved through a tapestry of cultures, cuisine, mouthwatering recipes, and magnificent photography. Bernard and Ron's passion for the deep blue ocean jumps off the page, bringing together the cook, the fisherman, and the fragile ecosystem."

—**Eric Ripert,** chef, author, and co-owner of Le Bernardin

"This book is a beautiful reflection of two chefs' life experiences and culinary journeys through forty-five countries. It showcases the wondrous bounty of seafood found all over the world and how different countries express their culture through food. Interspersed throughout the book are anecdotes and short stories that convey the chefs' love for the sea and passion for the craft."

—**Roy Yamaguchi,** chef, author, and founder
of Roy's Restaurant and Hawaiian fusion cuisine

"Refreshing and well organized! Travel the world through the experiences of two great chefs with awesome pictures, even better recipes, and a tribute to our environment."

—**Rick Moonen,** chef, author, educator, and owner of
Rick Moonen's RM Seafood and Rx Boiler Room

"My friends Bernard and Ron's insatiable appetite—for travel, for seafood, and for life—comes across on each page of this vibrant cookbook. Their thoughtful anecdotes and world-class recipes make *Two Chefs, One Catch* a must-have for anyone who cares to learn more about the ocean and the way we consume all the bounty it provides."

—**Jose Garces,** chef, restaurateur, author, James Beard
Award winner, Iron Chef, and founder of the Garces Group

"*Two Chefs, One Catch: A Culinary Exploration of Seafood* captures the incredible natural beauty and extensive bounty of what thrives under the waves. Chefs Bernard and Ron explore these unique seafoods, framed in their natural splendor and seasoned with the complimentary local flavors that have shaped these indigenous cuisines. The inspiring presentations excite your cooking skills to try every recipe, while embarking on a global journey of taste that never tires."

—**Jimmy Schmidt,** executive chef at Morgan's in the Desert,
James Beard Award winner, and author of *Cooking for All Seasons*

"The wealth of knowledge that Bernard and Ron share in this book is a direct passport to delicious seafood."

—**Gavin Kaysen,** chef/owner of Merchant Minneapolis
and head coach of Team USA Bocuse d'Or

"Bernard Guillas and Ron Oliver's amazing new book, *Two Chefs, One Catch: A Culinary Exploration of Seafood,* is far more than even its subtitle suggests. It is a complete guide for every variety of fish and seafood in our seven seas, along with detailed instructions on how to prepare and serve each of them. The fabulous photographs for every recipe are extraordinary. This magical book is a 'must have' for anyone who loves seafood or just wants a complete education on our oceans and their bounty."

—**Jeanne Jones,** author and syndicated Cook It Light columnist

"For years I have drooled over the delicious photos posted on social media that are created by Chefs Bernard and Ron. Every time I surf the pages, there is one word that comes to mind each and every time: Sexy! Sexy delicious food! Bernard and Ron's passion for fresh seafood translates into absolutely delicious dishes that will tantalize your senses. A book to feed your soul, your friends, and family. A seafood masterpiece! It be tasty!"

—**Ted Reader,** chef, author, and producer of Ted's World Famous BBQ products

"It takes a lot of hard work putting together the details needed to help people guide their way through seafood cookery. To demystify seafood and take the scare factor out of its preparation is a huge service to the home cooking community. Chef Bernard and Chef Ron have really done an amazing job compiling a thorough series of interesting and simple-to-follow recipes that will guide you through the world under the sea. My motto has always been to 'live a life in liquid,' and these guys are doing it!"

—**Dean James Max,** chef, restaurateur, and president of DJM Restaurants Inc.

"Chef Bernard and Chef Ron have written one of the best seafood cookbooks of the century. The culinary creativity and details in this sensational book bring out the 'true wonders and flavors of the sea.' Having developed many commercial recipes for the production of consumer seafood myself, I was totally impressed with the contents of *Two Chefs, One Catch.* This book will educate readers and delight foodies everywhere. I can't wait for the sequel! Thank you for enlightening me and your continued contribution to the culinary world. 'Stay Hungry, My Friends!'"

—**Rick Tarantino,** celebrity, research chef, and president of Tarantino Food Group, LLC

"Chef Bernard and Chef Ron's award-winning debut cookbook, *Two Chefs, One World,* is like that amazing appetizer that leaves you craving the next course. In their usual mouthwatering fashion and impeccable style, the chefs deliver another tasty winner in *Two Chefs, One Catch.*"

—**Pierre Chambrin,** executive chef of the Saint Louis Club and past executive chef of the White House (1990-94)

Two Chefs, One Catch

A Culinary Exploration of Seafood

Bernard Guillas
Ron Oliver

Photography by
Marshall Williams

LYONS PRESS
Guilford, Connecticut
Helena, Montana
AN IMPRINT OF ROWMAN & LITTLEFIELD

Lyons Press is an imprint of Rowman & Littlefield

Distributed by NATIONAL BOOK NETWORK

British Library Cataloguing-in-Publication Information available

Library of Congress Cataloging-in-Publication Data

Oliver, Ron (Chef)
 Two chefs, one catch : a culinary exploration of seafood / Ron Oliver, Bernard Guillas ; photography by Marshall Williams.
     pages cm
 Includes index.
 ISBN 978-0-7627-9140-8
 1. Cooking (Seafood) I. Guillas, Bernard. II. Title.
 TX747.O365 2014
 641.6'92—dc23
                                                                2014015148

∞™ The paper used in this publication meets the minimum requirements of American National Standard for Information Sciences—Permanence of Paper for Printed Library Materials, ANSI/NISO Z39.48-1992.

Beneath the surface of the azure waters lies an expansive array of edible treasures. Nothing tastes as pure and delicious as seafood plucked straight from its native waters. This is reflected in the diets and food cultures of the world's coastal communities. To preserve this enjoyment for generations to come, it is everyone's responsibility to care for our oceans, support sustainable fishery, and make well-informed decisions when purchasing seafood.

We dedicate this book to everyone who gets involved and makes a difference.

Contents

Thanks/Merci

One of the most important ingredients in writing this cookbook was the selfless participation and support from our family, friends, and peers in the industry. Our sincerest thanks and gratitude go to your generous contributions. The success of this project is stamped with your special spirit.

La Jolla Beach & Tennis Club
"Merci beaucoup" to our friend, General Manager John Campbell, for his vision, experience and guidance. By encouraging us to travel and learn, this book became possible. Thank you to all of the owners and the Board of Directors of the La Jolla Beach & Tennis Club for supporting our creativity and culinary endeavors.

Macy's School of Cooking at San Diego's Macy's West
Thank you for generously welcoming us into your kitchen to shoot the chefs in action.

San Diego Seafood Company
Thank you for your unwavering commitment to provide the freshest fruits of our local and global oceans.

Specialty Produce, owned by the Harrington Brothers
Special thanks to our favorite produce girl, Julie Hosler, for embracing our project like it was her own, gathering the best ingredients from our local farms, and delivering them with a smile.

Introducing Our Superstar Team . . .

Director of Photography
Marshall Williams

Digital technician
Ken Sadlock

Kitchen Photo Shoot Team
Euphemia Ng
Carlos Olguin
Satoe Turner
Clarissa Flamenco
Chloe Williams
Ella Williams

Photography Assistants
Zachary Barron
Shawn Cullen
Andy Wilhelm
Chris Park
Mick Morley

Makeup and Hair Stylist
Natalie Bohlin

Seven Seas

When you sail without boundaries or the fear of failure and are guided by your unquenchable thirst for the knowledge of discovery and sharing it with those you meet along the way, that passion is contagious. It is an exciting, unpredictable, and rewarding voyage.

Seventy percent of the earth's surface is covered by a giant body of salted water, home to a vast living ecosystem. Large communities of fish and sea creatures inhabit every corner of its seven seas and four oceans. The ocean plays an integral role in supporting the life of nearly half of the species on planet earth. Just like on land, the oceans' communities are divided by geography and environmental conditions. The culture and cuisine of each coastal region is influenced by the local harvest, making fishermen an important link in the ecosystem. As the population of the earth grows, so does the demand on the ocean to produce quickly, placing a toll on popular species.

Humans are creatures of habit. It is essential to broaden our horizons and introduce new species that are plentiful in our ocean to the world market. Nowadays, aquaculture has brought a more abundant and diverse selection of seafood to the global market. Farming provides a source of seafood that, over the long term, isn't dependent upon what Mother Nature can provide from wild fisheries, allowing some wild fish stocks to rebound. But this has come with its own set of challenges and controversy.

It is everyone's responsibility to be caretakers of our oceans and good educators of future seafood lovers. Searching for and sharing information will bring strength and knowledge for generations to come. Sustainability is the key to the future growth and well-being of our oceans, rivers and lakes. You can contribute to sustainability by following three easy steps. One, always ask your fishmonger the

> **It is everyone's responsibility to be caretakers of our oceans and good educators of future seafood lovers.**

origin and harvest method of your seafood; "local," "just out of the water," and "caught by hook and line" have always been our favorite answers. Two, eat small fish often and large fish occasionally. Three, step outside your comfort zone and try new species—it's a delicious way to maintain a balanced ocean dynamic and get hooked on fish.

We are both avid travelers guided by food as a compass to foreign lands. Writing this book is our way to invite you on a maritime exploration of different cultures, told through recipes and life stories. This is one of the core values behind our cookbook series *Flying Pans*. We are energized by the beauty of life, the art of cooking, the discovery of travel, and the passion of the human race. We have a burning desire to share those revelations with as many people as will listen.

Author Bios and Philosophy

BERNARD

The ocean—I was born by it, I live near it, I eat from it, I sail on it, and I swim in it. I grew up on the coast of Brittany with a family of fishermen, butchers, bakers, and farmers. At the helm of our family was my grandmother, who was an exquisite cook. She taught me how to respect the bountiful opportunities bestowed upon me with the ocean at my feet and the resources available to us. The ocean was a large part of my daily life. Every month, with a kiss of the breeze, at the highest tides, following the moon's cycle, our family would gather in the Baie de Morlaix in Roscoff to harvest oysters, mussels, clams, crab, shrimp, and Brittany's prized *haricots de mer,* "sea beans." It was wonderful what the sea gave us along the Brittany coast of natural wonders.

At an early age, I knew that my path was in the kitchen because cooking came naturally to me. I knew this would be a great craft and would be my passport to travel the world and discover what abounds in the oceans and beyond. And travel I did.

I ate fish in the raw in Japan, sizzling octopus barbecued on the back of a bicycle in China, oyster ceviche in the mountains of Ecuador, *poisson cru* in Raiatea in the Society Islands, and candied smoked salmon hanging from rafters in the wilderness of Alaska. I had a close encounter with a great white shark while windsurfing with the chief of police's son to Devil's Island, French Guyana, in one of the world's largest populations of great whites. I have sailed the ocean discovering the fishing ports of the Seychelles, Bali, Italy, Spain, Bay of Biscay, Australia, Thailand, and the beautiful coastal village of Al Fujairah in the United Arab Emirates. I discovered ancient fishing nets in Kochin, India, with my friend Jean-Michel Cousteau.

The philosophy of ocean to kitchen has been embedded in me as the core value of my cuisine. My mentor Chef Georges Paineau, from his coveted restaurant Le Bretagne, taught me the artistic aspects of culinary craft and allowed me to learn hands-on at the tender age of fifteen. Every Friday morning at 2 a.m. we would drive two hours to La Criée fish market where *les petits pêcheurs* would auction their prized catch to the highest bidder, including wild sea bass (*bar de ligne*) as well as the outrageously plump *langoustine,* aka Brittany gold! The soul of any coastal community, great or small, is its market. The markets provide a snapshot of a people, their environment, and their resources.

Nothing is better than the freshest shellfish, taken right from the sea, either cooked in the simplest possible way or served raw. Sharing a *plateau de fruits de mer* on my native coast of Brittany with family and friends at home, with freshly baked bread from my Uncle Gilbert and *fleur de sel*–infused butter, is a phenomenal feeling that brings me inner happiness.

Having globe-trotted all over the planet, I am able to take all of life's experiences and place those memories and discoveries on every plate that I create. Life's postcards from journeys past is a magnificent voyage. As a traveler it can be phenomenal, burdensome, and challenging in many ways. As my grandmother would say, take a bite out of life and savor the moment!

Water has the power to wash away the negative and infuse your mind with spirit.

RON

The ocean runs through my bloodline. My great-grandfather, a seafaring man, built his life from the abundance of sardines in Turkish waterways. His fishing boats were the sultans of the Dardanelles. His mansion on the ocean's edge, financed by fish, is where my grandfather Nate was born and raised. As a young man in the Turkish navy, it was certain that Nate's destiny was to be transported by sea to an untimely battle death. But, by a twist of fate, he was spared and lived to cross the ocean in a more fulfilling sort of journey—emigration to the United States. Nate's daughter, my mom, was born in Los Angeles and grew to worship the ocean, spending many days at the beach with friends and family. Watching the sunset over the blue-green horizon was a treasured ritual, and perhaps the only one in life that is always as good as the first time. My family feels a special connection to the ocean. Swimming in the waves is one of life's best therapies. Invigorated and energized, one exits the salty water ready to face the day. Water has the power to wash away the negative and infuse your mind with spirit.

I grew up listening to the maritime tales of my great-grandfather, witnessing my grandfather emerge from a jaunt in the waves a new man again and again, and watching my mom's eyes flutter at the sight of many a setting sun. Once your life is touched in that way, it is hard to venture inland. I have always made it a point to live with access to the coast, from South Carolina, Rhode Island, and Florida in the East to Pacific Grove, Ventura, and San Diego in the West. Each region is proud of its local delicacies, whether it be sand dabs, spotted prawns, or soft-shell crabs, creating excitement and anticipation as each season begins.

When I was a child, my family's obsession with tasty food and our habit of gathering in the kitchen inspired me to start cooking. Years before I was tall enough to see above the countertops, I would spend hours absorbing the sounds, aromas, and orchestrated movements surrounding me. Those experiences started the curiosity and excitement I still feel every time I step into a kitchen. I can close my eyes and revisit those very first impressions of cooking—the rhythmic tapping of efficient knife work, the steel-on-steel swoosh of hand-whipped cream, or the clinking of dishes as the table is prepared in anticipation.

Seafood cookery is a great way to synergize a love for the ocean, a passion for cooking, and an appetite for travel. My culinary excursions around the world have done more than allow me to discover native ingredients and cooking methods. The perspective I've gained toward life from one destination is fortified at the next. The idea that food is a gift from the earth, that cooking is an act of love, and that eating is socially unifying are all concepts I've learned through travel. Having discovered, dined on, and cooked seafood in my own country and abroad is a privilege that I never take for granted. But being able to share those experiences with others is the best part.

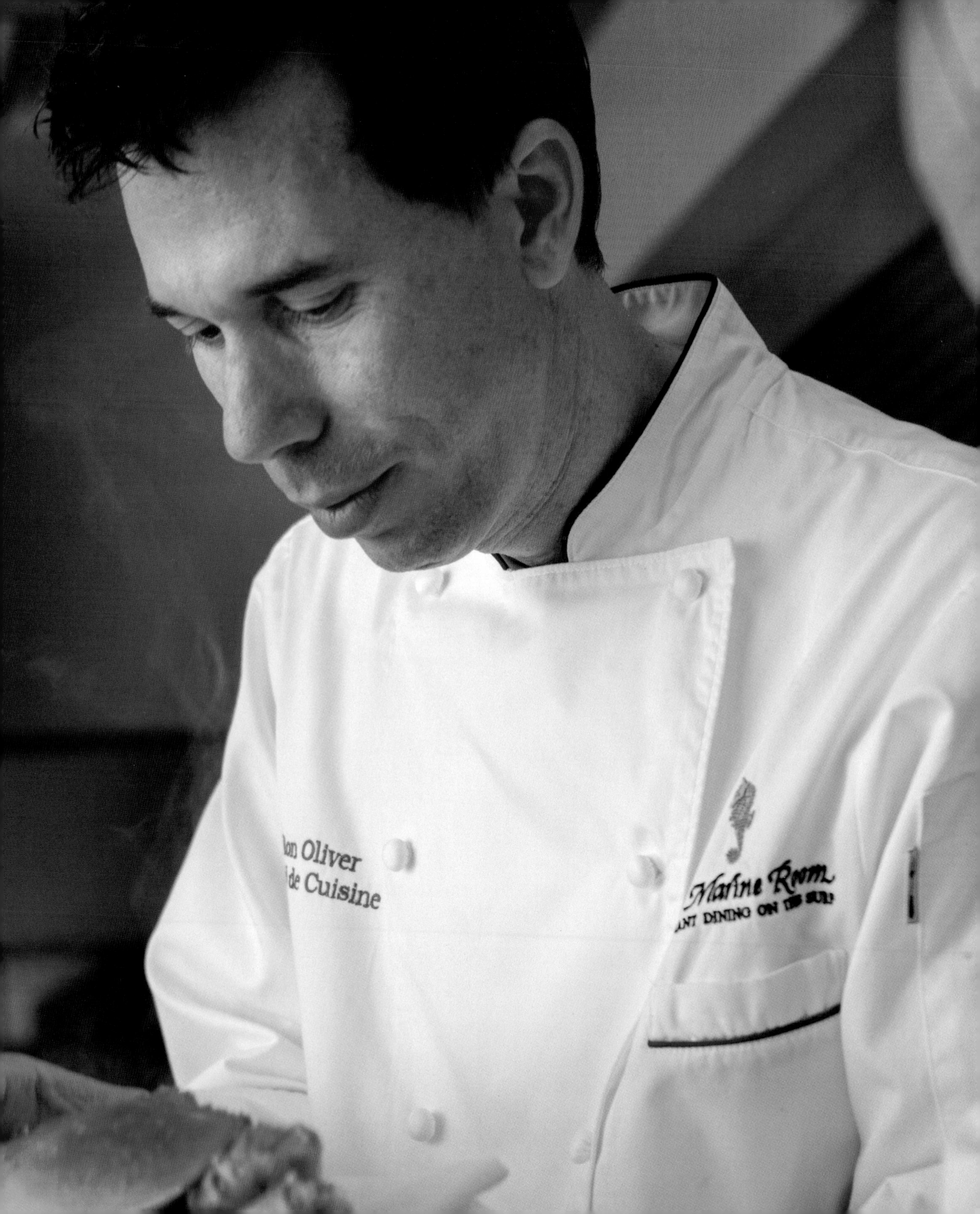
Oliver
de Cuisine
Marine Room
DINING ON THE SURF

Ocean 101

It is ideal to present fish and shellfish early in a meal's progression, when lighter, palette-teasing dishes are most welcome. Many cooking methods showcase the natural flavors of seafood. Curing adds saltiness while infusing the aromas of blended herbs and spices. Smoking adds an underlying warmth and richness. Pickling contributes a pronounced brightness and tart intensity. All of these processes were developed as preservation techniques in times when refrigeration was not an option. What was invented out of necessity is now practiced almost purely for pleasure!

Freshness, quality, and safety are paramount when purchasing seafood. To ensure you get all three, it's important to seek out reliable sources. Once you've located quality fishmongers, get to know them. They have their fingers on the pulse of the local waters, knowing which fish and shellfish are in season. Ask them which varieties represent the best of each day's catch. You'll gain a friend in the business and the peace of mind that you have the absolute freshest, best-tasting seafood possible.

Here are all of the fish in this book (and more) categorized by their characteristics:

Large Flake: seabass, striped bass, snapper, halibut, grouper, orange roughy, bluefish, cod, salmon

Thin and Delicate: sole, fluke, flounder, John Dory, orange roughy, trout

High Oil Content: salmon, trout, arctic char, steelhead, cod, pompano, pomfret, mackerel, yellowtail, kampachi, tuna, oysters, mussels, sardines, anchovies

Shells: clams, cockles, mussels, scallops

Meaty: mahi mahi, monkfish, swordfish, shark, tuna, yellowtail, ono, scallops

Sea Creatures: octopus, squid

Sweet and Nutty: shrimp, lobster, crab, scallops, oysters, monkfish

Here are our favorite fish and shellfish for each cooking method:

In the Raw: tuna, kampachi, salmon, yellowtail, scallops, shrimp, mackerel, arctic char, halibut, oysters, clams, ono

Barbecued: swordfish, mahi mahi, tuna, salmon, yellow tail, shrimp, lobster, halibut, shark, scallops, squid, octopus, ono

Slow Cooked: monkfish, stuffed squid, salmon, swordfish, cod, stuffed sole, mackerel, octopus

Smoked: arctic char, trout, salmon, cod, tuna, swordfish, mackerel, yellowtail, kampachi, mussels, oysters, scallops, ono

Deep-Fried: shrimp, squid, oysters, grouper, orange roughy, sole, shark, salmon, John Dory, mahi mahi, halibut, cod

Oil Poached: arctic char, cod, halibut, salmon, swordfish, tuna, yellowtail, kampachi, lobster, scallops, shrimp, ono

Liquid Poached: halibut, fluke, scallops, shrimp, lobster, octopus, salmon, flounder, orange roughy

Kebabs: mahi mahi, monkfish, salmon, shark, swordfish, tuna, grouper, yellowtail, squid, octopus, shrimp, scallops, ono

En Papillote: sole, fluke, flounder, halibut, salmon, arctic char, striped bass, cod, pompano, John Dory, salmon, swordfish, orange roughy, trout

Steamed: salmon, fluke, grouper, orange roughy, shrimp, clams, cockles, mussels, crab, lobster, oysters, bass, halibut, John Dory, snapper, sole, flounder, cod

Pan Roasted: arctic char, bass, striped bass, cod, halibut, pompano, monkfish, salmon, shark, swordfish, tuna, snapper, sole, flounder, fluke, grouper, orange roughy, scallops, shrimp

How to Select and Store

When it comes to fish, think cold! Seafood is very sensitive to temperature. When buying fish we recommend having a small cooler with ice packs to keep a safe temperature during transport. At home, refrigerate your purchase immediately at 34°F to 38°F. Try to buy fish the same day you will cook it. Trust your senses when shopping and look for these signs of freshness:

Fish

- Clear eyes that are not sunken
- Bright red gills
- Tight flesh that springs back to the touch
- Vibrant-colored flesh with no discoloration
- Glistening, moist skin
- Smells fresh like the sea with no ammonia or strong odor
- Whole fish displayed *in* ice, fillets and steaks displayed *on* ice
- Pat dry with absorbent paper, tightly wrap with plastic wrap, and store on ice. Do not allow fish to sit in water or even in its own natural moisture.

Shellfish

- Tightly closed shells
- Information tag with origin and harvest date on bins of shellfish
- No cracked or broken shells
- Slightly opened shells close up when tapped
- Pleasant smell of the sea
- Oysters: creamy color and clear liquid when opened
- Store loosely in an open container and covered with damp cloths or paper towels. Place a bag of ice loosely atop. Do not store live shellfish in a sealed container or in water.

Live Crab, Shrimp, Lobster

- Alive and kicking, literally—must have moving legs
- Store loosely in an open container that they can't escape from, then cover with damp cloths or paper towels. Place a bag of ice loosely atop. Do not store in a sealed container or they will die.

Shrimp Tails, Crabmeat, Lobster Tails

- Uniform light-colored tail
- No discoloration, sliminess, or strong smell
- No black spots on the flesh
- Whole, undamaged shells
- As a rule consume as soon as possible after purchase, but not later than forty-eight hours. Rinse shrimp and lobster under cold running water then pat dry before cooking. Crabmeat from a can should be transferred to a nonreactive container after it's opened.

CHAPTER 1

Chill Out

SMALL BITES FROM AROUND THE WORLD

FIJI
Ahi Tuna Tiger Eye
spicy cashew sauce

NORWAY
Steelhead Caraway Gravlax
buckwheat blini, salmon roe

SPAIN
Cíes Islands Clam Crudo
chorizo, pumpkin seeds

PERU
Máncora Beach Oysters
fuyu persimmons, pink grapefruit
pisco granita

MEXICO
Wild Baja Shrimp Cocktail
cumin tortilla chips

SOUTH AFRICA
**Port Shepstone Mahi Mahi
Escabeche**
grated carrot sambal

FRANCE
Finistère Bar Sea Bass Tartare
sunny-side-up quail egg

JAPAN
Shime Saba Mackerel
wasabi tangelo vinaigrette

UNITED STATES
Hawaii Ono Sashimi
eggplant sunomono

Fish and shellfish, dwellers of the nippy sea, always seem most comfortable on a bed of ice, a cold platter, or a chilled vessel allowing the mineral flavors and delicate textures to land on your tongue with a tingly chill. Whether it's sweet crab, raw tuna, buttery diver scallops, or freshly shucked oysters, seafood boasts an expansive array of potent and altogether scrumptious sensations. These unique qualities are reflected in the diets and food cultures of the world's coastal communities.

"Chill out" could have been a term used by one of our favorite authors of the nineteenth century, Jean Anthelme Brillat-Savarin, a French politician whose passion for gastronomy led him to pen the most famous book on the art of cooking, *Physiology of Taste*. To truly experience the palate and its pleasures, one must be relaxed, in a heightened state of sensory awareness.

Each coastal region's indigenous food resources lends its distinctive flavors and essence that form the base of their cuisine. Communities from around the world embrace these same unique values essential to everyday life.

Suva, a harbor on a mangrove-lined peninsula, is Fiji's capital and main gateway to the open sea. Legendary fishermen native to the archipelago can tell which fish are feeding in the ocean just by looking toward the sky. A large flock of birds circling and diving signals the presence of big-game fish such as yellowfin and striped tuna. At the fish market, select ahi with a vibrant ruby-red color and firm flesh. Seasoned seaweed salad is usually found in the Asian section of supermarkets, or it can be substituted with a mixture of mint and basil leaves. —BERNARD

Ahi Tuna Tiger Eye
Spicy Cashew Sauce
SERVES 6

TUNA

12 ounces sushi-grade ahi tuna loin, 1 inch thick
2 sheets nori (dry seaweed sheets)
1 mango, peeled, seeded, cut into 2 x ¼ x ¼-inch strips
½ cup seasoned seaweed salad

Place ahi on cold clean surface. Carefully slice ahi into ¼-inch-thick slices. Place one sheet nori on work surface. Lay half of the ahi slices side by side to line half of the surface of nori. Arrange half of the mango strips atop ahi in one line from left to right, 1 inch from the closest edge. Do the same with ¼ cup of the seaweed salad. Roll tightly. Place in freezer 15 minutes. Repeat process with the remaining ingredients.

SPICY CASHEW SAUCE

3 tablespoons mirin
1½ tablespoons soy sauce
2 tablespoons seasoned rice vinegar
2 tablespoons cilantro leaves
1 tablespoon chopped ginger
½ teaspoon sambal chile sauce
½ cup toasted cashews

Place first six ingredients in blender. Turn on to low speed. Add cashews a few at a time. Turn to high speed. Blend until thick and smooth.

TEMPURA

2 quarts corn or grapeseed oil for frying
½ cup all-purpose flour
½ cup cornstarch
1 teaspoon baking soda
1 teaspoon baking powder
½ teaspoon sea salt
1 teaspoon honey
1 large egg
¾ cup cold water
2 tablespoons sesame seeds
1 tablespoon finely minced chives
1 teaspoon lemon zest

Add oil to deep fryer or heavy-bottomed pot fitted with thermometer. Oil should be at least 5 inches deep. Preheat to 365°F. Sift flour, cornstarch, baking soda, baking powder, and salt into mixing bowl. In separate bowl, combine honey, egg, and water. Add to flour mixture. Whisk until smooth. Stir in remaining ingredients. Set aside. Dip ahi roll in prepared tempura mix. Deep fry 7 seconds. Drain on paper towel. Refrigerate immediately.

PRESENTATION

Cut ahi tuna roll into six ½-inch medallions. Add ½ teaspoon of Spicy Cashew Sauce to six Asian spoons. Stand tuna medallions atop sauce. Transfer remaining sauce to serving dish.

Gravlax, glistening in its translucent, oily red glory, is sliced precisely and laid atop griddled buckwheat cakes called blini in this recipe, a synergy between land and sea. Gravlax can be thought of as Nordic charcuterie, which originated in Middle Ages Scandinavia. It was prepared by fishermen who buried salmon in the sand while it cured, hence the name gravlax, which translates to "salmon in the grave." It is equally delicious prepared with steelhead or arctic char. Fillets over 1 inch thick require an additional twenty-four hours of curing. —RON

Steelhead Caraway Gravlax
Buckwheat Blini, Salmon Roe
MAKES 12

STEELHEAD
¼ **cup** dried parsley flakes
2 **tablespoons** dried dill
1 **tablespoon** caraway seeds, toasted
2 **pounds** steelhead fillets, center-cut, skinless, boneless
1 lemon, zested
1 **teaspoon** olive oil
2½ **tablespoons** kosher salt
2 **tablespoons** granulated sugar

Add parsley, dill, and caraway seeds to coffee grinder. Process to fine powder. Transfer mixture to flat plate. Rub surface of steelhead with lemon zest and olive oil. Place atop spice mixture. Flip to coat both sides. Mix salt and sugar together. Sprinkle half onto large piece of plastic wrap. Place steelhead on top. Sprinkle remaining mixture over fish. Wrap tightly. Refrigerate 24 hours. Turn over. Refrigerate another 24 hours. Unwrap. Dry thoroughly with paper towels. Refrigerate overnight.

BUCKWHEAT BLINI
1 **cup** buckwheat flour
½ **cup** all-purpose flour
1½ **teaspoons** baking powder
½ **teaspoon** sea salt
3 large eggs
1 **cup** milk
¾ **cup** sour cream
¼ **cup** (½ stick) unsalted butter, melted
1 **tablespoon** honey
as needed canola oil spray

Sift flours, baking powder, and salt into large mixing bowl. In another bowl, whisk the eggs, milk, sour cream, melted butter, and honey. Pour milk mixture over flour mixture. Whisk to combine. Place nonstick skillet over medium heat. Spray with canola oil. Spoon 1 tablespoon batter onto griddle. Cook until dry around the edges. Flip over. Cook additional 20 seconds.

PRESENTATION
½ **cup** crème fraîche
1 **tablespoon** lemon juice
to taste sea salt
to taste ground black pepper
3 **ounces** salmon roe

Whip crème fraîche and lemon juice in mixing bowl to form stiff peaks. Season with salt and pepper. Transfer to serving dish. Thinly slice steelhead across grain using sharp knife. Serve with Buckwheat Blini, crème fraîche, and salmon roe.

The Cíes Islands, off the coast of Galicia, are reachable only by boat. Turquoise waters are a castaway's paradise. The sandbanks facing the Vigo estuary are a treasure chest of clams awaiting that squeeze of citrus and dash of Xeres, a signature sherry vinegar from the city of Jerez de la Frontera. The sweet-sour juiciness invigorates the clam to be eaten *crudo,* or raw, with a hint of spicy chorizo. Island paradise, Spanish style. —BERNARD

Cíes Islands Clam Crudo

Chorizo, Pumpkin Seeds

MAKES 12

CRUDO

16 cherrystone clams, scrubbed, rinsed
¾ cup orange juice
1 small hot red chile, stemmed, seeded, minced
3 tablespoons minced red onion
¾ cup finely diced tomatillos
2 tablespoons chopped cilantro
3 tablespoons extra-virgin olive oil
1½ tablespoons sherry vinegar
to taste sea salt
to taste ground black pepper

Using a thick towel, grip clam in palm of hand with hinged side of clam facing outward. Hold pointed clam knife in other hand. Keeping clam level, insert the tip of knife between the shell halves at the hinge. Twist to pry shell apart until you hear a snap. Twist knife to open shell. Cut clams out of shell and into a bowl with their juice. Save 12 of the best shell halves. Refrigerate shells. Remove the clams from juice. Discard any shell fragments. Cut into small pieces. Transfer to mixing bowl. Strain 3 tablespoons clam juice into bowl. Fold in remaining ingredients. Season to taste. Refrigerate 3 hours.

ASSEMBLE

2 ounces Spanish chorizo
3 tablespoons toasted pumpkin seeds

Cut chorizo into thin slices. Cut slices into fine matchsticks. Spoon the crudo into clam shells. Garnish with chorizo. Sprinkle with pumpkin seeds.

Like an oyster tucked tight in its shell, Peru's Máncora Beach took refuge from all but the most ambitious intruders—surfers from the capital Lima, spurred by rumors of world-class waves that crash on virgin sand. As the legend grew, so did access to the town, now famous not only for her surf but for the delicacies it brings. Máncora's oysters, plump and briny, are perfect with the fragrant sweetness of persimmons and grapefruit ice. —RON

Máncora Beach Oysters

Fuyu Persimmons, Pink Grapefruit Pisco Granita
SERVES 6

PINK GRAPEFRUIT PISCO GRANITA
2 cups pink grapefruit juice (about 3 grapefruits)
1 tablespoon honey
¼ cup pisco brandy
2 teaspoons grated ginger
pinch cayenne pepper

Combine all ingredients in mixing bowl. Stir to dissolve honey. Let stand 30 minutes. Pour mixture into an 8 x 8-inch glass baking dish. Cover. Freeze overnight.

FUYU PERSIMMONS
1 fuyu persimmon, trimmed, finely diced
2 tablespoons finely diced, seeded cucumber
1 tablespoon lime juice
12 small mint leaves, julienned
1 teaspoon safflower oil
to taste sea salt
to taste ground black pepper

Combine all ingredients in mixing bowl. Season with salt and pepper.

OYSTERS
18 oysters
as needed crushed ice

To shuck oysters, cover palm of hand with folded kitchen towel. Place oyster in center. Thrust point of oyster knife into hinge of shell. Run knife around oyster, forcing it open. Once oyster is open, remove shell fragments. Detach oyster from shell. Discard any debris, retaining as much seawater as possible inside shell. Fill serving bowl with crushed ice. Arrange oysters on top. Garnish with persimmon mixture. Scrape surface of granita with tines of fork until fluffy. Spoon atop oysters. Serve immediately.

San Felipe, gateway to the Sea of Cortez, is renowned as the shrimp epicenter of the Baja peninsula. The color of the giant shrimp is a reflection of San Felipe's gorgeous blue water. Just like in all Mexican coastal towns, the *malecón,* or waterfront promenade, is the heartbeat of the community where friends and family gather. Wild shrimp plucked from the waters, served chilled and spicy, is a refreshing way to cool down on a hot Mexican afternoon. —BERNARD

Wild Baja Shrimp Cocktail
Cumin Tortilla Chips
MAKES 12

COCKTAIL SAUCE
YIELDS 1½ CUPS
½ cup tomato ketchup
1 tablespoon Dijon mustard
½ cup lime juice
2 tablespoons lemon juice
¼ cup tequila
⅛ teaspoon granulated garlic
½ teaspoon sea salt
2 teaspoons olive oil
½ teaspoon Worcestershire sauce
⅛ teaspoon ground black pepper
1 teaspoon hot chile sauce

Add all ingredients to large mixing bowl. Whisk to combine. Refrigerate.

SHRIMP
½ teaspoon sea salt
12 shrimp, size U-15
½ cup Cocktail Sauce
¼ cup chopped cilantro
½ cup diced avocado
3 spring onions, white part only, shaved crosswise
¼ teaspoon lime zest
½ teaspoon minced serrano chile, seeded, deveined
6 sprigs cilantro
2 red radishes, cut into matchsticks

Bring 2 quarts of water and salt to simmer in large pot over medium heat. Add shrimp. Cook 2 minutes or until slightly underdone. Transfer shrimp to ice bath. Peel and devein shrimp, saving tails for garnish. Cut shrimp into ¼-inch pieces. Transfer to mixing bowl. Add Cocktail Sauce. Toss to coat. Fold in chopped cilantro, avocado, spring onions, lime zest, and serranos. Spoon into ramekins. Garnish with cilantro sprigs, reserved shrimp tails, and radish matchsticks.

CUMIN TORTILLA CHIPS
½ teaspoon smoked paprika
½ teaspoon ground cumin
½ teaspoon sea salt
4 (8-inch) corn tortillas
1 cup vegetable oil

Mix paprika, cumin, and salt in small ramekin. Set aside. Cut tortillas into 1½-inch-wide strips, then cut strips in half diagonally to make long triangles. Add oil to 10-inch skillet over medium heat. When hot, add tortilla strips. Fry until golden and crisp. Transfer to paper towel–lined plate. Sprinkle with spice mixture. Transfer to serving dish.

During hot African summers, the famous Mozambique Current carries warm water down south to Port Shepstone in the coastal region of Kwazulu-Natal, bringing dorado, tuna, king mackerel, and blue marlin. Dorado are also called dorrie, mahi mahi, and dolphin fish, though there is no relation to the dolphin. Hooking a dorado on a fly-fishing rod is a thrilling battle with a majestic opponent. When breaking the surface of the water with spectacular aerial leaps, dorado show off their metallic rainbow-colored flanks in the shining sun. Fish *escabeche* is a pickling method classically prepared hot and served cold. In this recipe we cool the pickling liquid before adding the mahi mahi to maintain the flavor profile of the fish. —BERNARD

Port Shepstone Mahi Mahi Escabeche
Grated Carrot Sambal
SERVES 6

ESCABECHE
1 stalk lemongrass
1 cup blood orange juice
1 tablespoon white wine vinegar
1 teaspoon black peppercorns
2 cloves garlic, crushed
1 teaspoon celery seeds
3 bags rooibos or Earl Grey tea
½ teaspoon sea salt
1 pound mahi mahi fillet, skinless, boneless

Cut lemongrass into 3-inch-long pieces, discarding the hard bottom root. Crush pieces with mallet. Add lemongrass, blood orange juice, vinegar, peppercorns, garlic, celery seeds, tea, and sea salt to saucepan over medium heat. Bring to simmer. Remove from heat. Cool to room temperature. Strain through fine sieve into baking dish. Cut mahi mahi into ¼-inch slices. Add to marinade. Cover. Refrigerate 2 hours.

CARROT SAMBAL
1 cup Sauvignon Blanc wine
1 tablespoon malt vinegar
1 tablespoon finely grated ginger
1 tablespoon honey
½ teaspoon anise seeds
¼ teaspoon dried orange peel
¼ teaspoon ground cardamom
⅛ teaspoon red chile flakes
1 pound carrots, peeled, grated
2 spring onions, white part only, thinly sliced
1 tablespoon safflower oil
2 tablespoons chopped mint
to taste sea salt
to taste ground black pepper

Add first eight ingredients to nonreactive sauce pot over medium heat. Bring to simmer. Reduce by two-thirds. Add carrots. Cook, stirring occasionally, until all liquid evaporates. Transfer to mixing bowl. Refrigerate to chill. Fold in remaining ingredients. Season with salt and pepper.

PRESENTATION
¼ teaspoon celery seeds
6 sprigs mint

Mound Carrot Sambal in middle of individual serving dishes. Place mahi mahi beside it. Sprinkle with celery seed. Garnish with mint sprig. Spoon 1 teaspoon marinade onto plate.

Pointe de la Torche beach juts out from the southern end of the Bay of Audierne in Finistère, a province in southwestern Brittany. Despite the pounding of the Atlantic, communities have thrived here for centuries. In September, the sea and wind stir the cobalt water to a sandy brown, creating deep water corridors for bar fish to hunt. Cousins of the sea bass family, and well-known for their predatory voracious behavior, bars move in small schools of the same age and build. They are the most sought-after game fish in France. Catching one is a "bar fight"! —BERNARD

Finistère Bar Sea Bass Tartare
Sunny-Side-Up Quail Egg
MAKES 12

TARTARE
3 tablespoons extra-virgin olive oil, divided
1 cup finely diced butternut squash
to taste fleur de sel or flaky sea salt
pinch ground white pepper
1 pound sea bass fillet, center-cut, sashimi quality, skinless, boneless
1 teaspoon brown mustard seeds
1 tablespoon minced shallots
1 tablespoon minced chives
½ teaspoon Meyer lemon zest
1 tablespoon Meyer lemon juice

Add 1 tablespoon olive oil to small skillet over medium heat. Add butternut squash. Season with salt and pepper. Cook 5 minutes or until al dente. Transfer to plate. Refrigerate. Cut sea bass into ¼-inch cubes. Transfer to chilled mixing bowl. Combine with 2 tablespoons olive oil, mustard seeds, shallots, chives, and lemon zest and juice. Season with salt and pepper.

PRESENTATION
12 quail eggs
to taste sea salt
to taste ground black pepper
3 tablespoons olive oil
2 tablespoons pomegranate seeds
2 tablespoons chopped, toasted pistachios
12 sprigs chives

Crack quail eggs into 12 small ramekins. Add oil to nonstick skillet over low heat. Add eggs to skillet two at a time. Cook sunny-side up. Season with salt and pepper. Transfer to cutting board. Cut with 1-inch ring, keeping the yolk intact. Add butternut squash to mini cocktail glass. Top with sea bass tartare. Sprinkle with pomegranate seeds and pistachios. Garnish with quail egg and chive sprig.

The Japanese word for mackerel, *saba*, is written 鯖 in Japanese, a combination of two kanji characters that mean "fish" and "blue." In Japan, a gift from the sea brings happiness to the kitchen. The fishermen of Yaizu, an ancient fishing village, harvest their prized catch along the shore bordering Suruga Bay, with Mount Fuji ever present in the background. Even Japan's hardcore sushi aficionados will agree that raw saba is only considered a delicacy after curing with vinegar and salt, traditionally called *shime* saba. —RON

Shime Saba Mackerel
Wasabi Tangelo Vinaigrette
MAKES 12

MACKEREL
½ **cup** seasoned rice vinegar
½ **cup** sake
1 **teaspoon** grated ginger
½ **teaspoon** sea salt
¼ **teaspoon** shichimi togarashi pepper
2 fresh mackerel fillets, boneless (6 ounces each)

Combine rice vinegar, sake, ginger, sea salt, and togarashi in nonreactive baking dish. Place mackerel, skin side up, into marinade. Cover. Refrigerate overnight. Transfer fillets to paper towel–lined plate.

VINAIGRETTE
¾ **cup** tangelo juice
1 **teaspoon** tangelo zest
¼ **cup** rice vinegar
2 **teaspoons** wasabi paste
¼ **cup** avocado oil
to taste sea salt

In a small saucepan over medium heat, reduce tangelo juice, zest, and rice vinegar by two-thirds. Transfer to mixing bowl. Whisk in wasabi and avocado oil vigorously to emulsify. Season with salt.

PRESENTATION
¾ **cup** diced avocado
2 **tablespoons** finely sliced green onion
1 **tablespoon** lemon juice
to taste sea salt
to taste shichimi togarashi pepper
1 **cup** diced, drained cherry tomatoes
1 **teaspoon** minced ginger
¼ **teaspoon** sesame oil
½ **teaspoon** sambal olek
¾ **cup** finely diced mango
1 (2½-**ounce**) package daikon sprouts

In small bowl combine avocado, green onion, and lemon juice. Season with sea salt and togarashi. In separate bowl combine tomatoes, ginger, sesame oil, and sambal. Season with sea salt. Transfer mackerel to cutting board. Cut fillets crosswise into ¼-inch-thick slices. Place 1-inch ring in center of chilled serving dish. Fill with equal amounts of avocado mixture, tomato mixture, and mango. Sprinkle with togarashi. Remove ring. Arrange mackerel slices beside. Garnish with daikon sprouts. Spoon vinaigrette into each dish.

Ono is a tropical warm-water fish whose name in Hawaiian means "delicious." Also called wahoo in the Caribbean, ono are vicious predators with majestic bluish-green striped, lean bodies. They are agile and fast swimmers that can reach speeds of fifty miles per hour, with teeth as sharp as a sushi knife. The best way to enjoy their rich, clean-tasting flesh is nice and slow with a chilled locally brewed lager. —RON

Hawaii Ono Sashimi
Eggplant Sunomono
SERVES 6

ONO

3 tablespoons toasted sesame seeds
½ teaspoon black peppercorns
1 tablespoon smoked sea salt
1 pound ono, center-cut, sashimi-quality, skinless, boneless

Add sesame seeds and peppercorns to spice grinder. Process to coarse powder. Add smoked sea salt. Pulse to incorporate. Transfer to plate. Roll ono in sesame mixture to coat thoroughly. Wrap tightly in plastic wrap. Refrigerate 2 hours. Transfer to cutting board. With plastic wrap intact, cut crosswise into thin slices. Peel plastic wrap from each slice. Transfer to serving platter.

EGGPLANT SUNOMONO

1 tablespoon wakame (dried seaweed)
2 medium Japanese eggplant, peeled, cut into ¼-inch dice
1 clove garlic, thinly sliced
1 tablespoon chopped ginger
2 tablespoons soy sauce
1 tablespoon miso paste
¼ cup sake
4 teaspoons packed brown sugar
1 tablespoon sesame oil
1 tablespoon seasoned rice vinegar
1 Asian pear, cored, diced

Place wakame in bowl with 1 cup water. Soak 10 minutes. Drain. Squeeze dry. Finely chop. Combine eggplant, garlic, ginger, soy sauce, miso paste, sake, and brown sugar in large mixing bowl. Let sit 10 minutes. Add to nonstick skillet over medium heat. Cook, stirring occasionally, until liquid is reduced to glaze consistency. Fold in wakame, sesame oil, and rice vinegar. Cook additional 30 seconds. Set aside to cool. Fold in Asian pear. Transfer to six ramekins.

CHAPTER 2

Shells

SCALLOPS, CLAMS, OYSTERS, MUSSELS

Scallops

ISRAEL
**Almond Milk Poached
Akko Bay Scallops**
pasta pearls, roasted
cherry tomatoes

UNITED STATES
**Dill and Orange Peel Scented
Sea Scallops**
beluga lentil casserole

AUSTRALIA
**Abrolhos Island Diver
Scallops Crudo**
sesame brittle

FRANCE
**Coquilles St. Jacques
Île d'Ouessant**
cauliflower puree, truffle oil

TAIWAN
Plum Miso Candied Scallops
green tea noodles

NEW ZEALAND
**Hazelnut Dukkah Spiced
Diver Scallops**
blood orange reduction

Clams

MALAYSIA
Kam Heong Spicy Clams
golden fragrance sauce

FRANCE
Brittany Cockles Marinière
parsnips, white wine, garlic

PORTUGAL
Pork and Clam Stew
linguiça, root vegetables

UNITED STATES
**Jerusalem Artichoke
Clam Chowder**
celery salt popped corn

Oysters

JAPAN
Crispy Oysters Tempura
tangerine ponzu

GLOBAL
Drunken Oysters
vodka pomegranate, pisco lime,
aquavit apple

UNITED STATES
Rockin' Stellar Oysters
mustard seed cream

ITALY
Prosciutto Wrapped Oysters
fennel chile butter

CHINA
Oyster Sugar Pea Stir-Fry
szechuan black bean sauce

Mussels

MEXICO
Chilled Mussels on Half Shell
papaya, cotija cheese

SPAIN
Cast-Iron Black Mussels
sherry wine, chorizo, tomatoes

UNITED STATES
Bourbon Street Steamed Mussels
andouille, eggplant,
okra, baguette

NEW ZEALAND
Green-Lipped Mussel Bisque
celery seed orange croutons

FRANCE
Piperade Moules Provençale
fennel, garlic, rosé wine

INDIA
Goa Mussels Hot Pot
curry coconut broth

Scallops

Four hundred species of scallops populate the earth's waters, from intertidal zones to deeper ocean depths.

Scallops have long been associated with Saint James in Europe, as demonstrated in the German name *Jakobsmuschel* and the French *coquille St. Jacques*.

Scallops are mollusks that have ridged, or scalloped, shells. The single white, round muscle that opens and closes the shell is the part we eat. The muscle usually comes with a small tendon attached, which has a rubbery texture and is removed simply by peeling it off.

The reproductive glands of the scallop, called the "coral," are a delicacy prized in Europe but consumed less frequently in North America.

Besides humans, the most prolific hunters of scallops are starfish. They pull the shells apart by wrapping their arms around the scallop and suctioning it open.

In the Wild

Scallops are also called fan shells or comb shells. Their shells come in many different colors and can be bright red, purple, orange, yellow, or sandy white.

Atlantic sea scallops have a very large ratio of shell to meat with some shells reaching 9 inches in diameter.

Scallops are unusually mobile, propelling themselves in short bursts by expelling water from their shells.

Here are some of our favorite kinds of scallops:

Maine Diver Scallops
Harvested in Georges Bank, Maine

Meat or "nut" can be 2 ounces in weight

Calico Scallops
Harvested by divers in Peru

Calicos are similar to bay scallops but found in deeper waters. Instead of being shucked by hand, they are steamed briefly to open the shells, causing the meat to have whitened edges where they are slightly cooked from the steaming.

Spiny Scallops
Harvested in Canada

Also called swimming scallops or singing scallops, as they make a popping sound by flapping their shells together

Lion-Paw Scallops
Known in Spanish as *mano de leon,* these are harvested in Baja California Sur.

Bigger and more chewy than Maine scallops, they are best for raw preparation.

Bay Scallops
The best known are harvested on the US island of Nantucket.

About 4-inch shells have a marshmallow-shaped meat with a sweet aroma of fresh corn.

Weathervane Scallops
Harvested in Alaska's waters

Hokkaido Scallops
Harvested on the Japanese island of Hokkaido

SCALLOP SIZES

In the United States, scallops are sold by count. This is a rating of the size and weight of the scallop. The count represents the number of scallops in a pound. The numbers are typically a range; for example, a count of 10/20 means—on average—there are between 10 and 20 scallops in a pound. The *U* in the scallop sizes stands for "under." For example U-10 means under 10 scallops per pound.

In the Kitchen
Scallops are best when slightly undercooked, warm but not hot in the middle, and still translucent inside. Overcooking scallops ruins their voluptuous texture. The tendon on bay scallops does not need to be removed. Scallops need high heat and a hot surface to caramelize their natural sugars, so do not overcrowd the pan; instead cook them in smaller batches. These are the most common ways to prepare scallops:

- **Sashimi style**—scallops are luscious when eaten raw.

- **Wrapped in bacon**—the salty bacon plays on the sweet scallop.

- **Poached in aromatic broth**—then use the broth as a cooking liquid.

- **Seared in butter**—this provides maximum caramelization.

Valuable Nutrients from Scallops
- Choline: assists in proper cell function, prevents osteoporosis, reduces inflammation

- Magnesium: maintains healthy blood pressure and strong bones, relaxes nerves

- Omega-3 fatty acids: prevent cardiovascular disease

- Phosphorus: builds healthy bones and strong teeth

- Potassium: promotes healthy heart and kidneys, reduces stress

- Selenium: antioxidant, prevents arthritis

- Vitamin B_{12}: promotes healthy blood cells, prevents anemia, eases migraines

- Zinc: controls acne, boosts immune system

Fun Facts

Scallop shells are a common element in the art of various cultures and are often used as a religious symbol. The ancient Greeks claimed the goddess Aphrodite was born from a scallop shell. Botticelli's *Birth of Venus*, one of the most famous paintings in the world, depicts Venus (the Romans' name for Aphrodite) floating to shore in a scallop shell. The original fifteenth-century painting currently hangs in the Uffizi Gallery in Florence, Italy.

Scallops have about sixty brilliant blue eyes that peek out from their shells to detect light and motion.

Scallop shells make a perfect eating utensil and were used as spoons or dishes by primitive civilizations.

Akko, a city in Israel's Haifa Bay, was built on a narrow strip of land jutting into the sea and surrounded with water. Its name comes from the Greek word *ake,* which means "to cure." Greek mythology tells that Heracles healed himself with medicinal herbs found in the vicinity. The city was first settled in 3000 BC and has been highly sought after as a strategic coastal gateway to the Eastern Mediterranean ever since. Over the course of time, it was protected by massive walls but still was the backdrop for many a greedy and bloody siege, yet all the while the scallops remain blissfully under the water. Israeli couscous is toasted pasta in the shape of small pearls. Called *ptitim,* it was created in the 1950s as a substitute for rice when the newly established Israel faced money and food shortages. Scallops infuse the almond milk, which in turn cooks the pasta pearls, creating a full circle of flavor. —RON

Almond Milk Poached Akko Bay Scallops
Pasta Pearls, Roasted Cherry Tomatoes
SERVES 6

ROASTED CHERRY TOMATOES
2 tablespoons grapeseed oil
1 pound red cherry tomatoes on vine
3 cloves garlic, thinly sliced
¼ teaspoon cumin seeds
to taste sea salt
to taste ground black pepper

Add oil to large skillet over medium high heat. When hot, add tomatoes, garlic, and cumin. Cook, tossing constantly, until tomatoes plump and their skins break, about 1 minute. Season with sea salt and ground black pepper. Set aside.

SCALLOPS
1 pound bay scallops
3 cups almond milk
1 large pinch saffron threads
½ cup white wine
6 sprigs thyme
½ teaspoon sea salt
⅛ teaspoon ground white pepper

Place scallops in single layer in casserole dish. Add almond milk, saffron, wine, thyme, sea salt, and pepper to saucepan over medium-high heat. Bring to boil. Pour liquid over scallops. Stir once. Cool to room temperature. Strain liquid back into saucepan. Transfer scallops back to casserole dish. Set aside. Return saucepan to medium heat. Reduce almond milk mixture by half. Set aside.

PASTA PEARLS
2 tablespoons extra-virgin olive oil
1½ cups Israeli couscous
1 cup sliced leeks, white and light
   green part only
⅔ cup toasted pistachios
to taste sea salt
to taste ground black pepper
1 tablespoon chopped parsley

Add olive oil to saucepan over medium heat. Add couscous. Cook 1 minute, stirring constantly. Stir in leeks. Cook 1 minute. Stir in reduced almond milk mixture from Scallops. Cover. Cook 8 minutes at low simmer or until couscous is tender and liquid is absorbed. Fold in pistachios and scallops. Season with salt and pepper. Transfer to serving dish. Garnish with Roasted Cherry Tomatoes. Sprinkle with parsley.

The black beluga lentils have an air of sophistication about them. Shiny like black onyx, tiny and round like black caviar, they are the fashionable members of the lentil family, retaining their intense black color and swanky round shape even after cooking. But their appearance is a facade for a down-to-earth, nutty flavor and high nutritional status—rich in protein, iron, and fiber. Black lentils pair well with the sweet, briny flavor of roasted Maine sea scallops. You can substitute green or brown lentils in this recipe by doubling their cooking time. —RON

Dill and Orange Peel Scented Sea Scallops
Beluga Lentil Casserole
SERVES 4

DILL ORANGE PEEL CRUST
1 cup panko bread crumbs
½ tablespoon dried orange peel
2 tablespoons dried parsley
½ tablespoon dried dill
⅛ teaspoon sea salt
1 tablespoon extra-virgin olive oil

Preheat oven to 250°F. Spread bread crumbs onto cookie sheet. Toast 20 minutes or until golden brown. Transfer to mixing bowl. Add orange peel, parsley, dill, and salt to coffee grinder. Process until fine powder. Add to bread crumbs. Toss with olive oil.

SCALLOPS
8 large sea scallops, size U-10, tendon removed
to taste sea salt
to taste ground black pepper
2 tablespoons grapeseed oil
2 teaspoons extra-virgin olive oil

Preheat oven to 375°F. Season scallops on both sides with salt and pepper. Add grapeseed oil to large cast-iron or nonstick skillet over high heat until very hot. Add scallops, spaced evenly in pan. Sear 30 seconds on each side to golden brown. Place 2 scallops atop lentils in each casserole dish. Sprinkle seasoned panko crust generously atop each scallop. Bake 5 minutes or until just warm in the center. Drizzle with olive oil.

BELUGA LENTIL CASSEROLE
2 tablespoons olive oil
½ cup diced red onion
½ cup finely diced carrots
½ cup finely diced celery
4 cloves garlic, chopped
2 bay leaves
to taste sea salt
to taste ground black pepper
2 tablespoons balsamic vinegar
2 cups chicken stock
1 cup black beluga lentils
2 sage leaves

Add olive oil to saucepan over medium heat. Add onion, carrots, celery, garlic, and bay leaves. Season with salt and pepper. Cook 2 minutes, stirring often. Add balsamic vinegar and chicken stock. Bring to a boil. Add lentils and sage. Reduce heat. Simmer uncovered 15 minutes or until tender. Adjust seasoning. Divide among four casserole dishes. Set aside.

Western Australia's Abrolhos Islands, located in the Indian Ocean and surrounded by coral reef communities, are one of the highest latitude reef systems in the world. Saucer scallops, also known as moon scallops in Asia, are found in deep water on the sandy ocean floor, in sheltered areas of the island. Their shape is almost round, and their smooth, flat-top shell is adorned with reddish-brown concentric circles. At fish markets around Australia, saucer scallops are generally sold on the half shell. The key to success of any *crudo* ("uncooked") is the quality of the ingredients. The firm flesh of scallops at the peak of freshness is a way to highlight its flavor profile! This scallop crudo takes minutes to assemble and can be made anywhere in the world where live scallops are harvested. —BERNARD

Abrolhos Island Diver Scallops Crudo
Sesame Brittle
SERVES 4

SESAME BRITTLE
2 tablespoons white sesame seeds
2 tablespoons black sesame seeds
½ teaspoon ground cumin
1 teaspoon smoked paprika
½ cup (1 stick) unsalted butter
1 cup light corn syrup
2 tablespoons miso paste
1 tablespoon roasted sesame oil
½ cup sifted all-purpose flour

Heat oven to 350°F. Combine sesame seeds, cumin, and paprika in a small bowl. Add butter and corn syrup to small saucepan over low heat. Melt. Do not boil. Set aside. Add miso and sesame oil, stirring constantly. Fold in flour until well combined. Fold in sesame mixture. Drop 1 teaspoon batter at 5-inch intervals on a baking sheet lined with a silicone baking mat. Bake 5–6 minutes or until edges of brittle are lightly brown. Let cool completely. Transfer to wire rack.

SCALLOP
¾ pound diver sea scallops, tendon removed
2 tablespoons finely chopped shallots
2 tablespoons extra-virgin olive oil
2 tablespoons lemon juice
1 tangerine, juiced, zested
2 tablespoons chopped parsley
⅓ cup seeded, diced Roma or plum tomatoes
1 hot red chile pepper, seeded, veins removed, thinly diced
to taste sea salt
to taste ground black pepper

Finely dice scallops. Place in chilled container. Gently whisk shallots, olive oil, lemon juice, and tangerine juice and zest together in small bowl. Combine with scallop. Fold in parsley, tomatoes, and chile. Season with sea salt and ground black pepper. Transfer to serving dishes. Garnish with sesame brittle.

The harvest of coquilles St. Jacques in the three main Côtes d'Armor fishing ports is highly regulated to two days a week for forty-five minutes each day. To protect sustainability, the season halts prior to the development of the roe in order to ensure reproduction. During the season the scallops are bundled up in burlap sacks, dipped in ocean water, and sent to the local fish markets. Cooking scallops in butter and *fleur de sel* is the classic approach in Brittany, as it caramelizes the natural sugar in the scallops. Cauliflower puree and truffle oil bring a delicate balance to the crown jewels of Brittany. —BERNARD

Coquilles St. Jacques Île d'Ouessant

Cauliflower Puree, Truffle Oil

SERVES 4

CAULIFLOWER PUREE

1 small head cauliflower
(about 1½ pounds)
1 cup heavy cream
to taste sea salt
to taste ground white pepper
¼ teaspoon lemon zest

Trim cauliflower leaves. Cut florets off inner stalk. Rinse florets under cold water. Pat dry. Add cauliflower, cream, and salt and pepper to saucepan over medium heat. Cover. Bring to low simmer. Cook until cauliflower is very soft, about 20 minutes. Transfer cauliflower mixture to blender. Add lemon zest. Process until smooth. Season with additional salt and pepper.

SCALLOPS

8 large sea scallops, size U-10, tendon removed
to taste ground black pepper
3 tablespoons unsalted butter
1 teaspoon chopped thyme leaves
to taste fleur de sel

Season scallops on both sides with pepper. Melt butter in large skillet over high heat until foamy and lightly brown. Add scallops, spaced evenly in pan. Cook 1 minute. Turn over. Sprinkle with thyme. Cook 1 more minute, or until slightly underdone, spooning butter over scallops as they cook. Sprinkle scallops with fleur de sel.

PRESENTATION

1 teaspoon black truffle oil
¼ cup watercress leaves
4 sprigs chives

Spoon Cauliflower Puree in center of warm serving plate. Place Scallops atop. Drizzle with truffle oil. Garnish with watercress leaves and chives.

A strong winter storm sweeps through the Mituo Nanliao fishing port. At dawn the winds calm down. A group of children flies kites above a fleet of colorful fishing boats that bob in the agitated harbor. Fishermen trade their catches with local villagers while visitors browse the seafood restaurants along the wooden trail. My friend Huang orders the house specialties: hot-coal-grilled shrimp skewers and steamed scallops on a bed of fried-egg tofu. A charismatic gray-haired woman tends the cast-iron wok, cooking handfuls of tiny scallops, caramelized to perfection. She hands me a bowl . . . tastes like candy! —BERNARD

Plum Miso Candied Scallops
Green Tea Noodles
SERVES 4

NOODLES

¼ **pound** snap peas

8 large shiitake mushrooms, stemmed

8 ounces dry green tea noodles

⅓ **cup** finely diced yellow bell pepper

¼ **cup** sliced scallions on the bias, white part only

3 red radishes, thinly sliced

1 tablespoon julienned mint leaves

2 tablespoons apple cider vinegar

2 tablespoons plum wine

1 tablespoon soy sauce

1 tablespoon sesame oil

1 lemon, zested

SCALLOPS

2 tablespoons red miso

¼ **cup** plum wine

1 tablespoon seasoned rice vinegar

1 tablespoon sesame oil

2 teaspoons soy sauce

2 teaspoons grated ginger

1 teaspoon minced garlic

⅛ **teaspoon** shichimi togarashi pepper

1 pound bay scallops

1 tablespoon grapeseed oil

2 teaspoons toasted sesame seeds

Add 2 quarts cold water to large sauce pot over medium-high heat. Bring to rolling boil. Add snap peas and shiitake mushrooms. Cook 1 minute. Transfer peas to ice bath and shiitakes to plate. Cut peas in half on bias. Slice shiitake mushrooms. Add noodles to boiling water. Cook 5 minutes or until al dente. Drain in colander. Rinse thoroughly under cold running water. Drain. Transfer to mixing bowl. Toss with remaining ingredients. Set aside.

Whisk miso, plum wine, vinegar, sesame oil, soy sauce, ginger, garlic, and togarashi in a mixing bowl. Add scallops. Toss to coat. Marinate 30 minutes. Drain marinade. Pat scallops dry with paper towel. Heat oil in large nonstick skillet over high heat. Add scallops. Saute 2 minutes, or until scallops are caramelized and slightly underdone. Toss with noodles. Sprinkle with sesame seeds.

Throughout history people have observed that a scallop inside its shell resembles the setting sun. To propagate this ancient notion, we designed this dish, whose colors, flavors, and presentation pay tribute to that nightly miracle that all the world can see—sunset. In New Zealand's Bay of Plenty, as the sun disappears behind the scallop-laden waters, the sky turns deep red like a blood orange. The *dukkah,* a blend of nuts and seeds, is toasty, the scallop buttery, and the combination yummy. —RON

Hazelnut Dukkah Spiced Diver Scallops
Blood Orange Reduction
SERVES 4

HAZELNUT DUKKAH SPICE

¾ **cup** hazelnuts, skin removed
¼ **cup** sesame seeds
1 teaspoon coriander seeds
1 teaspoon cumin seeds
½ **teaspoon** fennel seeds
½ **teaspoon** fleur de sel
¼ **teaspoon** black pepper
¼ **teaspoon** paprika
pinch of cayenne pepper

Preheat oven to 350°F. Place hazelnuts and sesame seeds in single layer on baking sheet. Roast in oven 10 minutes. Transfer to food processor with remaining ingredients. Pulse until mixture is crumbly. Set aside.

DIVER SCALLOPS

12 size U-10 diver scallops
to taste sea salt
to taste ground black pepper
2 tablespoons olive oil
2 tablespoons butter

Preheat oven to 375°F. Season scallops on both sides with salt and pepper. Add 1 tablespoon each olive oil and butter to large skillet over medium-high heat until butter is foamy and lightly browned. Add 6 scallops, spaced evenly in pan. Sear 30 seconds on each side until golden brown. Transfer to baking sheet. Repeat process with remaining ingredients. Sprinkle dukkah generously atop each scallop. Bake 5 minutes or until just warm in the center.

BLOOD ORANGE REDUCTION

¼ **cup** sherry vinegar
2 cups blood orange juice
½ **cup** granulated sugar
1 teaspoon Spanish paprika
to taste sea salt
to taste ground black pepper

Add all ingredients (except salt and pepper) to small saucepan over medium heat. Bring to simmer. Reduce to syrupy consistency; about ¾ cup liquid remains. Season with salt and pepper. Cool. Transfer to squeeze bottle. Squeeze reduction onto warm serving plates in zigzag design. Place scallops atop.

Clams

Clams have been a tasty seafood treat for the world since prehistoric times and are currently being farmed worldwide.

Most clams inhabit shallow waters, where they are protected from wave action by the surrounding bottom.

True clams are bivalves with equal shells that are opened and closed by two abductor muscles situated at opposite ends of the shell.

Clams have a powerful, muscular, burrowing foot that they use both to move and stay put.

Two main types of clams exist—hard-shell clams and soft-shell clams. Hard-shell clams are marketed according to their size, from smallest to largest: countnecks, littlenecks, topnecks, cherrystones, and quahogs.

In the Wild

Hard-shell clams are found in saltier waters than soft-shell clams, at depths up to 60 feet. Here are our favorites:

Quahog Clams

Also called chowder clams

Found from the Arctic Ocean to the Bay of Biscay off France, and in North America from Newfoundland to North Carolina

Large and tough; suitable for chopping into soups and chowders

Manila Clams

Also called Venus clam and steamer clam

Native to Japan, live intertidal zone of the United States , China, Korea, and Japan

Small and tender; great for steaming

Pismo Clams

Native of the eastern Pacific and the coastline city of Pismo Beach, California

Largest Pacific coast clam

Great for making fried clams

Sunray Venus Clams

Found from North Carolina to Florida and as far south as Brazil

Beautiful shells turn pink when cooked

Small, tender meat

Cherrystone Clams

Native to Cherrystone Creek, Virginia

Delectable simply steamed or in pasta and clam sauce

Littleneck Clams
Native to Littleneck Bay, Long Island, New York

Smaller clam that is good for steaming in wine and butter

Butter Clams
Native to the Puget Sound area

Known as "moneyshells" by the native American Indians

Large clam with a butter-colored shell

Considered to be the best chowder clam

Cockles
Heart-shaped shells with radiating ribs

From northern Europe, Barents Sea, Norway, Korea, Malaysia, and as far south as Senegal

Tiny clams perfect for sautéing

Soft-Shell Clams
Also called sand gapers or longnecks

Introduced to California waters from the Atlantic Ocean around 1870 and gradually spread north to British Columbia

Called *manninose* by northeastern American Indians

Pacific Geoducks
Native to Washington State

Giant clam with an immense edible siphon that is often eaten as sashimi

Incredible soft, chewy texture and cucumber flavor

Razor Clams
Named after their long narrow shape

Found in North America, Canada, Belgium, the Netherlands, France, Germany, Britain, and Denmark

In the Kitchen
Clams are awesome in both Eastern- and Western-style cooking.

Use smaller clams for steaming and sautéing or any preparation where you will eat the clam meat whole. Larger clams are best for chopping in fritters, chowders, and sauces.

Clams need very little cooking and are ready virtually as soon as the shell opens. When cooking a large batch, it's best to remove the clams individually from the pan as each one opens, so as not to overcook them.

To purge live clams of sand, place them in a solution of cool water and sea salt and/or cornmeal for several hours or overnight in a cool part of the house (if you refrigerate them they'll close up and won't "spit out" the sand).

Valuable Nutrients from Clams

- Copper: for healthy metabolism and organ function

- Iron: vital to the production of energy and a healthy immune system

- Manganese: powerful antioxidant essential to healthy bones

- Potassium: for a healthy heart and kidneys, reduces stress

- Riboflavin: for healthy skin and healing

- Selenium: antioxidant, prevents arthritis

- Vitamin B_{12}: promotes healthy blood cells, prevents anemia, eases migraines

- Zinc: controls acne, boosts immune system

Fun Facts

The heaviest clam ever found weighed a hefty 750 pounds. It was pulled from the waters of Japan in 1956.

The oldest clam ever found was 570 years old—and it was still alive! Unfortunately the test that determined the clam's age also killed it.

In Great Britain, cockles, a small gem of a clam, were once a cheap and healthy snack for the masses. They were carted through the markets in wheelbarrows by hawkers calling out melodically, "Cockles and mussels alive-o" to passersby.

The cuisine of Malaysia reflects the multicultural layers of its country, bringing multiple ethnic ingredients, styles, and flavors together! Malay food is best characterized by its extensive use of spices and stir-frying method. *Kam heong* derives from the Cantonese dialect for "golden fragrance," a very popular Malaysian stir-fry combination of Chinese, Malay, and Indian ingredients renowned for the aromatics released during cooking. The explosion of flavors makes this seafood dish highly addictive. Bring a taste of Malaysia to your own kitchen by stir-frying your favorite ingredients with kam heong—amazingly delicious with octopus, prawns, mussels, and even chicken or eggplant. —BERNARD

Kam Heong Spicy Clams

Golden Fragrance Sauce

SERVES 4

GOLDEN FRAGRANCE SAUCE

1 cup diced mango

2 tablespoons premium oyster sauce

1 tablespoon miso paste

1½ teaspoons curry powder

½ teaspoon ground turmeric

Whisk all ingredients together in small mixing bowl. Set aside.

CLAMS

⅓ cup sea salt

¼ cup cornmeal

4 pounds manila clams, cleaned

3 tablespoons light sesame oil

1 cup sliced shallots, cut crosswise ⅛ inch

2 tablespoons chopped ginger

4 cloves garlic, thinly sliced

4 Kaffir lime leaves

2 bird's-eye chiles, seeded, chopped

Add 1 gallon cold water to large pot. Stir in salt and cornmeal. Add clams. Soak 45 minutes to purge sand. Remove clams from water. Transfer to colander. Drain. Add oil to wok over medium-high heat. Add shallots, ginger, garlic, and Kaffir lime leaves. Stir-fry 1 minute. Add clams. Cover wok. Cook 2 minutes. Stir in chiles and Golden Fragrance Sauce. Cover. Cook 3 minutes or until clams open. Transfer to serving bowl.

On the pink granite coastline of my native Brittany, the island of Bréhat was my childhood playground. Every summer my family reunited during the highest tides of the year to gather local sea creatures. Everyone had a mission. Uncle Jean Claude and my sisters collected mussels, sea snails, and crab. Uncle Bernard, my father, and I dug in the exposed seabed and other sandy strands, armed with pitchforks and buckets in search of clams, cockles, and *praire,* also called Venus clams. I have fond memories of my mother simmering shallots and garlic in her large cast-iron pot, awaiting our steamers! —BERNARD

Brittany Cockles Marinière

Parsnips, White Wine, Garlic

SERVES 6 FAMILY STYLE

COCKLES

2 tablespoons (¼ stick) unsalted butter

¼ **cup** chopped shallots

½ **teaspoon** fennel seeds

½ **cup** finely diced celery root

1 cup finely diced parsnips

3 cloves garlic, minced

1 bay leaf

4 sprigs fresh thyme

to taste sea salt

to taste ground black pepper

1 cup white wine

5 pounds cockles

½ **cup** crème fraîche

¼ **cup** brandy

¼ **cup** chopped flat-leaf parsley

1 (1-pound) loaf country bread,
    cut into 1-inch-thick slices, grilled

Add butter to dutch oven over medium heat. Add shallots, fennel seeds, celery root, parsnips, garlic, bay leaf, and thyme. Season with salt and pepper. Cook 3 minutes without browning, stirring often. Add wine and cockles. Cover. Cook 2 minutes or until liquid starts to boil. Uncover. Using slotted spoon, rotate cockles from bottom to top to ensure even cooking. Add crème fraîche and brandy. Cover. Cook additional 5 minutes or until shells open. Remove lid. Discard any cockles that do not open. Sprinkle with parsley. Transfer to large serving bowl. Serve family style with basket of warm grilled country bread.

In fourteenth-century Portugal, in the Algarve region, Olhao started as a small settlement of fishermen who lived in huts made from local straw and reeds. Three hundred years later their little place on earth grew important enough to need fortification and defense from pirates. The sea gives, but the sea also brings those who take away. Happily, the city thrived and grew, all the time relying on fishing as the main industry. Today Olhao's visitors are the welcome kind. You can stroll by the waterfront, through the cool gardens, and end up at an outside cafe dining on stunningly fresh clams. —RON

Pork and Clam Stew

Linguiça, Root Vegetables

SERVES 4

MARINADE

2 teaspoons smoked paprika
1 orange, zested, juiced
4 garlic cloves, minced
2 tablespoons olive oil
2 pounds boneless pork shoulder, fat trimmed

Combine paprika, orange zest and juice, garlic, and olive oil in large mixing bowl. Cut pork into 1-inch cubes. Add to marinade. Toss to coat. Cover. Refrigerate 24 hours.

STEW

¼ **pound** smoked bacon, cut into 1-inch pieces
2 tablespoons flour
2 cups Madeira wine
1 cup chicken stock
1 cup chopped tomatoes
1 cup sliced carrots
1 cup sliced red onion
1 pound new red potatoes, quartered
2 pounds manila clams, cleaned
6 ounces hot linguiça sausage, sliced ⅛-inch thick
1 lemon, halved
2 tablespoons chopped flat-leaf parsley

Add bacon to large dutch oven over medium heat. Cook until lightly browned and bacon fat is rendered. Transfer bacon to paper towel–lined plate. Raise heat to high. Add marinated pork to dutch oven. Sear on all sides until golden brown. Dust with flour. Cook 1 minute, stirring constantly. Add Madeira. Bring to simmer. Add chicken stock, tomatoes, carrots, onions, potatoes, and reserved bacon. Return to simmer. Cover. Cook 1 hour or until tender. Add linguiça. Top with clams. Cover. Cook 3 minutes or until clams open. Remove cover. Squeeze lemon juice atop. Sprinkle with parsley.

Chowder comes from the French word *chaudière,* a large, black, three-legged kettle normally associated with long stewing over an open flame. On the coastal villages of the English Channel, villagers waited shoreside with their large chaudières, ready to accept a penance from each fisherman upon return to steady land. The chaudière was then fired up, vegetables and seasonings added, and the stew prepared as a communal celebration. In America, *chaudière* became "chowder." While the natives ate clams like candy, discarding the empty shells into massive piles, the pilgrims only fed them to their hogs. But soon clams were added to chowder, as well as salt pork, and ship's biscuits were sprinkled on top. In this version, we use popped corn instead of biscuits in honor of the Native Americans' influence. Jerusalem artichokes, or sunchokes, were cultivated by the same Native Americans who loved clams. —RON

Jerusalem Artichoke Clam Chowder
Celery Salt Popped Corn
SERVES 4

CHOWDER

1 cup white wine
2 bay leaves
1 teaspoon black peppercorns
4 pounds littleneck clams, scrubbed, rinsed
1 tablespoon unsalted butter
4 strips bacon, chopped
3 tablespoons all-purpose flour
1 cup diced celery
1 cup sliced leek, white part only
1 tablespoon chopped garlic
⅓ **cup** sherry wine
1 cup diced, peeled Jerusalem artichokes
1 cup fresh corn kernels
1 cup vegetable stock
1 cup heavy cream
to taste sea salt
to taste ground black pepper
1 tablespoon chopped fresh parsley

Add wine, bay leaves, and black peppercorns to large pot over high heat. Cover. Bring to boil. Add clams. Cover. Cook 3 minutes without opening the lid. Then rotate clams from bottom to top using slotted spoon so they cook evenly. Cook additional 3 minutes. Using tongs, transfer clams to cookie sheet as they open. Discard all unopened clams. Strain broth through fine sieve. Set aside. Remove clam meat from shell. Coarsely chop. Refrigerate clams until needed. Add butter and bacon to large saucepan over medium heat. Cook until bacon fat is rendered. Add flour. Cook 1 minute, stirring constantly. Add celery, leeks, and garlic. Cook 3 minutes without browning, stirring often. Add sherry, Jerusalem artichokes, and 1 cup reserved clam broth. Bring to simmer. Add corn, vegetable stock, and cream. Return to low simmer. Cover. Cook 15 minutes. Fold in clams. Season with salt and pepper. Ladle soup into warm bowls. Garnish with popped corn and parsley.

CELERY SALT POPPED CORN

1 tablespoon corn oil
¼ **cup** popcorn kernels
2 tablespoons (¼ stick) melted unsalted butter
¼ **teaspoon** celery salt
to taste ground black pepper

Add oil and popcorn kernels to heavy-bottomed pot over medium heat. Cover. Cook, shaking pot often, until popping slows down. Turn off heat. Let sit 30 seconds. Uncover. Toss with butter, celery salt, and black pepper.

Oysters

Since antiquity, oysters have been a delicacy reserved for special celebrations. These small mollusks are perpetually surrounded by myths and magic. Theirs is a tale of exclusivity, of the fresh, pure taste of the sea, of lovers, and of potency. Anecdotes confirm the claim that oysters are a coveted aphrodisiac. Casanova allegedly ate fifty oysters every day, served ungarnished—au naturel you might say—by some dazzling beauty. Oysters take us on a metaphoric and literal journey to the sea and shore. But to benefit from their fragile environment, we must protect it.

In the early years of the United States, the "Oyster Line" brought oysters from the Atlantic westward via stagecoach. It was a lifeline to those who ventured into the wild frontier in search of new land, leaving everything behind, except their unquenchable thirst for the briny mineral flavors of the sea.

In the Wild

Nowadays oysters are farmed all over the world. Notable producers are France, England, Norway, Japan, and both coasts of the United States. Most oysters are named after the areas in which they are found. European oysters are grown on the seafloor, which makes for a rugged life but results in a hardy oyster. Oysters grown in suspended trays are the prima donnas of oysters, protected from predators, mud, sand, and silt. These oysters have brittle shells, tender meat, and a clean sweet flavor. One type of suspended-tray oyster, the highly coveted French Belon, only comes from the Belon River estuary of Brittany, in northern France. Apart from their cultivation method, salinity, minerality, and nutrient variations in the water influence an oyster's flavor profile. Besides the Belons, these are our favorite oysters:

Grassy Bar
From Morro Bay, California

Rich briny flavor and plump, juicy meat

Blue Point
Found near the town of Blue Point, Long Island, United States

Renowned Eastern oyster with distinctive salty flavor and meaty texture

Coromandel
Found in the Coromandel Peninsula, New Zealand

Brinier and crispier flavor than most Pacific oysters, with some citrus aroma

Fanny Bay

Found in Baynes Sound, British Columbia, Canada

Salty and sweet with cucumber flavors

Kumamoto

Originally from Japan, now farmed in Humboldt Bay, California, United States

Take several years to reach their small size

Deep cupped with salty-sweet flavor

Malpeque

Found in Malpeque Bay, Prince Edward Island, Canada

Considered one of the world's finest

Still harvested by traditional hand rakes

In the Kitchen

Like a sommelier of seafood, an oyster aficionado can often determine what region an oyster came from just by its flavor profile and texture.

Raw oysters should be eaten only by healthy individuals, but cooking oysters is a great option, too. They can be roasted, steamed, chowdered, fried, smoked, stewed, baked, stuffed, broiled, marinated, poached, and sautéed.

Purists insist on eating raw oysters without accoutrements, allowing their intrinsic, complex flavors to come through.

The flavor of oysters varies greatly among varieties and regions: sweet, salty, earthy, minerally, with notes of melon, green apple, citrus, or cucumber. The texture is soft and fleshy but crisp on the palate.

Valuable Nutrients from Oysters

- Calcium: maintains strong bones, prevents colon cancer
- Copper: for healthy metabolism and organ function
- Iron: vital to the production of energy and a healthy immune system
- Omega-3 fatty acids: prevent cardiovascular disease
- Vitamin A: for healthy eyes and vision
- Vitamin C: powerful antioxidant, prevents high blood pressure and cataracts
- Vitamin D: increases absorption of calcium and phosphorus, promotes healthy cell function
- Zinc: controls acne, boosts immune system

Fun Facts

Americans eat over 100 million pounds of oysters in a year. It may sound like a lot, but that's only ⅓ pound per person per year.

The myth that oysters increase sexual potency and keep you "up" all night has a true foundation: Eating oysters aids in the production of testosterone and estrogen.

Oysters are said to be of higher quality in months that have an R in their name. This is because the colder water of these nonsummer months produces a fattier, richer meat.

Oysters gather nutrients by filtering an amazing amount of ocean water—up to 50 gallons per oyster per day!

President Abraham Lincoln was an oyster lover—honestly!

Tempura is a Japanese cooking method where ingredients are battered lightly then deep-fried until golden and crisp. The Japanese perfected this method but did not create it. Portuguese missionaries who were quite fond of frying, especially shrimp, introduced this technique to Japanese culture. Even though the Portuguese called this *tempero,* meaning "spice mixture," the Japanese adopted it as a general term for frying and changed the pronunciation to "tempura." It did take the Japanese a couple hundred years to really warm up to the idea of frying, which previously was a very rare part of their culinary heritage. But by the 1800s restaurants and street carts specialized in the preparation, and now most of the world is familiar with tempura. Japanese oysters are plump and called "milk of the sea" due to the richness of their nutrients. Drying off the oysters prior to dipping allows the batter to stick better. —RON

Crispy Oysters Tempura
Tangerine Ponzu
SERVES 4

TANGERINE PONZU
1 cup strained tangerine juice
¼ cup honey
2 tablespoons soy sauce
1 teaspoon grated ginger
⅛ teaspoon shichimi togarashi pepper

Combine all ingredients in mixing bowl.

TEMPURA BATTER
½ cup all-purpose flour
½ cup rice flour
1 teaspoon baking soda
1 teaspoon baking powder
1 teaspoon granulated sugar
½ teaspoon sea salt
1 large egg
¾ cup sake wine
1 tangerine, zested, juiced

Sift flours, baking soda, baking powder, sugar, and salt into mixing bowl. In separate bowl, combine egg and sake. Add to flour mixture. Whisk until smooth. Stir in remaining ingredients. Set aside.

OYSTERS
1 quart canola oil
24 large oysters
1 cup sifted all-purpose flour
¼ cup nori flakes
1 teaspoon black sesame seeds
1 chile pepper, seeded, sliced paper-thin
to taste sea salt

Heat oil in deep fryer or large heavy-bottomed pot to 375°F. Shuck oysters. Discard shell fragments from meat. Detach oyster from shell. Transfer to paper towel–lined plate. Combine flour and nori flakes in baking dish. Dip in Tempura Batter. Dredge oysters in flour mixture. Deep-fry 6 oysters at a time, about 30 seconds or until golden brown. Drain on paper towel–lined plate. Transfer oysters to warm serving platter. Sprinkle with sesame seeds, chile pepper, and sea salt. Serve with Tangerine Ponzu.

The oyster cocktail was invented by a customer in a San Francisco restaurant around 1860. Returning from the minefields with pockets full of gold, he ordered whiskey and some oysters with tomato and horseradish. For some unknown reason, the chap mixed it all together, creating the first oyster shooter. Within weeks it was all the rage. Oyster shooters are popular because they're breathtakingly simple to prepare. We have created a tasting of oysters that reflects our travels around the world, from frigid Scandinavia to steamy South America. As a rule, always shuck oysters shortly before serving. The colder the oyster, the safer and the easier to shuck it is. —BERNARD

Drunken Oysters

Vodka Pomegranate, Pisco Lime, Aquavit Apple

EACH RECIPE MAKES 12 SHOOTERS

VODKA POMEGRANATE

12 oysters
½ **cup** vodka
¼ **cup** pomegranate juice
2 tablespoons honey
1 tablespoon finely minced shallots
1 teaspoon finely chopped tarragon
pinch cayenne pepper

Shuck oysters, straining their seawater into a mixing bowl. Discard all shell fragments. Detach oyster from shell. Transfer each oyster to one shot glass. Refrigerate until needed. Combine remaining ingredients with seawater in mixing bowl. Refrigerate 1 hour. Divide vodka mixture among shot glasses.

PISCO LIME

12 oysters
½ **cup** pisco
¼ **cup** fresh-squeezed lime juice
2 tablespoons granulated sugar
1 tablespoon finely chopped mint
2 tablespoons peeled, seeded, finely diced cucumber
2 tablespoons peeled, seeded, finely diced mango

Shuck oysters, straining their seawater into a mixing bowl. Discard all shell fragments. Detach oyster from shell. Transfer each oyster to one shot glass. Refrigerate until needed. Combine remaining ingredients with seawater in mixing bowl. Refrigerate 1 hour. Divide pisco mixture among shot glasses.

AQUAVIT APPLE

12 oysters
½ **cup** aquavit
¼ **cup** apple juice
2 tablespoons lemon juice
¼ **cup** finely diced green apple
1 tablespoon finely chopped cilantro
Pinch ground black pepper

Shuck oysters, straining their seawater into a mixing bowl. Discard all shell fragments. Detach oyster from shell. Transfer each oyster to one shot glass. Refrigerate until needed. Combine remaining ingredients with seawater in mixing bowl. Refrigerate 1 hour. Divide aquavit mixture among shot glasses.

This is our Southern California take on the famous New Orleans dish, oysters Rockefeller. Created in 1899, they were named after America's wealthiest man, John D. Rockefeller, a title that foreshadows the richness of the sauce. Antoine's restaurant in New Orleans has been serving the original version of this dish since its invention by Antoine's son, Jules. It is said that the dish has never been successfully replicated outside the walls of Antoine's, but you can have fun with new versions, such as this West Coast twist that we playfully call Rockin' Stellar Oysters. In our version, we whip the rich sauce to lighten it and stud it with spicy mustard seeds. —RON

Rockin' Stellar Oysters
Mustard Seed Cream
SERVES 4

OYSTERS
24 large oysters
3 tablespoons unsalted butter
⅓ cup finely chopped shallots
3 cloves garlic, chopped
2 cups finely chopped oyster mushrooms
½ cup sherry wine
to taste sea salt
to taste ground black pepper
3 cups packed stemmed, chopped swiss chard leaves
½ cup bread crumbs
½ cup grated gruyère cheese
1 tablespoon extra-virgin olive oil
¼ cup almond meal
pinch freshly ground nutmeg

Preheat oven to 375°F. Shuck oysters, discarding top shell and any shell fragments. Detach oyster but leave in shells. Refrigerate until needed. Melt butter in skillet over medium heat. Cook shallots and garlic until translucent. Add mushrooms. Cook 2 minutes, stirring often. Add sherry. Cook until all liquid evaporates. Season with salt and pepper. Fold in swiss chard. Cook until wilted. Combine bread crumbs, gruyère cheese, olive oil, almond meal, and nutmeg in mixing bowl. Place generous mound of mushroom mixture on each oyster. Sprinkle with bread crumb mixture. Transfer to baking sheets. Bake 8 minutes or until center is warm.

MUSTARD SEED CREAM
¾ cup crème fraîche
1 tablespoon sherry wine vinegar
1 lemon, zested
2 tablespoons chopped chives
2 teaspoons brown mustard seeds
to taste sea salt
to taste ground white pepper

Add crème fraîche, vinegar, and lemon zest to chilled large mixing bowl. Whisk until soft peaks form. Fold in remaining ingredients. Season with salt and pepper. Transfer to four individual serving dishes.

PRESENTATION
2 cups rock salt

Divide rock salt among four serving plates. Place 6 oysters atop. Serve with Mustard Seed Cream.

The ancient coastal city of Taranto is located on the Salentina Peninsula in Puglia (the region that forms part of the heel of Italy's boot), overlooking the bay, where three sides of land face inward on the Mar Grande, the Mar Piccolo, and the Ionian Sea. Because of its location and its fishing center, Taranto provides some of the country's best seafood. At Piazza Fontana, the small fishing port sells sea urchin, octopus, bream, mussels, and oysters farmed in the Mar Piccolo. Taranto's signature oyster preparation is *ostriche tarantine in tiella,* simply baked in the shell with bread crumbs, parsley, and olive oil. In our version we jazz it up by adding flavors of prosciutto, fennel, and chile. As the locals would say, "Se non amate la vita, non si può godere di un ostrica!"—"If you don't love life, you can't enjoy an oyster!" —BERNARD

Prosciutto Wrapped Oysters

Fennel Chile Butter

SERVES 4

¼ **cup** finely diced shallots

½ **cup** finely diced fennel

½ **cup** finely diced zucchini, green part only

¼ **teaspoon** chile flakes

½ **teaspoon** orange zest

2 **teaspoons** chopped oregano leaves

¾ **cup** (1½ sticks) unsalted butter, room temperature

to taste sea salt

to taste ground white pepper

24 oysters

12 **paper-thin slices** prosciutto ham

¼ **cup** chopped, toasted Marcona almonds

2 **ounces** Parmesan cheese

Preheat oven to 375°F. Combine shallots, fennel, zucchini, chile flakes, orange zest, oregano, and butter in mixing bowl. Season with salt and pepper. Mix until mixture forms a ball. Set aside. Shuck oysters, discarding top shell. Discard shell fragments from meat. Detach oyster from shell. Cut prosciutto slices in half lengthwise. Wrap each oyster in prosciutto. Return to shell. Transfer oysters to baking sheet. Divide butter mixture between oysters, about 2 tablespoons per oyster. Bake 5 minutes or until hot in center. Sprinkle with almonds. Shave Parmesan atop oysters.

Whether you spell it Szechuan or Sichuan, this central Chinese province, also known as "the Land of Abundance," has a rich culinary culture and history of spicy cuisine, highlighted by its own secret spice blend. Native to northern China, the Szechuan pepper—not related to black pepper—displays citrus characteristics that create a subtle tingling and numbing effect on the tongue. In 2011 the United Nations Educational, Scientific, and Cultural Organization (UNESCO) named the Szechuan city of Chengdu "a city of gastronomy" for its sophisticated cuisine. Szechuan black bean sauce, made from fermented black beans and garlic, is a key ingredient in many Szechuan dishes and the perfect foundation for your stir-fried oysters. —BERNARD

Oyster Sugar Pea Stir-Fry
Szechuan Black Bean Sauce
SERVES 4

SZECHUAN BLACK BEAN SAUCE

¼ **cup** sesame oil

1 **cup** minced red onion

6 **cloves** garlic, minced

¼ **cup** julienned ginger

1 **teaspoon** crushed Szechuan peppercorns

4 **teaspoons** honey

3 **tablespoons** soy sauce

2 **tablespoons** red wine vinegar

½ **cup** sake wine

6 **tablespoons** fermented black bean sauce

½ **cup** chopped cilantro

2 scallions, finely sliced on bias

Add oil to small saucepan over medium heat. Add onion, garlic, and ginger. Cook 1 minute without browning, stirring often. Add peppercorns, honey, soy sauce, vinegar, and wine. Bring to simmer. Stir in black bean sauce. Cook 1 minute. Remove from heat. Stir in cilantro and scallions. Set aside.

STIR-FRY

24 large oysters

2 **tablespoons** peanut oil

½ **cup** quartered water chestnuts

1 **cup** quartered button mushrooms

1 **cup** sugar snap peas, trimmed, cut in half on bias

½ **cup** diced red bell pepper

1 **tablespoon** toasted sesame seeds

¼ **cup** chopped, toasted peanuts

Shuck oysters, straining their seawater into a mixing bowl. Discard all shell fragments. Detach oyster from shell. Transfer oysters to small dish. Refrigerate.

Add peanut oil to large skillet over medium-high heat. Add water chestnuts, mushrooms, snap peas, and bell peppers. Stir-fry 2 minutes. Reduce heat to low. Stir in Black Bean Sauce and oysters. Raise heat to high. Cover. Cook 30 seconds or until oysters are as done as you like them. Transfer to serving bowl. Garnish with sesame seeds and peanuts.

Mussels

Cultivated mussels have been around for almost nine hundred years, though wild mussels are one of the earth's oldest animal species. Mussels are found all over the world and are especially popular in European countries, particularly France and Italy. Spain is currently the leading producer of cultivated mussels. In North America, wild mussels have been harvested since the early 1900s. Suspended cultivation of blue mussels began in Washington State in the 1970s and became very successful. In this method the mussels are hanging from ropes as opposed to sitting on the ocean floor.

Male mussels are light tan to cream-colored, while females are orange.

In a moist, cool environment, mussels can live out of water up to twelve days by gaping open and breathing. To see if a gaping mussel is alive, try tapping the shell lightly; if the shell starts to close, the mussel is still alive.

Mussels use their "beards" (the fibrous strands connected to the flesh) to attach themselves to reefs, poles, and rocks. Based on this practice, a cultivation technique used around the world was inadvertently invented when a shipwrecked sailor on the coast of France stuck poles in the water to hold his fishing net. When he checked the net, he noticed mussels had attached themselves to the poles.

Of the seventeen edible types of mussels, two are the most common—blue mussels and green mussels.

In the Wild

In Australia you will find blue mussels that are almost identical to Mediterranean and North Atlantic mussels. New Zealand is the native home to the green-lipped mussel. The California mussel is indigenous to the Pacific coast of North America and has an orange flesh. They are susceptible to contamination in periods of algal bloom, a phenomenon known as red tide.

Blue Mussels

Sometimes called black mussels, these usually are bluish-black in color but can also be purple or brown.

Blue mussels account for the largest percentage of mussels sold around the world. They grow wild in clusters in intertidal waters.

Green Mussels

Also known as green-lipped mussels, these are not only native to New Zealand in the wild but also cultivated there extensively. They are larger than blue mussels with a sweeter, more delicate flavor.

In the Kitchen

On average, 30 percent of a mussel's weight is edible meat.

When cooking mussels we usually figure on 1 pound per person.

By pinching the shells together, the whole empty shell of one mussel can be used like a utensil to extract the meat of the other mussels.

Mussels should be consumed very shortly after purchase. In the meantime, store the mussels loosely with a damp towel atop, then covered with ice, allowing the melted ice to drain away.

Mussels are known as *muurugai* when prepared for sushi.

Some of our favorite ways to prepare mussels include:

- **Mussel bisque**—with crispy celery seed scented croutons

- **Chilled on half shell**—great on a summer day

- **Roasted in cast iron**—spiked with chorizo, Spanish style

- **Steamed** with wine, shallots, parsley, and butter—simple and delightful

Valuable Nutrients from Mussels

- Calcium: maintains strong bones, prevents colon cancer

- Magnesium: maintains healthy blood pressure and strong bones, relaxes nerves

- Omega-3 fatty acids: prevent cardiovascular disease

- Phosphorus: builds healthy bones and strong teeth

- Potassium: for a healthy heart and kidneys, reduces stress

- Selenium: antioxidant, prevents arthritis

- Vitamin A: for healthy eyes and vision

- Vitamin B_{12}: promotes healthy blood cells, prevents anemia, eases migraines

Fun Facts

Mussels became popular in the United States during World War II as a cheap and tasty alternative to red meat.

Said to have been around since the creation of the earth, mussels are the best source of omega-3 fatty acids in the shellfish world.

Cotija is a hard, aged cow's cheese from the town of Cotija in Michoacán, a state in central Mexico. Cotija is made two ways. *Tajo* style resembles feta and can be sliced. It has a higher percentage of milk fat and less salt. "De Montaña"(Spanish for mountain style) is dry and salty and used as a taste enhancer that accentuates flavor. Because of salt's ability to preserve, Cotija de Montaña is more likely to be exported. It is an artisan cheese produced at high altitudes from July to October, when the mountain grass is enriched by autumnal rains. The cow's diet gives the cheese its unique flavor. During handcrafting, curds are milled into smaller pieces and then pressed and aged. It crumbles willingly and, when grated on a Microplane, blankets your dish with light flakes, adding a mineral brininess that is perfect on mussels. —RON

Chilled Mussels on Half Shell

Papaya, Cotija Cheese

SERVES 4

MUSSELS

3 tablespoons olive oil
⅓ cup finely diced red onion
½ teaspoon cumin seeds
4 cloves garlic, finely diced
1 cup diced tomatoes
¼ cup orange juice
2 pounds large black mussels, debearded, scrubbed

Add oil to large pot over medium heat. Add onion, cumin seeds, and garlic. Cook 15 seconds. Add tomatoes, orange juice, and mussels. Cover. Cook 3 minutes or until liquid starts to boil. Uncover. Using slotted spoon, rotate mussels from bottom to top to ensure even cooking. Cover. Cook 3 minutes or until all shells open and mussel meat is plump. Using tongs, transfer mussels to shallow platter and refrigerate. Lower heat to medium. Reduce tomato liquid by three-fourths. Transfer to shallow bowl. Refrigerate at least 1 hour. Remove mussel meat from shells, saving shells for presentation.

PRESENTATION

1 tablespoon sherry vinegar
½ cup finely diced jicama
½ cup finely diced papaya
2 tablespoons chopped parsley
1 tablespoon finely minced, seeded jalapeño pepper
to taste sea salt
to taste ground black pepper
2 ounces Cotija cheese

Add vinegar, jicama, papaya, parsley, and jalapeño to refrigerated tomato mixture. Gently fold in mussels. Season with salt and pepper. Fill each shell with mussel mixture. Transfer to large serving platter. Grate Cotija cheese atop.

Jerez is a sherry-producing region of Spain located halfway between the coast and the mountains, as if it were the heartbeat of the Andalusian topography. And since Phoenician times, sherry has been the blood that breathes life through the veins of the elegant city. Sherry is everything. It gives the city its name, its income, its identity. Bodegas (wineries) summon you with a steady whiff of evaporating sherry carried on the dissipating breeze, Mother Earth's fair share. Streets are lined with palm trees and eateries, most serving one or more dishes *a la jerezana,* or laced with sherry. Mussels are very popular throughout Spain, and their canoe-shaped shells bring the sherry broth straight to your lips. —RON

Cast-Iron Black Mussels
Sherry Wine, Chorizo, Tomatoes
SERVES 4

2 tablespoons olive oil
¾ cup finely diced Spanish chorizo
1 cup diced onion
4 cloves garlic, thinly sliced
¼ teaspoon red chile flakes
1 teaspoon Spanish smoked paprika
1 cup sherry wine
4 pounds black mussels, debearded, scrubbed
12 cherry tomatoes, halved
to taste ground black pepper
1 valencia orange
¼ cup chopped flat-leaf parsley

Preheat oven to 400°F. Heat olive oil in large cast-iron skillet over medium heat. Add chorizo, onion, garlic, chile flakes, and paprika. Cook without browning 3 minutes. Add sherry wine. Reduce by half. Fold in mussels. Arrange tomatoes atop mussels. Transfer to oven. Cook 10 minutes. Using tongs, carefully pull mussels in bottom center of skillet to the top to ensure even cooking. Cook 5 minutes or until all shells open and meat is plump but not overcooked. Add pepper. Zest orange atop the mussels. Sprinkle with parsley.

When New Orleans was built under French rule in the 1720s, most streets were named in honor of France's royal houses and patron saints. The royal House of Bourbon gave its name to "Rue Bourbon," later renamed Bourbon Street by the Americans. The infamous street is trampled nightly by free-spirited souls who toss beads and make toasts side by side with the ghosts of indulgence. Beyond all the debauchery lies a rich history of architecture, jazz music, and Creole cuisine, garnished with wrought iron and neon signs. Turns out a quintessential American whiskey also takes its name from France's House of Bourbon—bourbon. This dish is inspired by the multinational heritage that New Orleans is famous for. —RON

Bourbon Street Steamed Mussels

Andouille, Eggplant, Okra, Baguette

SERVES 4

1 baguette
¼ **cup** extra-virgin olive oil
to taste sea salt
to taste ground black pepper
2 tablespoons (¼ stick) unsalted butter
1 cup thinly sliced red onion
½ **pound** andouille sausage, sliced
2 cups diced eggplant
1 cup quartered brown button mushrooms
1 bay leaf
½ **teaspoon** sassafras (filé powder)
1 cup hard apple cider
¼ **cup** bourbon
8 okra pods, cut in half lengthwise
½ **teaspoon** Tabasco sauce
¼ **cup** crème fraîche
4 pounds black mussels, debearded, scrubbed
¼ **cup** chopped green onion

Preheat broiler to medium high. Cut bread into 1-inch-thick slices. Drizzle with olive oil. Sprinkle with sea salt and pepper. Toast under broiler on both sides until golden. Transfer to bread basket. Keep warm. Add butter, onion, and andouille sausage to large stock pot over medium heat. Cook 2 minutes or until lightly browned. Add eggplant, mushrooms, bay leaf, and sassafras. Cook 4 minutes, stirring often. Add cider, bourbon, okra, Tabasco sauce, crème fraiche, and mussels. Cover. Cook 3 minutes or until liquid comes to boil and steam escapes from lid. Uncover. Use slotted spoon to rotate shells from top to bottom to cook evenly. Cook 5 minutes or until shells open and meat is plump but not overcooked. Sprinkle with green onion. Serve family style.

To reach the seaside town of Kerikeri, I had to drive through the mountainous area of New Zealand's North Island. The oldest wooden and stone buildings, weathered by the ocean, have survived since the 1820s, bringing character to the entire region. At the local supermarket there, large, transparent glass bins house the giant emerald-green mussels found only on the coast of New Zealand. I gathered a few kilograms of this magnificent creature with veggies and herbs and made delicious, silky bisque on a chilly night. As I fell asleep my mind drifted to my grandmother's medieval house on the emerald coast of Brittany, where the family would gather during violent storms, sipping hot creamy soups and playing card games. Comfort food it is! —BERNARD

Green-Lipped Mussel Bisque
Celery Seed Orange Croutons
SERVES 4

BISQUE
¼ **cup** olive oil

1 cup chopped celery

1 cup chopped white onion

1 cup sliced leek

4 cloves garlic, crushed

4 sprigs thyme

2 bay leaves

¾ **teaspoon** ground turmeric

1 cup Sauvignon Blanc wine

4 pounds green-lipped mussels, debearded, scrubbed

1 quart heavy cream

1 tablespoon cornstarch

2 tablespoons peach schnapps

to taste sea salt

to taste cayenne pepper

Add olive oil to large stock pot over medium heat. Add celery, onion, leek, garlic, thyme, and bay leaves. Cook 5 minutes without browning, stirring often. Add turmeric, Sauvignon Blanc, and mussels. Cover. Cook 5 minutes or until liquid comes to boil and steam escapes from lid. Uncover. Use slotted spoon to rotate shells from top to bottom to cook evenly. Cook 5 minutes or until shells open and meat is plump but not overcooked. Using tongs, transfer mussels to baking sheet to cool quickly. Return pot to stovetop. Bring cooking liquid to boil. Add cream. Bring to simmer. Reduce by one-fourth. Dilute cornstarch in 2 tablespoons cold water. Whisk into cream. Cook 1 minute. Strain through fine sieve into blender. Add peach schnapps. Puree until smooth. Season with sea salt and cayenne pepper.

CELERY SEED ORANGE CROUTONS
2 tablespoons olive oil

1 orange, zested

½ **teaspoon** celery seeds

2 teaspoons minced chives

¼ **teaspoon** sea salt

6 slices sourdough bread, crust removed, cubed

Preheat oven to 275°F. Combine olive oil, orange zest, celery seeds, chives, and salt in large mixing bowl. Add sourdough cubes. Toss gently to coat. Transfer to baking sheet. Bake 15 minutes or until golden and crispy.

PRESENTATION
3 teaspoons avocado oil

6 sprigs dill

to taste ground black pepper

Divide mussels between soup tureens. Pour soup atop. Drizzle with avocado oil. Garnish with croutons, dill, and black pepper.

La Ciotat is a small town on the edge of the Mediterranean, southeast of Marseille and Cassis. It is where the Lumière brothers invented the cinema in 1895. At the *vigie,* the highest point in town, you can admire the *calanques,* a spectacular series of jagged diamond-shaped limestone rock formations snuggled in the folds of the mountain range that looms over the colorful fishing village. At the *vieux port,* people eat overflowing bowls of steamed blue-black mussels with their fingers. The garlic is fragrant, the wine rosé, and the baguette crusty. —BERNARD

Piperade Moules Provençale

Fennel, Garlic, Rosé Wine

SERVES 4

3 tablespoons unsalted butter
1 small bulb fennel, cored, halved, thinly sliced
½ **cup** thinly sliced shallots
6 cloves garlic, sliced
½ **cup** diced, seeded red bell peppers
½ **cup** diced, seeded yellow bell peppers
2 sprigs oregano
to taste sea salt
to taste ground white pepper
1 cup rosé wine
1 cup quartered cherry tomatoes
5 pounds black mussels, cleaned, beards removed
2 lemons, peeled, seeded, flesh diced
16 black olives, pitted, quartered
¼ **cup** chopped basil
¼ **cup** crushed smoked almonds
2 tablespoons extra-virgin olive oil
1 freshly baked baguette

Heat butter in large stockpot over medium heat. Add fennel, shallots, and garlic. Cook 1 minute. Add bell peppers and oregano. Season with salt and pepper. Cook 2 minutes without browning, stirring often. Add rosé wine, tomatoes, and mussels. Cook 5 minutes or until liquids start to simmer. Uncover. Add lemons, olives, and basil. Use slotted spoon to rotate shells from top to bottom to cook evenly. Cook 5 minutes or until shells open and meat is plump but not overcooked. Transfer to large serving bowl. Sprinkle with smoked almonds. Drizzle with olive oil. Serve with baguette.

In the late fifteenth century, while looking for a direct sea route from Europe to India for the spice trade, the Portuguese discovered Goa on the southwestern coast of India. Goan cuisine blends the pungent spice of Indian food with the influences garnered from over four hundred years of Portuguese colonialism. On the river banks, simmering pots of seafood curries including fish, clams, crab, prawns, black mussels, and longish green mussels called *shinnaneo* steam away, tended to by local fishermen and their families. The powerful aromatic broth, curry paste, garlic, cumin, coriander, and cinnamon bark are tamed by the creaminess of coconut milk, bringing a beautiful balance to the broth. Cooked within five minutes or so, the mussels are served on the go during the hustle and bustle of the morning rush! —BERNARD

Goa Mussels Hot Pot

Curry Coconut Broth

SERVES 4

2 tablespoons olive oil

1 cup diced red onions

2 tablespoons finely chopped ginger

1 small lemongrass stalk, crushed, cut in 3-inch pieces

1 teaspoon curry powder

½ **cup** pineapple juice

1 cup coconut milk

4 pounds green mussels, scrubbed

1 lime

2 tablespoons chopped fresh cilantro

¼ **cup** finely sliced scallions

1 small hot chile pepper, seeded, thinly sliced

Add olive oil to large stockpot over medium heat. Add onions, ginger, lemongrass, and curry powder. Cook without browning, stirring often, for 2 minutes. Add pineapple juice and coconut milk. Reduce by half. Add mussels. Cover. Raise heat to high. Cook 3 minutes or until liquid starts to simmer. Uncover. Use slotted spoon to rotate shells to cook evenly. Cook 5 minutes or until all shells open and meat is plump but not overcooked. Uncover. Zest and juice lime over the mussels. Sprinkle with cilantro, scallions, and hot chile pepper.

CHAPTER 3

Sea Creatures

SHRIMP, CRAB, LOBSTER, OCTOPUS, SQUID

Shrimp

MEXICO

Tomatillo Shrimp Cazuela
pumpkin seed crema

KOREA

Seoul Street Food Shrimp Pajeon
pear red chile sauce

UNITED STATES

**Shrimp Andouille
Sausage Lollipops**
saffron artichoke sauce

INDONESIA

Lemongrass Shrimp Satay
cashew mint sauce

TUNISIA

"Shop Owner's" Shrimp
tomato marmalade, ras el hanout

URUGUAY

**La Costa Shrimp and
Corn Soufflé**
honey coriander vinaigrette

Crab

SINGAPORE

**Singapore Finger-Licking
Sticky Crab**
sesame broccoli rabe

VIETNAM

Kaffir Lime Asian Crab Risotto
plum wine, ginger, coconut milk

UNITED STATES

Blue Crab Quiche
buckwheat black pepper crust

Maryland Soft-Shell Crab Fritter
sun-dried cherry grits, smoked
ham vinaigrette

MEXICO

Stone Crab Cake
walnut nogada sauce

BELGIUM

Blue Crab Soufflé
frisée lardon salad, walnuts

Lobster

ITALY

Lobster Minestrone
pearl barley, pecorino romano

UNITED STATES

Vinalhaven Island Lobster Roll
bibb lettuce, green apple,
brioche bun

CAYMAN ISLANDS

Rum Point Roasted Lobster Tails
scotch bonnet herb butter

ENGLAND

Blue Lobster Saint Aubin
melon nectar

FRANCE

Brittany Lobster Fricassee
oyster mushrooms, leek,
peach brandy

MEXICO

Puerto Nuevo–Style Spiny Lobster
orange pico, almond salsa

Octopus

JAPAN

Octopus Takoyaki
candied garlic dipping sauce

GREECE

Cyprus Pickled Octopus
feta, mushrooms, oregano

Squid

FRANCE

Petit Syrah Braised Calamar
champignon, pearl onions, fennel

SPAIN

Paprika Chorizo Squid
almond saffron bomba rice

CHINA

**Szechuan Pepper
Wok-Fried Squid**
water chestnuts, orange
hoisin sauce

TUNISIA

Date Spinach Stuffed Squid
tomato chile sauce

Shrimp

Shrimp are found abundantly in the Gulf of Mexico, Asia, Latin America, Alaska, California, and off the Atlantic and Pacific seaboards in sandy-bottomed inshore waters. Since shrimp are available year-round due to farming and freezing, it's easy to forget that there is a shrimp season that runs from May to October. Ninety-five percent of wild shrimp are caught in the warm waters of the South Atlantic and Gulf of Mexico.

More than three hundred species of shrimp have commercial value globally, but in the United States, only a few species are important to the market. They generally come under three categories: cold-water shrimp, warm-water shrimp, and freshwater shrimp. It is common for large shrimp to be mistakenly called prawns, which are actually in the lobster family.

Shrimp can be wild-caught or farm-raised. Shrimp that are caught in their natural habitats (bays, estuaries, and oceans) are far superior in quality to their farm-raised counterparts. The methods for catching shrimp must be scrutinized to ensure the safety of other endangered species, such as sea turtles.

Most shrimp spawn offshore in deep water from early spring through early fall. They reproduce rapidly, with one female shrimp releasing thousands of eggs that hatch within twenty-four hours. Young shrimp are carried by currents into coastal estuaries to mature. When water temperatures are warm, shrimp grow very fast. Shrimp grown in aquaculture are also known as pond-raised or maricultured.

SHRIMP SIZES

In the United States, shrimp are sold by count. This is a rating of the size and weight of the shrimp. The count represents the number of shrimp in a pound. The numbers are typically a range; for example, a count of 16/20 means—on average—there are between 16 and 20 shrimp in a pound. They also may be sold by a name such as "jumbo" or "extra-large." Shrimp should always be labeled both ways to help you determine the size you are buying.

The *U* in the shrimp sizes stands for "under." For example U-10 means under 10 shrimp per pound.

In the Wild

We have two favorites that are caught in the wild and are considered to have low environmental impact:

Gulf Shrimp

There are five species of wild-caught shrimp commercially harvested in the Gulf of Mexico and South Atlantic. Four of them are named after their natural shell color: pink, white, brown, and royal red. The fifth is named after the toughness of its shell: rock shrimp, a deepwater cousin of the previous four.

Pink shrimp make up the bulk of shrimp harvested in Florida. They have light pink shells with a pearl-like texture, and some have a pink dot on the head. When cooked, the shells turn a deeper shade of pink. They are the largest Gulf species and can reach 11 inches and live up to twenty-four months. The peak harvest season is in the spring and the fall.

Spot Prawns

Not actually a prawn, these are the largest shrimp on the West Coast, found from Alaska to California.

Spot prawns are caught with traps that have a low impact on the ecology. Traps are submerged wire or wood cages that attract the shrimp and hold them alive until fishermen return to haul in the catch.

In the Kitchen

The flavor and texture of each type of shrimp are influenced by the waters they come from and what they eat. Wild shrimp feed on seaweed and crustaceans, which gives them a rich flavor and thick shells. Their ability to swim freely also produces a firm, robust meat.

Shrimp are one of the most versatile members of the seafood world. Small shrimp can be used on salads, pizza, pasta, and stuffings. Large shrimp are great to skewer and grill, sauté scampi style, broil, deep-fry, or poach.

Shrimp should always be cooked quickly and at lower temperatures to preserve their sweet, delicate flavors. Most shrimp cook in as little as three minutes; as a rule, when they're pink, they are done.

Valuable Nutrients from Shrimp

- Choline: assists in proper cell function, prevents osteoporosis, reduces inflammation
- Iron: vital to the production of energy and a healthy immune system
- Niacin: increases good cholesterol levels
- Omega-3 fatty acids: prevent cardiovascular disease
- Phosphorus: builds healthy bones and strong teeth
- Selenium: antioxidant, prevents arthritis
- Vitamin B_{12}: promotes healthy blood cells, prevents anemia, eases migraines
- Zinc: controls acne, boosts immune system

Fun Facts

Shrimp has been a food staple in China since the seventh century AD. Even Marco Polo was astonished by the abundance of these delicious creatures in Chinese markets.

About 80 percent of shrimp consumed in the United States each year is eaten in restaurants, but you can change that with this book!

It's no mistake that "shrimpy" is used to refer to things that are small. The word *shrimp* evolved from the Middle English word *shrimpe,* which means "pygmy."

In Mexico, *cazuela* is a word that refers to both a casserole-style meal and the pan in which it is cooked. Traditionally made from terra cotta, the cazuela pan is one of the oldest types of cookware. Today, cazuelas can be made in a variety of materials, especially cast iron. The defining concept of cazuela is to cook protein and vegetables in the pan, rendering juices that harmonize into a thick stock. Tomatillos, one of the most underutilized ingredients in the global kitchen, have a pleasant sweet-and-sour flavor and juicy pectinous texture when heated. Combined with the renderings of the cooked shrimp, this creates a flavorful foundation for the finished cazuela. Mexican wild shrimp are plump and maintain their size and juiciness when cooked. —RON

Tomatillo Shrimp Cazuela

Pumpkin Seed Crema

SERVES 4

PUMPKIN SEED CREMA

¼ **cup** hulled pumpkin seeds
⅛ **teaspoon** white peppercorns
1 cup sour cream
to taste sea salt

Add pumpkin seeds and peppercorns to skillet over medium heat. Toast 1 minute or until fragrant, tossing constantly. Transfer to spice grinder. Pulse to a fine meal. Transfer to mixing bowl. Whisk in remaining ingredients.

CAZUELA

8 shrimp, size U-15, peeled, deveined
1 tablespoon olive oil
2 tablespoons lime juice
1 small red onion, sliced
½ **pound** tomatillos, husked, quartered
1 cup cubed feta cheese
½ **teaspoon** cumin seeds
½ **teaspoon** chile powder
1 teaspoon ground coriander
1 large avocado, halved, seeded, peeled, chopped
¼ **cup** cilantro leaves
to taste sea salt
to taste ground black pepper

Preheat broiler. Combine shrimp in mixing bowl with oil, lime juice, red onions, tomatillos, feta cheese, cumin, chile powder, and coriander. Season with salt and pepper. Toss to coat. Refrigerate 30 minutes. Place large cast iron skillet over medium high heat. When pan is very hot, add shrimp mixture in even layer. Immediately transfer to oven. Bake 4 minutes or until shrimp are slightly underdone. Remove cazuela from oven. Garnish with avocado and cilantro leaves. Add salt and pepper. Serve with Pumpkin Seed Crema.

While exploring the Gyeongdong Market located in Seoul, the aroma of roasted chestnuts, barbecued meats, fish fritters, and the ever-popular *pajeon* wafts through the air. Pajeon is a traditional Korean-style pancake loaded with slivered green onions. Endless variations include kimchee, beef, and pork, but the cooked-to-order shrimp and octopus pajeon, golden crisp on the outside yet soft and doughy in the middle, gets my vote. Locals enjoy this dish with a glass of milky, effervescent Korean rice wine called *makgeolli*. Eating local street food is a great way to immerse yourself in the culture. —BERNARD

Seoul Street Food Shrimp Pajeon
Pear Red Chile Sauce
SERVES 4

PANCAKES
¾ **pound** shrimp, size 16/20, peeled, deveined

1 **cup** all-purpose flour

½ **teaspoon** fine sea salt

⅛ **teaspoon** ground white pepper

¼ **teaspoon** ground turmeric

1 large egg, lightly beaten

6 **tablespoons** sake wine

¾ **cup** water

½ **cup** chopped green beans

½ **cup** finely sliced oyster mushrooms

½ **cup** grated carrots

⅓ **cup** finely sliced scallions

1 **tablespoon** toasted sesame seeds

¼ **cup** light sesame oil

PEAR RED CHILE SAUCE
¼ **cup** soy sauce

2 **tablespoons** rice vinegar

½ **cup** chopped onion

1 **teaspoon** minced garlic

1 **cup** chopped, peeled Asian pear

1 **teaspoon** Korean red chile paste (gojuchang)

Combine all ingredients in mixing bowl. Cover. Refrigerate 1 hour. Transfer to serving bowl.

Cut shrimp into ½-inch pieces. Sift flour, salt, pepper, and turmeric into large mixing bowl. Make a well in the center of the flour mix. In a separate bowl, whisk egg, sake, and water. Pour in center of well. Using wire whisk, stir small circles in the center of the well, moving progressively outward until you have a smooth batter. Fold in green beans, mushrooms, carrots, scallions, sesame seeds, and shrimp. Add ½ tablespoon oil to cast-iron or nonstick skillet over medium heat. Ladle ¾ cup batter into skillet. Cook 2 minutes or until golden brown. Flip. Cook 1 more minute or until golden. Transfer pancake to serving platter. Repeat process with remaining batter. Serve with Pear Red Chile Sauce.

Andouille sausage originated in the French region of Normandy. In earlier times, this rustic sausage utilized all the butchered parts of a pig, including the tripe and the stomach, with garlic and fresh herbs. French immigrants to the Americas brought the recipe for andouille sausage with them, which later melded with Cajun cuisine. The rich, spicy andouille is often smoked over sugarcane and pecan and alder wood. Andouille plays a major role in dishes such as gumbo and jambalaya, flavors that define Louisiana cooking, and sausage and shrimp celebrate the flavors of New Orleans. This delicious sausage can also be made of chicken, turkey, beef, or tofu—all good substitutes for the pork. —BERNARD

Shrimp Andouille Sausage Lollipops
Saffron Artichoke Sauce
SERVES 4

SAFFRON ARTICHOKE SAUCE
2 large artichokes
1 egg yolk
½ tablespoon Dijon mustard
½ tablespoon white wine vinegar
1 teaspoon minced garlic
Large pinch saffron threads
1 teaspoon lemon zest
2 tablespoons lemon juice
1 cup extra-virgin olive oil
pinch cayenne pepper
2 tablespoons chopped basil
to taste sea salt
to taste ground black pepper

Place artichokes in steamer. Steam 30 minutes or until tender. Cool. Remove leaves. Using spoon, scoop out fuzzy choke and discard. Finely chop hearts. Set aside. Add egg yolk, mustard, vinegar, garlic, saffron, lemon zest, and lemon juice to mixing bowl. Whisk thoroughly. Add olive oil in slow steady stream, whisking vigorously until fully emulsified. Fold in remaining ingredients. Season with salt and pepper. Transfer to serving bowl.

LOLLIPOPS
12 (6-inch) bamboo skewers
1 link andouille sausage (about ½ pound)
12 shrimp, size U-15, peeled, deveined, tail-on
2 tablespoons grapeseed oil
1 tablespoon finely chopped thyme leaves
to taste sea salt
to taste ground black pepper
1 tablespoon finely chopped chives

Soak skewers in water at least 30 minutes. Cut andouille into twelve ½-inch-thick slices. Wrap 1 shrimp around each sausage slice. Insert 1 skewer through shrimp tail, sausage, and back through shrimp to create lollipop shape; repeat for each skewer. Add oil to skillet over medium high heat. Season lollipops with thyme, salt, and pepper. Sauté 1 minute on each side. Sprinkle with chives.

PRESENTATION
2 large lemons
bouquet fresh garden herbs

Cut lemons in half. Place cut side down on serving platter. Insert 3 skewers into each. Garnish with garden herbs. Serve with Saffron Artichoke Sauce.

INDONESIA

The tropical island of Java is renowned as one of the most heavenly spice destinations in the world. A unique combination of exotic flavors is layered throughout its cuisine. The Javanese love using coconut milk, ginger, and lemongrass as well as a chile-shrimp paste called *sambal*. One of the most popular cooking methods is called *bakar,* or grilling, using fresh fish, shrimp, or lobster. Grilling shrimp in their shells imparts a roasted element to their flesh while keeping them moist. Spiny lobster can be grilled in the same fashion by butterflying the tail. In a Javanese kitchen you will find peace and harmony, the key elements of Indonesian cuisine. —BERNARD

Lemongrass Shrimp Satay
Cashew Mint Sauce
SERVES 4

SHRIMP + MARINADE

12 shrimp, size U-15,
    peeled, deveined, tail-on
2 stalks lemongrass
1 cup coconut milk
1 lime, zested, juiced
1 small Thai red chile,
    seeded, deveined, chopped
1 tablespoon brown sugar
2 teaspoons chopped garlic
2 tablespoons chopped ginger
1 tablespoon sesame oil

Using sharp serrated knife, butterfly shrimp by cutting lengthwise through the upper shell down to—but not through—the bottom shell. Remove the vein and discard. Place shrimp in single layer, cut side up, onto baking sheet. Remove and discard outer layers of lemongrass. Slice thinly crosswise. Add coconut milk, lime, chile pepper, brown sugar, garlic, ginger, sesame oil, and lemongrass to blender. Puree 30 seconds. Strain through fine sieve into shallow nonreactive container. Add shrimp. Toss to coat. Cover. Refrigerate 1 hour.

CASHEW MINT SAUCE

½ cup chopped mint leaves
½ cup chopped basil leaves
3 tablespoons seasoned rice vinegar
1 tablespoon soy sauce
1 small Thai red chile,
    seeded, deveined, chopped
1 tablespoon grated ginger
1 tablespoon lime juice
¼ cup chopped cashew nuts
¼ cup safflower oil
to taste sea salt
to taste ground black pepper

Place mint, basil, rice vinegar, soy sauce, red chile, ginger, lime juice, and cashew nuts in blender. With blender running, slowly drizzle in safflower oil until well incorporated. Season with salt and pepper. Transfer to serving bowl.

PRESENTATION

2 tablespoons grapeseed oil
8 sprigs cilantro
2 tablespoons toasted coconut flakes

Preheat grill to medium-high heat. Coat grates with grapeseed oil. Place shrimp on hot grill, flesh side down. Cook 30 seconds. Flip over. Generously brush flesh side with remaining marinade. Close lid. Cook 2 minutes or until slightly underdone. Transfer to serving platter. Sprinkle with coconut flakes. Garnish with cilantro sprigs. Serve with Cashew Mint Sauce.

In North Africa, *ras el hanout,* meaning "head of the shop," is the shop owner's coveted spice blend that can include more than thirty ingredients. Spice blending is a competitive craft in the medina, the heart of Tunisia's capital. The honor of having a highly desirable blend is the goal of each merchant. With several hundred different spices, dried flowers, and other exotic ingredients in their repertoire, the final blend varies greatly from merchant to merchant and region to region. Special customers may even receive blends that include Spanish fly (dried green beetles). Ras el hanout, a warming spice blend, is not typically used with seafood, but when mixed with almonds and dusted on shrimp, we found the result to be intoxicating. —RON

"Shop Owner's" Shrimp

Tomato Marmalade, Ras el Hanout

SERVES 6

TOMATO MARMALADE

1 tablespoon extra-virgin olive oil
¼ cup finely julienned, peeled ginger root
4 cups diced vine-ripened tomatoes
1 tablespoon red wine vinegar
1 lemon, zested, juiced
1½ tablespoons honey
1 small red chile pepper, seeded, chopped
1 teaspoon sea salt
½ teaspoon ground black pepper

Add oil to saucepan over medium heat. Add ginger. Cook 1 minute, stirring often. Add remaining ingredients. Bring to simmer. Cook 30 minutes, stirring often, to a marmalade consistency. Adjust seasoning with salt and pepper if needed. Transfer to serving dish.

RAS EL HANOUT

1 tablespoon coriander seeds
1 teaspoon cumin seeds
½ teaspoon black peppercorns
2 pods green cardamom
½ cup sliced almonds
1 teaspoon paprika
⅛ teaspoon ground allspice
¼ teaspoon ground turmeric
½ teaspoon sea salt

Add coriander, cumin, peppercorns, cardamom, and almonds to skillet over medium heat. Toast until fragrant, tossing constantly. Transfer to mixing bowl. Add remaining ingredients. Process in small batches in coffee grinder to a coarse meal. Store in airtight container.

SHRIMP

2 quarts water
1 cup dry white wine
1 teaspoon black peppercorns
1 bay leaf
1 teaspoon sea salt
6 sprigs thyme
18 shell-on shrimp, size U-15
1 tablespoon almond oil

Combine water, wine, peppercorns, bay leaf, sea salt, and thyme sprigs in stock pot. Bring to a simmer over medium high heat. Simmer 5 minutes. Add shrimp. Cook 3 minutes or until shrimp is opaque in center. Drain in colander. Transfer shrimp to bowl of ice water until well chilled. Remove shell, leaving tail intact. Devein. Pat dry. Toss in bowl with almond oil. Sprinkle with Ras el Hanout to taste.

As I approached José Ignacio (the town, not the man) after a long hiatus from visiting Uruguay, dreamy memories of quaint tranquility were interrupted by a new reality, a stunning makeover that leaves return guests with one question: What happened? The answer is simple. The fashionable, chic, and celebrity types have outgrown Punta del Este, Uruguay, South America's version of Saint Tropez twenty miles to the south, and they are now spilling into José Ignacio, adopting the city as the new jet-setters' playground. Despite all the transformation, the cuisine and the town still hold on to their fishing village values. —RON

La Costa Shrimp and Corn Soufflé

Honey Coriander Vinaigrette

SERVES 4

HONEY CORIANDER VINAIGRETTE

1 tablespoon minced shallots
1 tablespoon chopped cilantro
1 tablespoon chopped tarragon
2 tablespoons sherry vinegar
1 tablespoon honey
1 teaspoon coriander seeds, roasted, crushed
⅓ cup extra-virgin olive oil
to taste sea salt and ground black pepper

Whisk all ingredients together in small mixing bowl.

CORN SOUFFLÉ

½ tablespoon softened unsalted butter
2 tablespoons unsalted butter
2 tablespoons all-purpose flour
1 cup milk
½ cup fresh corn kernels
2 medium eggs, separated
⅓ cup self-rising cornbread mix
to taste sea salt and ground black pepper

Brush four 4-ounce ramekins with softened butter. Place on baking sheet. Set aside. Preheat oven to 350°F. Add butter to saucepan over medium heat. When melted, whisk in flour. Cook 2 minutes, stirring constantly, until foamy and lightly browned. Add milk in ¼-cup increments, whisking until smooth after each addition.

Transfer to blender. Add corn. Puree until smooth. Transfer to large mixing bowl. Whisk in egg yolks and cornbread mix. Season to taste with salt and pepper. In clean large mixing bowl, whip egg whites until stiff peaks form. Fold into egg yolk mixture. Divide batter equally between prepared ramekins. Place in oven. Bake 15 minutes or until puffed and golden brown.

SHRIMP

2 tablespoons olive oil, divided
5 ounces queso fresco, crumbled
2 tablespoons chopped parsley
to taste sea salt and ground black pepper
12 shrimp, size U-15, peeled
12 thin strips applewood smoked bacon
12 (6-inch) skewers, soaked in water at least 1 hour
2 tablespoons unsalted butter

Combine 1 tablespoon olive oil, cheese, and parsley in small mixing bowl. Season with salt and pepper. Set aside. Using a paring knife, slice shrimp down the backs. Remove and discard the veins. Deepen the incisions to butterfly shrimp. Spoon cheese mixture stuffing into each shrimp. Fold shrimp back to original shape. Wrap each stuffed shrimp with bacon. Secure with skewer. Heat remaining tablespoon olive oil and butter in large skillet over medium heat. Sauté wrapped shrimp 2 minutes on all sides for 8 minutes total. Transfer to large serving platter. Spoon Honey Coriander Vinaigrette atop. Serve with Corn Soufflé.

Crab

The world's oceans are populated by over four thousand different types of crab! Most live in the sea. Even land crabs, which are abundant in tropical countries, start their life in the sea and make a return visit every now and then. The river crab of southern Europe is an example of freshwater crabs found in most of the warmer regions of the world.

Most species of crabs are caught in pots or traps that are designed to reduce bycatch and habitat damage.

The oldest crab industry in the United States is the blue crab industry of the Chesapeake Bay, dating back almost to the early 1600s.

In the Wild
The most sought after edible crabs are found in the coastal regions of Europe, North America, Indo-Pacific, Sea of Japan, Bering Sea, and Alaska.

Snow Crabs
Found in the western North Atlantic Ocean from Greenland to Newfoundland to the Gulf of Maine.

In the North Pacific, snow crabs are distributed on the continental shelf of the Chukchi and Bering Seas. Sweet, delicate snow-white meat.

Florida Stone Crabs
Found in the western North Atlantic and Gulf of Mexico, from North Carolina to Texas, including Cuba and the Bahamas.

Fishermen are only allowed to take the large front claws of the stone crab, which regenerate fully. This ensures sustainability of the species.

Stone crab meat is mild and sweet like lobster.

Dungeness Crabs
These are found in the western North Pacific, from Alaska to central California.

They have one of the highest ratios of meat to shell.

Red King Crabs
In Asia, they occur from the Sea of Okhotsk and the Shelf of Kamchatka in eastern Russia to the Aleutian Islands.

In North America, they are distributed from the Bering Sea to the Gulf of Alaska.

The main source of red king crabs is the Russian Federation.

The succulent meat is snow white with bright red highlights.

Blue King Crabs
These are found in the North Pacific, from British Columbia to the Bering Sea and from the Aleutian Islands to the Sea of Japan.

They are as sweet as red king crab with a milder flavor.

Blue Crabs

These are the key commercial species in the Chesapeake Bay. They are native to the western Atlantic from Nova Scotia, Canada, to northern Argentina, including Bermuda and the Caribbean.

They have been introduced into Europe and Asia and often are eaten as soft-shells.

Peekytoe Crab

These are rock or sand crabs from the coast of Maine.

The pink meat has a sweet, delicate flavor.

The name *peekytoe* comes from Maine slang for "pointed toe."

In the Kitchen

Soft-shell blue crabs are lightly battered and fried until crisp on the outside and steamy and juicy inside.

In Asian cultures, the roe of the female crab is also eaten; in Japan it is called *masago*.

Alaskan king crab and snow crab legs are so delectable that they are best served "old school"— simply boiled and served with clarified butter.

Crab cakes are an American dish, and a good one is loaded with high quality crabmeat.

Crabs are also used in bisque, a French soup popular around the world.

Dungeness crabmeat is incredibly versatile and can be made into crab cakes, and added to omelettes, soups, salads, and soufflés.

Adding aromatic spices, as they do in Singapore or on the Maryland seashore, is a good way to jazz it up.

Valuable Nutrients from Crab

- Copper: for healthy metabolism and organ function

- Folate: for a healthy pregnancy

- Omega-3 fatty acids: prevent cardiovascular disease

- Phosphorus: builds healthy bones and strong teeth

- Selenium: antioxidant, prevents arthritis

- Vitamin B_{12}: promotes healthy blood cells, prevents anemia, eases migraines

- Vitamin C: powerful antioxidant, prevents high blood pressure and cataracts

- Zinc: controls acne, boosts immune system

Fun Facts

The United States is home to more varieties of crab than any other country.

One Alaskan king crab can provide over 6 pounds of sweet, delicious meat.

The Japanese spider crab has a 12-foot leg span.

The superstars of the blue crab industry in the United States are Louisiana, Maryland, North Carolina, and Virginia. These four states account for 100 million pounds plus of blue crab landings each year.

Blue crab is the official state crustacean of Maryland.

Dungeness crab is the official state crustacean of Oregon.

Only one other state, Louisiana, has an official crustacean, but it's not a crab. In case you are wondering, it's a crayfish.

When Madam Cher Yam Tian and her husband, Mister Lim, invented "chilli crabs" in the 1950s, it was the beginning of a Singaporean institution. At first Madam Cher simply steamed the crabs that her policeman husband brought home from the beach, but later she stir-fried them with tomatoes and hot chiles to please her husband's assertive taste buds. When we travel to Singapore, it is our tradition to dive into a big bowl of spicy crabs chased with ice-cold beer. —BERNARD

Singapore Finger-Licking Sticky Crab

Sesame Broccoli Rabe

SERVES 4

CRAB

6 quarts water
2 tablespoons sea salt
2 live Dungeness crabs (1½ pounds each)

Bring water and salt to boil in large stockpot over high heat. Add crabs. Cook 2 minutes. Transfer to ice bath. Remove legs from body by twisting and pulling off. Place body on counter with bottom shell up. Remove the triangular flap that is tucked into the bottom shell. Place fingers under the edge of the top hard shell to pry it off. Remove the gills found on both sides of the body; they can be identified by their brown color, feathery texture, and crescent shape. Rinse crab under cold running water. Cut the bodies in half crosswise using a sharp chef's knife. Transfer to mixing bowl along with legs. Pat dry with paper towels.

SAUCE

3 tablespoons soy sauce
¼ **cup** ketchup
12 ounces dark beer
1 tablespoon lemon juice
1 tablespoon cornstarch
1 tablespoon oyster sauce
½ **tablespoon** honey

Combine all ingredients in a mixing bowl. Set aside.

SESAME BROCCOLI RABE

2 tablespoons cornstarch
5 tablespoons sesame oil, divided
3 tablespoons minced ginger
5 cloves garlic, finely sliced
¼ **cup** chopped shallots
2 red chile peppers, pounded with seeds
¾ **pound** broccoli rabe, trimmed, washed
4 green onions, sliced thinly on bias
1 tablespoon toasted sesame seeds

Toss crab with cornstarch. Add 4 tablespoons oil to wok over high heat. Add crab. Fry until shells turn red, about 4 minutes. Remove from the wok and transfer to platter. Return wok to medium heat. Add remaining 1 tablespoon oil. Add ginger, garlic, shallots, and chiles. Stir-fry 15 seconds. Stir in Sauce. Place crab over sauce. Toss. Cover wok. Cook 3 minutes. Add broccoli rabe on top of crab. Cover. Cook 5 minutes. Transfer to serving platter. Garnish with green onions and sesame seeds.

Kaffir limes are bumpy, green, juiceless citrus fruits with the most intoxicating exotic citronella aroma. The leaves are used in Vietnamese cuisine to perfume soups, rice, seafood, and chicken dishes. The unique double leaves are attached at a point like love bugs, making a distinctive hourglass shape. They can be used fresh, dried, or frozen. At my friend's home in Saigon, the fragrance of Vietnamese cuisine escapes the kitchen, arriving at the table ahead of the dish like a trumpeter announcing the appearance of a king. All your senses perk at the first sniff of Kaffir leaves, lemongrass, toasty sesame oil, and crab. If you cannot find Kaffir lime leaves, use 1 teaspoon lime zest. —RON

Kaffir Lime Asian Crab Risotto

Plum Wine, Ginger, Coconut Milk

SERVES 4

BROTH

5 cups vegetable stock
½ **teaspoon** sambal chile sauce
1 teaspoon green curry paste
3 stalks lemongrass, crushed
6 Kaffir lime leaves

Combine all ingredients in sauce pot over medium heat. Simmer 10 minutes. Strain through fine sieve. Return to pot. Place over low heat to keep hot.

RISOTTO

2 tablespoons light sesame oil
2 tablespoons unsalted butter
1 cup chopped celery
4 cloves garlic, minced
½ **cup** minced shallots
1½ **cups** Arborio rice
¾ **cup** plum wine
1 cup coconut milk
3 tablespoons lime juice
¼ **cup** freshly grated Parmesan cheese
½ **pound** jumbo lump crabmeat, shelled
¼ **cup** chopped flat-leaf parsley
¼ **cup** chopped cilantro leaves
1 tablespoon grated ginger
to taste sea salt
to taste ground black pepper

Add sesame oil and butter to large pot over medium heat. Add celery, garlic, and shallots. Cook 1 minute without browning, stirring constantly. Stir in rice. Cook 1 minute, stirring constantly. Add plum wine. Cook 1 minute, stirring often. Add 1 cup hot Broth. Cook, stirring occasionally until liquid is absorbed and a clear wake is left behind the spoon. Repeat process three times, cooking until rice is al dente. Total cooking time should be 15–20 minutes. Remove from heat. Fold in coconut milk, lime juice, Parmesan, crabmeat, parsley, cilantro, and ginger. Season with salt and pepper. If necessary, stir in more hot stock to achieve a creamy texture. Transfer to lidded serving dish.

For the last twenty years we have been celebrating the rhythm of the high tides with the waves crashing on the windows of the Marine Room Restaurant on the seashore of La Jolla, California. This is Mother Nature's best show. Our sous chef Felix and the culinary team meet at 5 a.m. for our ritual preparation of the breakfast harvest. Felix is the master of the quiche recipe and the only one in the kitchen who holds its secrets. As I walk through the restaurant in the early morning, the excitement of waves crashing against the glass and the wow of everyone tasting Felix's quiche resonate through the room. —RON

Blue Crab Quiche
Buckwheat Black Pepper Crust
SERVES 6

BUCKWHEAT BLACK PEPPER CRUST

½ **cup** all-purpose flour
½ **cup** buckwheat flour
½ **teaspoon** sea salt
½ **teaspoon** cracked black pepper
½ **teaspoon** lemon zest
½ **tablespoon** fresh thyme leaves
⅓ **cup** cold unsalted butter, cut in 5 pieces
2 **tablespoons** ice-cold water, plus more if needed
1 large egg white, beaten

Preheat oven to 375°F. Combine flours, salt, pepper, lemon zest, and thyme in mixing bowl. Using fork tines or pastry cutter, cut in butter until crumbly. Gently mix in water, adding a little more if necessary, until dough forms a ball. Turn onto floured surface and knead gently until dough is smooth. Wrap in plastic wrap. Refrigerate at least 1 hour or until firm. Remove dough from refrigerator. Form into round disk. Place on floured surface. With cold wooden rolling pin, begin at edge of dough and roll to opposite edge, applying even pressure. Pick up dough, rotate quarter turn, making sure surface is floured. Continue rolling and rotating until dough is an even 10½-inch circle. Place rolling pin on edge of dough and roll dough up on pin. Place rolling pin over 9-inch pie dish and unroll, so dough fits loosely into pan. Trim overhanging edges. Prick dough with tines of fork. Brush lightly with egg white. Refrigerate at least 1 hour.

FILLING

2 **tablespoons** (¼ stick) unsalted butter
1 **cup** chopped leeks, white part only
¾ **cup** chopped fennel
to taste sea salt
to taste ground black pepper
1½ **tablespoons** all-purpose flour
⅛ **teaspoon** baking powder
6 large eggs, beaten, divided
1¼ **cups** grated white cheddar, divided
1 **cup** chopped spinach leaves
1 **cup** blue crab meat
1¼ **cup** heavy cream
2 **teaspoons** chopped thyme
pinch freshly grated nutmeg

Preheat oven to 350°F. Melt butter in skillet over medium heat. Add leeks and fennel. Cook 3 minutes without browning, stirring often. Season with salt and pepper. Set aside. Sift flour and baking powder into large mixing bowl. Whisk in ¼ cup eggs until smooth. Whisk in remaining eggs. Add 1 cup cheese, reserved leeks and fennel, and remaining ingredients. Season again with salt and pepper if necessary. Pour into prepared pastry shell. Sprinkle with remaining ¼ cup cheese. Bake 50 minutes or until set. Let rest 5 minutes before serving.

As warmer water temperatures rise in Chesapeake Bay in early May, the blue crabs crawl out from the seafloor, shedding their hard outer shells. The crabs are shipped live to local markets and restaurants around country, wearing only a thin, edible shell covering. Soft-shell crabs are a delicacy and one of nature's greatest gifts. The harvest usually runs from May through September. It's best to buy live soft-shells whenever possible, and make sure the shell is still truly soft. Quickly deep-fried, you will relish every crispy bite! Soft-shells are sold in five sizes, increasing in ½-inch increments from the smallest to largest: mediums, hotels, primes, jumbos, and whales. —BERNARD

Maryland Soft-Shell Crab Fritter
Sun-Dried Cherry Grits, Smoked Ham Vinaigrette
SERVES 4 AS MAIN COURSE OR 8 AS APPETIZER

SOFT-SHELL CRABS
1 quart canola oil
2 cups buttermilk
1 teaspoon lemon zest
1 tablespoon chopped thyme
½ teaspoon celery seeds
8 medium soft-shell crabs
2 cups all-purpose flour
½ cup cornstarch
2 tablespoons Cajun spice mix
to taste sea salt

Preheat oven to 250°F. Heat oil in deep fryer or large heavy-bottomed pot to 375°F. Combine buttermilk, lemon zest, thyme, and celery seeds in large mixing bowl. Add crabs. Refrigerate at least 15 minutes. Combine flour, cornstarch, and Cajun spice mix in casserole dish. Working with 2 at a time, remove crabs from buttermilk. Dredge in flour mixture. Carefully place into fryer. Fry 2 minutes. Carefully flip over. Cook 1 minute or until crispy and golden brown. Transfer to parchment paper–lined platter. Place in oven to keep warm. Repeat process with remaining crabs.

SUN-DRIED CHERRY GRITS
1 tablespoon grapeseed oil
½ cup diced red onion
¼ cup chopped sun-dried cherries
½ cup sherry wine
4 cups vegetable stock
1 cup stone-ground grits
½ cup chopped pecans
½ cup crumbled goat cheese
pinch cayenne pepper
to taste sea salt
to taste ground black pepper

Add oil to saucepan over medium heat. Add onions and cherries. Cook 2 minutes, stirring often. Add sherry and vegetable stock. Bring to simmer. Slowly stir in grits. Return to simmer. Cook 5 minutes or until soft and creamy, stirring often. Remove from heat. Fold in pecans and goat cheese. Season with cayenne, salt, and pepper. Cover to keep warm.

SMOKED HAM VINAIGRETTE

¼ cup finely diced smoked ham

⅓ cup olive oil

1 tablespoon whole grain mustard

2 tablespoons apple cider vinegar

2 tablespoons minced red onion

1 tablespoon chopped tarragon

to taste sea salt

to taste ground black pepper

Add first six ingredients to mixing bowl. Whisk to emulsify. Season with salt and pepper.

PRESENTATION

24 sprigs thyme

Spoon Sun-Dried Cherry Grits into 3-inch ring placed in center of warm serving plate. Remove ring. Top with crab. Spoon Smoked Ham Vinaigrette around. Garnish each crab with 3 thyme sprigs.

Nogada, or walnut cream sauce, was originally invented by convent nuns in Puebla in the 1800s to accompany stuffed poblano chiles that were garnished with pomegranate seeds. The trio of ingredients represented the patriotic colors of Mexico's flag. When the great hero of Mexico's war for independence, Augustín de Iturbide, visited Puebla, the nuns served their new creation in his honor. Ironically, walnuts, poblanos, and pomegranates are all in season in September, the month of Mexico's independence. Nogada is a versatile sauce that can be used for many dishes. We love it with crab cakes, especially those made with sweet Mexican stone crab meat. —RON

Stone Crab Cake
Walnut Nogada Sauce
SERVES 4

CRAB CAKES

2 tablespoons olive oil
¼ cup chopped white onion
¼ cup chopped celery
¼ cup chopped seedless green chiles
pinch cayenne pepper
⅛ teaspoon ground cumin
¼ teaspoon paprika
3 tablespoons sesame seeds
to taste sea salt
to taste ground black pepper
1 pound stone crab meat, shelled
1 egg, beaten
¼ cup crème fraîche
5 tablespoons toasted bread crumbs
2 tablespooons (¼ stick) unsalted butter

Add oil to skillet over medium heat. Add onions, celery, and chiles. Cook 2 minutes without browning. Add cayenne, cumin, paprika, and sesame seeds. Season with salt and pepper. Transfer to large mixing bowl. Cool. Fold in crab, egg, crème fraîche, and bread crumbs. Divide mixture into 4 portions. Shape into patties about ¾ inch thick and 3 inches in diameter. Refrigerate, loosely covered, at least 1 hour or overnight. Melt butter in large skillet over medium heat. Add crab cakes. Cook 2 minutes or until golden brown. Flip carefully. Cook additional 3 minutes or until golden brown and center is hot.

NOGADA

1 cup chopped, toasted walnuts
1 cup milk
1 cup crème fraîche
4 ounces queso fresco
¼ cup sherry wine
½ tablespoon sherry vinegar
1 teaspoon granulated sugar
¼ teaspoon sea salt

Add walnuts and milk to bowl. Cover. Refrigerate at least 12 hours. Drain in colander. Rinse under cold water. Transfer to blender. Add remaining ingredients. Puree.

PRESENTATION

8 fresh cherries
½ cup tender inner celery leaves
¼ cup finely diced celery hearts
1 tablespoon toasted pepitas (hulled pumpkin seeds)
4 teaspoons walnut oil
to taste sea salt
to taste ground black pepper

Pit and quarter cherries. Add to mixing bowl celery leaves, celery hearts, pepitas, and walnut oil. Toss. Season with salt and pepper. Spread 2 tablespoons Nogada sauce onto center of warm serving plate. Place crab cake atop. Top with cherry celery salad.

Soufflé may be a chic French word for "puffed-up," but don't fret, this is an easy savory recipe. Although Belgian cuisine is highly influenced by the French love affair with butter, cream, and herbs, it creates its own identity from the many diverse regions that are packed into this tiny country. From the North Sea coast, the fondness for seafood spills throughout the rest of the land as if carried by the tide itself. Brown crabs are a prized crustacean. Bitter Belgian leaves such as endive and chicory accompany the sweetness of the crab in a stroke of harmony. Cooking local ingredients in a soufflé is Belgian at heart and a tip of the cap to the country below. —RON

Blue Crab Soufflé

Frisée Lardon Salad, Walnuts

SERVES 6

THE DISHES

1 tablespoon unsalted butter

Preheat oven to 350°F. Butter six 6-ounce soufflé dishes. Transfer dishes to baking sheet. Set aside.

SALAD

½ pound frisée leaves (French curly endive)
½ cup chopped, toasted walnuts
¼ cup diced sun-dried apricots
3 slices thick-cut bacon
¼ cup chopped shallots
¼ cup red wine vinegar
¼ cup walnut oil
to taste sea salt
to taste ground black pepper

Tear frisée into bite-size pieces and put in a large serving bowl with walnuts and apricots. Cut bacon slices crosswise into ¼-inch-thick sticks (lardons). Add bacon to heavy skillet over medium heat. Cook until golden and crispy, stirring occasionally. Discard all but ¼ cup bacon drippings. Add shallots, red wine vinegar, and walnut oil. Remove from heat. Pour hot dressing over frisée. Toss immediately. Season with salt and pepper.

THE SOUFFLÉ

3 tablespoons unsalted butter
¼ cup minced shallots
1 teaspoon lemon thyme leaves
3 tablespoons all-purpose flour
¾ cup half-and-half
½ cup crumbled soft, fresh goat cheese
½ teaspoon sea salt
⅛ teaspoon paprika
pinch cayenne pepper
4 large eggs, separated
½ cup shelled lump blue crab meat, patted dry
½ teaspoon cream of tartar

Melt butter in saucepan over medium heat. Add shallots and thyme. Cook 1 minute, stirring often. Add flour. Cook 1 minute stirring constantly. Whisk in half-and-half. Cook 3 minutes, whisking constantly. Remove from heat. Transfer to large mixing bowl. Immediately add goat cheese, salt, paprika, and cayenne pepper. Combine well. Whisk in egg yolks, one at a time. Fold in crabmeat. Set aside. In a separate bowl, beat egg whites with cream of tartar to stiff peaks. Fold one-fourth of egg whites into crab mixture. Gently fold in remaining egg whites with rubber spatula, ensuring that batter does not deflate. Divide mixture equally into soufflé dishes, three-fourths full. Bake 20 minutes in center of oven until nicely puffed and golden brown.

Lobster

Dining on lobster has long been a status symbol for the upper class. From the great "lobster palaces" of the Gilded Age to the dining rooms of luxury cruise lines, "I'll have the lobster" subliminally means "I have a lot of money." But when the English settled the New World, lobsters were so accessible and abundant that they were considered fodder for the poor. In those days it may have been common at the poor family's dinner table to hear, "Not lobster again!" Lobsters have bad eyesight but a fantastic sense of smell that leads them to feast on fresh clams, mussels, and crabs. They are gourmands, too!

In the Wild
There are many different species of lobster in our oceans, but they fall into basic categories:

True Lobsters
The true lobster lives in the cold waters of northeastern North America and Europe, populating the coasts of Maine, Canada, and Brittany. They have two large claws.

True lobsters can have different shades but are mostly rusty brown in color.

Being from cold water, the true lobster has sweeter and more tender meat than warm-water lobsters.

Spiny Lobsters
Also called rock lobster, Baja lobster, or Caribbean lobsters, spiny lobsters are found in the Caribbean and Mediterranean Seas, Asia, and along the Pacific coast of North America. They have spines on their body with yellow, brown, orange, and blue markings and long spiny antennae.

Spiny lobsters have five pairs of legs but do not have claws, so the only edible meat is in the tail.

The spiny lobster has hooked horns over their eyes, making them look mean.

Rock Lobsters

They are also called spiny lobsters, even though true spiny lobsters are different.

Australians may call them crayfish, sea crayfish, or crawfish.

Rock lobsters are found in warm waters around the world, including off the coast of Australia, South Africa, and New Zealand.

In the Kitchen

Tropical rock lobsters are considered the best for sashimi.

To cook whole spiny lobsters, place them head first into boiling salted water. Return water to very light simmer, then cook 8 minutes. The shell of a spiny lobster turns a bright red-orange when cooked.

To cook lobster tails, pull the flesh from the shell, season with your favorite spices and herbs, and roast in the oven.

To heat cold cooked lobster, place whole lobster or tails on a rack over a small amount of boiling water in a covered saucepan or steamer. (Do not immerse rack in water.) Steam just long enough to heat thoroughly.

Cooking lobsters 10 to 12 minutes under a hot broiler or a barbecue, depending on size, is usually enough.

Valuable Nutrients from Lobster

- Calcium: maintains strong bones, prevents colon cancer
- Copper: for healthy metabolism and organ function
- Omega-3 fatty acids: prevent cardiovascular disease
- Phosphorus: builds healthy bones and strong teeth
- Riboflavin: for healthy skin and healing
- Selenium: antioxidant, prevents arthritis
- Vitamin B_{12}: promotes healthy blood cells, prevents anemia, eases migraines

Fun Facts

During the American colonial period, lobsters were regarded as barely more than rodents and were fed to prisoners. That's a far cry from the status symbol of luxury and opulence they enjoy today.

Spiny lobsters march in single file, forming a line over one thousand lobsters long as they migrate from shallow to deep water. What's even more amazing is they actually have a true ability to navigate, a talent that is very unique amongst invertebrates. No GPS needed.

About 45 million pounds of lobster are caught in US waters each year; 90 percent of that comes from the coast of Maine.

The word *minestrone* in Italian means "the big soup"—the one that contains a lot of goodies and is eaten as a meal in itself. There is not a classic set recipe for minestrone; the preparation is driven by the region and the season. From the soup's early pre–Roman Empire origins until the seventeenth century, minestrone was made from the scraps of other recipes. Two major events transformed the soup into its modern version: First was the introduction of tomatoes from the Americas; second, was the practice of gathering ingredients specifically for the dish. This recipe is still based on the humble principles of the *cucina puvera* ("poor man's kitchen"), but since it is supposed to be the soup with the goodies, we just had to add some nuggets of lobster. —RON

Lobster Minestrone
Pearl Barley, Pecorino Romano
SERVES 6

LOBSTER
8 sprigs thyme
1 cup chopped carrots
1 lemon, sliced
1 teaspoon sea salt
2 live lobsters (1¼ pounds each)

Bring 2 gallons water to boil in large stockpot with thyme, carrots, lemon, and sea salt. Add lobsters. Cook 8 minutes. Transfer lobsters to ice bath. Reserve cooking water. Chill lobsters thoroughly. Separate tails and claws from the heads. Crack claws and knuckles. Remove meat from shell. Using sharp chef's knife, cut tail in half lengthwise. Remove meat from shell. Devein. Dice meat. Set aside. Rinse head cavity under cold water. Return all shells to cooking liquid in pot. Simmer 15 minutes. Strain lobster stock through fine sieve. Reserve.

MINESTRONE
½ cup pearl barley
2 tablespoons olive oil
1 cup diced pancetta
1 cup peeled, diced red onions
4 cloves garlic, finely chopped
1 cup chopped celery
½ cup dry white wine
2 cups diced vine-ripened tomatoes
8 cups reserved lobster stock
1 cup diced, peeled butternut squash
½ cup diced zucchini
1 cup seashell pasta
2 cups baby spinach leaves
¼ cup chopped fresh basil leaves
to taste sea salt
to taste ground black pepper
2-ounce piece pecorino
   Romano cheese
2 tablespoons extra-virgin olive oil

Rinse barley in colander under cold running water. Set aside. Add olive oil and pancetta to heavy-bottomed stockpot over medium heat. Cook until fat renders and pancetta is crisp. Add onions, garlic, and celery. Cook 3 minutes or until vegetables are soft, stirring often. Add white wine, tomatoes, barley, and lobster stock. Bring mixture to low simmer. Cook 30 minutes. Add butternut squash, zucchini, and seashell pasta. Cook 10 minutes or until pasta is tender, adding more stock if needed. Remove from heat. Stir in spinach, basil, and reserved lobster meat. Season to taste with salt and pepper. Ladle soup in serving bowls. Grate pecorino Romano atop. Drizzle with extra-virgin olive oil.

The setting in which we eat contributes a large amount of flavor to the dining experience. Take lobster rolls for example. Part of the culinary heritage of Maine, good ones and excellent ones can be found up and down the coast, like pushpins on a map. They are simple in structure: Boiled lobster is lightly dressed with mayonnaise and then slapped on a toasted bun, but highly seasoned with a secret ingredient—Maine's coastal ambience. Our favorite spot is Vinalhaven, an island-town, dressed in northeastern charm, accessible only by sea. Sitting on a porch overlooking Vinalhaven's harbor and watching rays of sunlight electrify the blue-green water is Maine's second greatest pleasure. The first is her lobster rolls. —RON

Vinalhaven Island Lobster Roll

Bibb Lettuce, Green Apple, Brioche Bun

SERVES 4

LOBSTER

¼ **cup** sea salt

1 ear sweet corn

2 live lobsters (1¼ pounds each)

¼ **cup** mayonnaise

½ **teaspoon** lemon zest

1 tablespoon lemon juice

½ **teaspoon** minced garlic

1 tablespoon chopped tarragon

¼ **teaspoon** celery salt

¼ **teaspoon** Tabasco sauce

½ **cup** diced green apple

to taste sea salt

to taste ground black pepper

Bring 3 gallons water to boil in large stockpot with sea salt. Add corn. Cook 4 minutes. Transfer to side dish. Add lobsters. Cook 8 minutes. Transfer lobsters to ice bath. Chill thoroughly. Separate tails and claws from the heads. Crack claws and knuckles. Remove meat from shell. Using sharp chef's knife, cut tail in half lengthwise. Remove meat from shell. Devein. Set aside. Slice lobster into ¼-inch pieces. Transfer to mixing bowl. Slice corn kernels from cob. Add to lobster meat. Add mayonnaise, lemon zest, lemon juice, garlic, tarragon, celery salt, Tabasco sauce, and green apples. Season with sea salt and pepper. Refrigerate at least 1 hour.

THE ROLL

¼ **cup** unsalted butter, melted, divided

4 brioche hot-dog buns or bakery buns

1 head Bibb lettuce, washed, patted dry

1 tablespoon minced chives

1 lemon, cut into 4 wedges

Heat a griddle or cast-iron frying pan over medium-high heat. Brush some melted butter on the cut sides of the buns. Grill, buttered side down, 2 minutes or until golden crisp. Lay lettuce leaves on bun. Spoon lobster meat atop. Drizzle with remaining melted butter. Sprinkle with chives. Garnish with a lemon wedge.

My friend Debi grew up on a beautiful island in the Caribbean, enjoying the benefits of crystal-clear water and fresh, abundant seafood. During the local lobster season, between December and February, her family-fun excursion was to head out on the boat with a grill and catch a few spiny lobsters. The spiny lobster has a meaty, sweet-tasting tail but should not to be confused with its cold-water cousin, the Maine lobster, who wears a pair of claws. The local scotch bonnet pepper is a variety of chile pepper found mainly in the Caribbean. They have a wonderful flavor but are very hot, and not all peppers have the same intensity. Debi's dear friend and Caymanian legend in the kitchen, Miss Cleo, always warned, "Never cut a scotch bonnet pepper with your bare hands!" A mixture of fresh herbs and pepper blended with butter brings out the amazing flavors of lobster. —BERNARD

Rum Point Roasted Lobster Tails

Scotch Bonnet Herb Butter

SERVES 6

LOBSTER

1 cup (2 sticks) unsalted butter, room temperature

¼ cup chopped chives

1 teaspoon orange zest

2 tablespoons chopped Thai basil

4 cloves garlic, minced

1 small scotch bonnet pepper, seeded, finely diced

to taste sea salt

to taste ground black pepper

6 spiny lobster tails (8 ounces each)

In a small bowl blend butter, chives, orange zest, basil, garlic, and scotch bonnet pepper. Season with sea salt and black pepper. Set aside at room temperature. Make a lengthwise cut through the top of each lobster shell using kitchen shears, cutting to, but not through, lobster meat. Press shell open. Pull out meat and place on top of shell. Transfer to baking sheet. Generously coat each lobster tail with scotch bonnet herb butter. Cover. Refrigerate up to 2 hours. Reserve remaining herb butter for basting.

PRESENTATION

2 lemons, cut into 12 wedges

sprigs Thai basil

Preheat oven to 425°F. Place lobsters in oven. Cook 10 minutes or until the lobster meat turns opaque in the center. Meanwhile melt reserved herb butter in small saucepan over medium heat. Transfer lobster tails to serving platter. Spoon remaining herb butter atop lobster. Serve with lemon wedges and basil sprigs.

Saint Aubin's Harbour is located on the island of Jersey's south coast, opening to the Gulf of Saint-Malo and the English Channel. Fishermen returning from Canada with their newfound fortunes centuries ago would stop at the thriving little harbor village to feast on lobster. Fine merchants' seventeenth-century houses lining the embankments of the old cobbled High Street are witness to this heritage. Lobsters are still harvested by traditional methods in the rough seas around the island. Along the coastline, garden patches of zucchini blossoms and melons are kissed by the sun's rays on breezy summer days. Chilled melon nectar brings out the nutty essence of the lobster, a brilliant balancing act! —BERNARD

Blue Lobster Saint Aubin

Melon Nectar

SERVES 6

NECTAR

4 cups cantaloupe melon,
    peeled, seeded, diced
12 mint leaves
1 teaspoon sea salt,
    plus additional as needed
⅛ teaspoon chile powder
¼ cup apple juice
½ cup carrot juice

Add all ingredients to blender. Puree until smooth. Strain through fine colander. Adjust salt and chile powder if necessary. Refrigerate minimum 2 hours.

LOBSTER

5 sprigs lemon thyme
1 tablespoon pickling spices
1 teaspoon sea salt
1 (1½-pound) live lobster

Bring 2 gallons salted water to boil in large stockpot with lemon thyme, pickling spices, and salt. Simmer 5 minutes. Add lobster. Cook 10 minutes. Transfer to ice bath. Separate tails and claws from the heads. Crack claws and knuckles. Remove meat from shell. Using sharp kitchen shears, cut through shell but not through tail meat. Remove tail meat from shell. Devein. Slice tail into 1-inch thick medallions. Set aside. Dice claws and knuckles.

PRESENTATION

2 pears
6 sprigs tarragon
2 teaspoons mustard oil

Peel pears. Cut into ¼-inch-thick slices. Cut slices into 2 x ¼-inch sticks. Add Nectar to six chilled serving bowls. Arrange 6 pear sticks in tic-tac-toe pattern in center of nectar. Fill middle of pear sticks with claw and knuckle meat. Top with tail medallion. Garnish with tarragon sprig. Drizzle mustard oil around.

Roskoff is a town located at the westernmost portion of France, in the *département* (an administrative region) of Finistère, which literally translates as "end of earth." The wealth of shellfish, rich farmland, and bountiful orchards that curve around the coastline are the regional pride. The noble Breton lobster, recognized by its black shell with blue highlights that turn brick red when cooked, became the prince of crustaceans in the seventeenth century. In my grandmother's kitchen, *homard breton fricassé* is a traditional way to celebrate the harvest from forest, land, and sea. —BERNARD

Brittany Lobster Fricassee
Oyster Mushrooms, Leek, Peach Brandy
SERVES 4

LOBSTER

5 sprigs thyme

2 bay leaves

1 tablespoon fennel seeds

1 lemon, sliced

12 whole black peppercorns

¼ cup sea salt

4 live lobsters (1¼ pounds each)

Bring 2 gallons water to boil in large stockpot with thyme, bay leaves, fennel seeds, lemon, peppercorns, and salt for 5 minutes. Add 2 lobsters. Cook 6 minutes. Transfer to ice bath. Repeat process with remaining lobsters. Separate tails and claws from the heads by pulling and twisting with your hands. Crack claws and knuckles. Remove meat from shell. Using sharp chef's knife, cut tail in half lengthwise. Remove meat from shell. Devein. Reserve tail, knuckles, and claws for Fricassee.

FRICASSÉE

2 tablespoons olive oil

2 tablespoons (¼ stick) unsalted butter

1 pound oyster mushrooms

2 cups sliced leeks, white part only

½ cup chopped shallots

4 cloves garlic, minced

1 cup white wine

½ cup peach brandy

2 tablespoons thyme

1 cup crème fraîche

to taste sea salt

to taste ground white pepper

2 tablespoons finely minced chives

Add oil and butter to large skillet over medium-high heat. Add reserved lobster tails. Sear 30 seconds on both sides. Transfer lobster to platter. Add mushrooms to skillet. Cook 3 minutes. Fold in leeks, shallots, and garlic. Cook 3 minutes, stirring occasionally. Add wine, brandy, and thyme. Reduce by half. Add crème fraîche. Season with salt and pepper. Add reserved lobster tail, knuckles, and claw meat. Bring to simmer. Cook 1 minute or until lobster is heated. Adjust seasoning. Transfer to warm serving bowl. Sprinkle with chives. Serve immediately.

Spiny lobster, also called rock lobster or Baja lobster, is distinguished by the absence of claws, a rusty color, and striped legs. Prolific in Baja, their reputation helped build the town of Puerto Nuevo and make it famous. Americans were enticed to this spot, fifteen miles south of Rosarito Beach, by delectable lobsters, fish, and hospitable seafaring locals. They brought cookies, candy, and other delicious treats in exchange for a hitchhike on a fishing boat and an invite to their hosts' homes for a Mexican meal. Puerto Nuevo soon became known as the "lobster village." Today there seem to be as many restaurants as there are homes in the town, each one specializing in local lobster, split in half, grilled or seared in lard, and served with tortillas. —RON

Puerto Nuevo–Style Spiny Lobster

Orange Pico, Almond Salsa

SERVES 4

ALMOND SALSA

1 large red tomato
1 jalapeño pepper
1 small white onion, peeled, quartered
4 cloves garlic
¼ cup sliced almonds
¼ cup vegetable stock
1 cup diced peeled avocado
2 tablespoons lemon juice
½ cup cilantro leaves
to taste sea salt

Combine all ingredients except avocado, lemon juice, cilantro, and sea salt in saucepan over medium heat. Bring to simmer. Cover. Cook 10 minutes. Remove from heat. Cool 10 minutes. Transfer to blender. Add remaining ingredients. Puree until smooth.

LOBSTER

2 lemons, sliced
6 sprigs thyme
3 bay leaves
1 teaspoon black peppercorns
1 tablespoon sea salt
4 whole live Pacific spiny lobsters (1¼ pounds each)

Add 2 gallons water, lemons, thyme, bay leaves, peppercorns, and sea salt to large stockpot over high heat. Simmer 10 minutes. Add lobsters. Cook 5 minutes. Transfer to ice bath to stop cooking. Using a chef's knife, split lobsters in half lengthwise. Clean head cavity by rinsing under cold running water. Pat dry. Devein tails. Set aside.

RED ONION SALAD

2 oranges
1 cup thinly sliced red onion
¼ cup lime juice
1 cup sliced seedless cucumber
¼ cup cilantro leaves
2 tablespoons olive oil
to taste sea salt
to taste ground black pepper

Peel oranges. Cut into segments. Transfer to mixing bowl. Toss with remaining ingredients.

MARINADE

2 tablespoons olive oil
2 teaspoons smoked paprika
½ orange, zested, juiced

Preheat outdoor grill to medium-high heat. Combine all ingredients in bowl. Brush on the lobster meat. Place each lobster, meat side down on grill. Cook 3 minutes or until lightly charred. Turn over. Baste lobster meat with more marinade. Cook the shell side until lobster is heated through, about 5 minutes. Transfer to serving platter. Fill head cavity with Red Onion Salad. Drizzle lobster tail with remaining marinade. Serve hot with Almond Salsa.

Octopus

Octopuses have a level of intelligence and behavioral flexibility that is unseen in most invertebrates. Related to cuttlefish and squid, octopuses have two eyes and four pairs of arms that sprout from their head.

An octopus has a hard beak that is strategically located in the center of its arms to efficiently capture and crush hard-shelled delicacies such as abalone, crab, lobster, and other crustaceans.

An octopus is the chameleon of the sea, changing its skin color rapidly to blend in with its surroundings. People in the Mediterranean, East Asia, and other parts of the world have long considered them a culinary delight.

In the Wild

Primary octopus suppliers are the Philippines, Thailand, and Korea. Hawaii and California are domestic sources.

There are over 140 species in temperate and tropical waters throughout the world, ranging in size from a few ounces to over 100 pounds.

Larger octopuses can have a wingspan of almost 30 feet.

Octopuses are often caught near the shore in tide pools or at depths of several hundred feet, where they inhabit small, dark crevices in the ocean floor.

One method of catching an octopus is to use unbaited "habitat traps," into which the unsuspecting invertebrate willingly crawls. On the Tunisian island of Jerba, local people do this. Knowing the animals' habit of hiding in crevices at night, they put gray ceramic pots on the seabed. The next morning they are sure to find an octopus inside. Octopuses are smart, but not that smart.

In the Kitchen

Unlike squid, octopus must be cooked a long time to become tender.

Octopus meat has a unique texture that is smooth, but with a firm-to-chewy "bite."

The animal's diet of high-quality shellfish gives it a mild, sweet flavor.

The edible skin is purplish black and cloaks its milky white meat.

Octopus is a common ingredient in Japanese cuisine, including *takoyaki* (octopus fritters), which we love and make often!

Some octopus species are consumed live as sushi.

In the Galician region of Spain, *polbo á feira* ("county fair–style octopus") is a local favorite.

In the Greek islands, octopus hang from ropes, like laundry on a clothesline, waiting to be grilled as a meze and served with a glass of ouzo.

Valuable Nutrients from Octopus

- Iron: vital to the production of energy and a healthy immune system

- Omega-3 fatty acids: prevent cardiovascular disease

- Phosphorus: builds healthy bones and strong teeth

- Selenium: antioxidant, prevents arthritis

- Taurine: for healthy retina and cardiovascular function

- Vitamin B_6: for a healthy metabolism and immune system

- Vitamin B_{12}: promotes healthy blood cells, prevents anemia, eases migraines

- Zinc: controls acne, boosts immune system

Fun Facts

What is the plural of *octopus: octopuses* or *octopi?* Actually, both are correct!

The octopus is featured prominently in the art and history of ancient Peru.

Native Americans of Alaska believed that octopuses had the ability to influence the weather, which in turn played a role in the well-being and health of the local population.

According to Hawaiian creationism, the octopus is the sole survivor from a prior universe, which makes it the only link between us and a previous existence.

Takoyaki are Japanese octopus fritters (*tako* = octopus, *yaki* = griddled). This walnut-size snack was invented in Osaka by Tomekichi Endo, a *yatai* street vendor in 1935. Yatai are the small, mobile food stalls or pushcarts in Japan that line walkways and fill festivals, alluring passersby with enticing aromas from morning til night. A yatai typically specializes in one particular delight. In Osaka, takoyaki is the most popular yatai offering, sought after for its crispy outside; creamy, almost hollow interior; and pleasantly chewy nugget of octopus. To make them at home, a simple but unique takoyaki pan is needed; it can be found easily online or in Asian markets. —RON

Octopus Takoyaki
Candied Garlic Dipping Sauce
SERVES 4

CANDIED GARLIC DIPPING SAUCE

¼ cup peanut oil

⅓ cup garlic cloves

2 teaspoons miso paste

½ tablespoon chopped pickled ginger

¼ teaspoon sea salt

⅛ teaspoon wasabi powder

½ cup Japanese (or other) mayonnaise

Preheat oven to 300°F. Place oil and garlic in small casserole dish. Cover. Bake 25 minutes or until garlic is lightly browned and very soft. Transfer to blender with oil. Add miso, ginger, salt, and wasabi. Puree until smooth. Transfer to mixing bowl. Whisk in mayonnaise. Transfer to serving dish.

TAKOYAKI

10 ounces octopus legs

1 piece kombu (dried kelp), 3 inches square

½ cup dried bonito flakes

1¼ cups cake flour or all-purpose flour

¼ teaspoon sea salt

2 large eggs

1½ teaspoons soy sauce

½ cup finely chopped scallions

3 tablespoons minced pickled ginger

as needed high heat canola oil

Place octopus legs in stockpot. Cover with cold water. Place over medium heat. Bring to very low simmer. Cook 1½ hours. Rinse under cold water. Cut into ½-inch pieces, each containing a suction cup. Refrigerate. Rinse kombu under cold water to remove excess salt. Add 2 cups cold water and kombu to sauce pot over medium heat. Just before water begins to simmer, turn off heat. Discard kombu but reserve broth. Add bonito flakes to pot. Let stand 10 minutes. Strain through fine sieve. Refrigerate until well chilled. Combine flour and salt in large mixing bowl. In separate bowl, whisk 1¼ cups kombu broth, eggs, and soy sauce. Using whisk, stir egg mixture into flour just to combine. Fold in scallions and pickled ginger. Set aside. Place takoyaki pan over medium heat. Lightly brush entire surface of pan with oil. Add ¼ teaspoon oil to each hole. When oil is hot, pour batter in each hole, all the way up to the edge. Place 1 piece octopus atop. Using toothpick, immerse octopus into middle of the batter, which will overflow slightly. Cook 1 minute or until lightly browned. Using takoyaki pick or wooden skewer, poke tip into edge of fritter where the batter is cooked and push down to rotate it. You may turn fritter partially or fully. If you turn partially, allow to cook briefly in that position then proceed to complete the turn. Cook 4 minutes or until golden brown on outside and soft in the middle, turning often. Transfer to serving platter.

PRESENTATION

¼ **cup** premium oyster sauce

¼ **cup** dried bonito flakes

¼ **cup** daikon radish sprouts

1 tablespoon toasted sesame seeds

Mix oyster sauce with 2 tablespoons kombu broth (see above). Top each takoyaki with oyster sauce. Sprinkle with bonito flakes, radish sprouts, and sesame seeds. Serve with Candied Garlic Dipping Sauce.

Summer is the season to visit Cyprus, when you can dine seaside at an open-air, vine-covered taverna. Meze is the preferred style of service on the island, just like on the Greek mainland. The tabletop becomes a jigsaw of dishes, consuming every inch of real estate with olives, cheeses, stuffed vine leaves, hummus, sausages, vegetables, stewed meats, and pickled fish and octopus. All are piled high and ready to be sampled, the diners reaching for this dish and that and passing them around to the rhythm of a live Cypriot band. It is a culture of abundance, as rarely an empty dish is seen. Pickles, always present at a meze table, are a great way to preserve the bounty. —RON

Cypress Pickled Octopus

Feta, Mushrooms, Oregano
SERVES 4

POACHING LIQUID

½ **cup** white wine

4 dried bay leaves

1 **small sprig** rosemary

8 black peppercorns

6 **cloves** garlic, smashed

1½ **pounds** octopus tentacles

Add 3 cups water, wine, bay leaves, rosemary, peppercorns, and garlic to stockpot over medium heat. Bring to simmer. Turn off heat. Steep 15 minutes. Return to low simmer. Add octopus. Cook 1 hour or until tender. Transfer octopus to baking sheet, leaving poaching liquid in pot. Refrigerate octopus to chill quickly. Allow poaching liquid to sit until sediment settles. Pour 2 cups clear liquid from top. Reserve for Pickling Liquid.

PICKLING

¼ **cup** olive oil

12 small button mushrooms, trimmed

2 mild red chile peppers, halved lengthwise

3 **cloves** garlic, sliced

1 **cup** white wine

½ **cup** white wine vinegar

1 **teaspoon** dried oregano

1 **teaspoon** sea salt

1 lemon, thinly sliced crosswise

4 green onions, trimmed

1 **cup** Persian cucumbers, cut into ¼-inch slices

¼ **pound** feta cheese, cut into ½-inch cubes

Add oil to skillet over medium heat. Add mushrooms and chiles. Cook 2 minutes, stirring occasionally. Turn off heat. Add garlic, white wine, white wine vinegar, oregano, and salt. Stir to dissolve salt. Layer reserved octopus, lemon slices, onions, cucumbers, and feta cheese in resealable glass jar. Pour liquid along with mushrooms and chile peppers into jar. Seal jar. Refrigerate at least 2 days. To serve, arrange all ingredients in chilled serving dish. Spoon Pickling Liquid atop.

Squid

About five hundreds species of squid have been documented. They are found in coastal waters, oceans, and estuaries worldwide, but not in freshwater.

Squid have elongated tubular bodies and are among the most highly developed invertebrates, with eyes almost as complex as those of humans.

Squid have many adaptations that make them skilled predators. They capture their prey by wrapping their razor-sharp tentacles around the victim, then they use their small beak to shred the captive into smaller pieces.

Squid are also adept escape artists: Spraying a thick cloud of black ink in the water, they disappear like a magician.

The squid's life span is relatively short, making them a very sustainable species.

In the Wild

Little is known of the life history of squids, but one thing is for sure: They have been here for millions of years. You will find large numbers of them in almost all the major bodies of water, including the North Atlantic, Gulf of Mexico, Sea of Japan, North Pacific, Indian Ocean, and Bering Sea.

Some squid thrive in warm tropical waters while others prefer colder water.

Squid are highly flexible creatures, able to move and adapt quickly if their natural habitat is destroyed. Many believe this is why squid have survived and prospered during their millions of years in the ocean.

Common Squid
This species often travels in shoals and is found from Maine to the Carolinas, in Monterey Bay (California), along the Florida coast, and in the Caribbean.

Boston Squid
The Boston squid is found from Massachusetts to North Carolina and has also been caught from Nova Scotia to the coast of Venezuela.

Colossal Squid and the Giant Squid
Also called Humboldt squid, these are found in the oceans near Antarctica. Because they can survive in

these extremely cold temperatures, they can grow to be very large as they don't have any predators except for sharks.

They swim in shoals over one thousand members strong.

Japanese Flying Squid

This species is found in the waters of Japan, China, Alaska, and Vietnam.

Called flying squid for their unique ability to leap great distances out of the water, sometimes spanning a distance of 90 feet through the air. This is done to conserve energy or possibly to elude a predator.

In the Kitchen

Squid is a favorite food in East Asia and the Mediterranean area and is served in virtually every coastal cuisine around the globe.

Calamari is the Italian word for "squid." Most people think of calamari as breaded and fried rings and tentacles, but we also love to stuff calamari tubes and braise both tubes and tentacles.

Stir-fried squid is great due to the short cooking time.

Squid must be cooked quickly at high temperature or slowly at low temperature in order to be tender; there is no in-between. Squid can also be added to cioppinos or any seafood stew.

If you get a hold of some squid ink, save it. It has very little taste but adds a dramatic black color to foods like freshly made pasta and gnocchi.

Make squid stew using a favorite stew recipe, but substitute squid for the meat.

Cuttlefish, a close cousin, can be substituted in almost all recipes calling for squid or calamari.

The port town of Yobuko, near Karatsu City, Japan, is well-known for squid sashimi served still alive. The squid is masterfully butchered by highly skilled sushi chefs, rendering a beautifully transparent meat with an almost gelatinous, toothy bite.

Valuable Nutrients from Squid

- Magnesium: maintains healthy blood pressure and strong bones, relaxes nerves

- Niacin: increases good cholesterol levels

- Phosphorus: builds healthy bones and strong teeth

- Potassium: for a healthy heart and kidneys, reduces stress

- Riboflavin: for healthy skin and healing

- Selenium: antioxidant, prevents arthritis

- Vitamin B$_{12}$: promotes healthy blood cells, prevents anemia, eases migraines

- Zinc: controls acne, boosts immune system

Fun Facts

Squid have three hearts—that makes for a great dish on Valentines Day!

Some species of squid glow in the dark.

The Humboldt squid is known to attack sharks and humans when in the mood.

Squid swim backward, with their head in back. Try that next time you go swimming.

A squid's body (the tube) is more nutritious than the tentacles.

The giant squid has eyeballs the size of basketballs!

While traveling Mediterranean littorals, you will find many different versions of this classic preparation of calamari. The seaside village of Lavandou is a favorite place for vacationers to explore the fragrant lavender fields, fine sandy beaches, and dreamy fishing port. Every morning the fish market is bustling with people looking for the freshest seafood catch and prized local squid—aka *calamar*! There are only two foolproof techniques for cooking squid: hot and quick, or low and slow—it toughens in between. On the Cote d'Azur *la daube de calamars* is a favorite, as the classic beef stew preparation is replaced by local squid simmered in red wine and aromatics, braised until it is perfectly tender. Like red wine, squid are found all over the world and are very popular in many cuisines. —BERNARD

Petit Syrah Braised Calamar
Champignon, Pearl Onions, Fennel
SERVES 4

VEGETABLES

2 tablespoons olive oil

1 cup diced red potatoes

to taste sea salt

to taste ground black pepper

½ cup diced smoked ham

2 cups halved button mushrooms (champignon)

1 cup finely sliced fennel

Add oil to large nonstick skillet over medium-high heat. Add potatoes. Season with salt and pepper. Cook 5 minutes or until golden brown and tender, stirring often. Transfer to side dish. Add ham, mushrooms, and fennel to skillet. Season with salt and pepper. Cook 4 minutes or until lightly browned, stirring often. Return potatoes to skillet. Remove from heat. Set aside.

SQUID

2 pounds cleaned squid tubes and tentacles

2 tablespoons (¼ stick) unsalted butter

5 cloves garlic, crushed

24 pearl onions, peeled

4 sprigs thyme

to taste sea salt

to taste ground black pepper

1 cup Petit Syrah wine

1 cup tomato juice

2 bay leaves

2 tablespoons chopped fresh parsley

1 tablespoon extra-virgin olive oil

Slice squid tubes into ¾-inch-wide rings. Add butter to dutch oven over medium heat. Add garlic, onions, and thyme. Cook 2 minutes or until lightly browned. Add squid tubes and tentacles. Season with salt and pepper. Cook 2 minutes. Add wine, tomato juice, and bay leaves. Bring to low simmer. Cover. Cook 35 minutes. Uncover. Raise heat to medium. Cook 10 minutes or until sauce is reduced by one-third. Stir in reserved Vegetables mixture. Transfer to serving dish. Sprinkle with parsley. Drizzle with olive oil.

Bomba is an ancient strain of rice that matures very slowly and is almost unknown outside of Spain. It is grown around the town of Calasparra in the province of Murcia, where the cultivation of bomba rice is considered an art form. It is very hard to grow, even under ideal conditions. Its yields are far lower than the classic balilla rice. Bomba's flavor is very unique, as the rice can absorb a large quantity of liquid, expanding in width like an accordion rather than longitudinally, while remaining firm during the cooking process. Combining almond milk, sherry wine, saffron, and chorizo will enhance the richness of bomba. Cooked in the style of risotto, it is heaven on earth for sizzling squids. If using Arborio rice, stir occasionally instead of constantly. —BERNARD

Paprika Chorizo Squid
Almond Saffron Bomba Rice
SERVES 4

SQUID

1 pound squid
　　tubes and tentacles, cleaned
6 cups vegetable broth
2 bay leaves
6 cloves garlic, smashed

Slice squid tubes into ½-inch-wide rings. Place in casserole dish along with tentacles. Refrigerate until needed. Add vegetable broth, bay leaves, and garlic to saucepan over medium heat. Simmer 10 minutes. Stir in squid. Cook 30 seconds. Turn off heat. Transfer squid to baking sheet, leaving broth in saucepan. Place squid in freezer 5 minutes. Transfer to refrigerator. Reserve broth for rice recipe.

ALMOND SAFFRON BOMBA RICE

⅛ teaspoon saffron threads
2 tablespoons olive oil, divided
¼ cup sliced onion
1½ cups bomba or Arborio rice
¾ cup dry sherry
½ cup unsweetened almond milk
½ cup chopped almonds
2 tablespoons chopped tarragon
½ cup grated Manchego cheese
to taste sea salt
to taste ground black pepper
½ cup finely diced Spanish
　　chorizo sausage
1 teaspoon smoked paprika
1 lemon, halved
12-ounce piece Manchego cheese
　　for shaving
4 sprigs oregano

Add saffron to reserved broth from Squid recipe. Place over low heat. Add 1 tablespoon olive oil to large pot over medium heat. Add onions. Cook 2 minutes, stirring constantly. Add rice. Cook 1 minute, stirring constantly. Add sherry wine. Cook 1 minute, stirring often. Add 1 cup hot broth reserved from Squid recipe. Cook, stirring occasionally until liquid is absorbed and leaves a clear wake behind the spoon. Repeat process three times, cooking until rice is al dente. Total cooking time should be 15–20 minutes. Remove from heat. Fold in almond milk, almonds, tarragon, and cheese. Season with salt and pepper. If necessary, stir in more hot broth to achieve a creamy texture. Transfer to lidded serving dish. Cover to keep warm. Add remaining 1 tablespoon olive oil and chorizo to large skillet over medium high heat. Cook 2 minutes. Add squid. Season with smoked paprika, salt, and pepper. Saute 2 minutes or until lightly browned. Transfer to atop risotto. Squeeze lemon over squid. Spoon pan juices atop. Shave Manchego atop of rice. Garnish with sprigs of oregano.

The climate in Szechuan Province is often hot and humid, which contributes to a style of cuisine that differs significantly from other regions of China. Szechuan cuisine is known primarily for its hot and spicy dishes that include a variety of aromatic ingredients: Garlic, ginger, star anise, various types of peppers, and fragrant herbs are commonly used. Despite its popular name, the Szechuan pepper also called "flower pepper" or "mountain pepper," in reality, is a type of fruit that grows in the city of Chongqing. It produces a tingly, numbing sensation in the mouth called *má*. In Shanghai I had my first adventurous Szechuan-style barbecued squid on a stick, which was cooked by a street vendor over red-hot charcoal on the back of a bicycle. Delicious! —BERNARD

Szechuan Pepper Wok-Fried Squid

Water Chestnuts, Orange Hoisin Sauce

SERVES 4

SQUID

2 teaspoons Szechuan peppercorns

1 teaspoon sea salt

1 teaspoon orange zest

1 tablespoon granulated sugar

1 pound squid tubes and tentacles, cleaned

2 tablespoons sunflower oil

½ cup cornstarch

Add Szechuan peppercorns, salt, and orange zest to mortar or spice grinder. Process to coarse powder. Combine with sugar in mixing bowl. Set aside. Using sharp chef's knife, open squid tubes by cutting along one side and unfolding. Lightly score inside surface of squid in crisscross diamond pattern. Then cut scored squid into 1-inch-wide strips. Transfer to large mixing bowl along with tentacles. Thoroughly pat dry with paper towels. Add oil to wok over high heat. Sprinkle peppercorn mixture over squid, tossing to coat. Add cornstarch. Toss to coat. Shake off excess cornstarch. When oil in wok starts to smoke, add squid. Stir-fry 2 minutes or until squid is opaque. Transfer to side dish. Reserve.

VEGETABLES

2 tablespoons sesame oil

1 cup chopped, seeded red bell pepper

½ cup sliced shallots

1-inch piece ginger, thinly sliced

4 cloves garlic, sliced

¼ cup sliced water chestnuts

1 cup snow peas, cut in half on bias

2 tablespoons hoisin sauce

2 tablespoons soy sauce

½ cup orange juice

¼ cup chopped cilantro

4 spring onions, thinly sliced on the diagonal

Add oil to wok over high heat. Add bell pepper, shallots, ginger, garlic, water chestnuts, and snow peas. Stir-fry 2 minutes. Add hoisin sauce, soy sauce, and orange juice. Bring to simmer. Add squid. Stir-fry 1 minute or until hot and sauce thickens to glaze consistency. Toss in cilantro and spring onions. Transfer to warm serving dish.

Sousse is a white city. White sand, whitewashed houses, and white clouds are accented with blue trim, blue sea, and blue sky. Inside the fortified walls of the medina, in the covered bazaar, one finds scores of white squid shingled in blue strainer baskets, like a reflection of the city itself. A popular tradition is to grill seafood *tabil* style, sauced with a relish of chiles, red peppers, garlic, and seasonings. In this recipe, we bake the squid in a tabil-inspired sauce after stuffing it with dates and uncooked couscous, which absorbs the renderings of the squid while it cooks. This causes the couscous to expand in flavor but also in size, so make sure to leave some room for expansion when stuffing the squid. —RON

Date Spinach Stuffed Squid
Tomato Chile Sauce
SERVES 4

SQUID

1 large egg
2 tablespoons extra-virgin olive oil
¼ cup white wine
1 teaspoon curry powder
1 tablespoon sliced mint leaves
2 tablespoons minced shallots
to taste sea salt
to taste ground black pepper
⅓ cup uncooked Moroccan couscous
½ cup chopped dates
1 cup spinach leaves,
     tightly packed, chopped
8 large squid tubes, cleaned

Whisk egg, olive oil, wine, curry powder, mint, and shallots together. Season with salt and pepper. Stir in couscous. Fold in dates and spinach. Let stand 10 minutes. Stuff mixture into squid tubes, securing each with two toothpicks.

TOMATO CHILE SAUCE

2 dried ancho chiles, stemmed, seeded
2 tablespoons olive oil
¼ cup minced white onion
½ teaspoon coriander seeds
½ teaspoon caraway seeds
3 cups diced tomatoes
3 cloves garlic, minced
to taste sea salt
to taste ground black pepper

Preheat oven to 350°F. Tear ancho chiles into 1-inch pieces. Add oil to skillet over medium-high heat. Add onion, coriander, caraway, and chiles. Saute 2 minutes, stirring constantly. Add tomatoes and garlic. Bring to low simmer. Cook 10 minutes. Transfer to blender. Process until smooth. Season with salt and pepper.

PRESENTATION

½ cup bread crumbs
¼ cup shredded gruyère cheese
2 teaspoons dried parsley flakes
½ tablespoon olive oil

Transfer one-third of Tomato Chile Sauce to serving ramekin. Spread another third of sauce in bottom of baking dish. Place squid atop sauce. Ladle remaining third of sauce atop squid. Cover. Cook 15 minutes. Uncover. Combine bread crumbs, cheese, parsley flakes, and oil in small bowl. Sprinkle mixture atop squid. Cook 5 minutes or until golden brown and stuffing is hot in center. Remove toothpicks and serve.

CHAPTER 4

Little Fins

SNAPPER, ARCTIC CHAR, SOLE, POMPANO/POMFRET, JOHN DORY

Snapper
INDIA
Kerala Beach Snapper Curry
cashew date basmati

THAILAND
Crispy Skin Red Snapper
aromatic sticky black rice

MEXICO
Red Snapper Margarita
charred orange tomatillo salsa

UNITED STATES
Opakapaka Snapper Lomi Lomi
papaya seed dressing

FIJI
Wok-Steamed Whole Red Snapper
mango pickles

Arctic Char
ENGLAND
Horseradish Baked Arctic Char
parsnip puree, apples, asparagus

FINLAND
Orange Peel Pickled Arctic Char
beet root jam, cucumber salad

CANADA
Pan-Roasted Arctic Char
black-eyed pea succotash

UNITED STATES
Blue Corn and Sunflower Crusted Arctic Char
apricot kasha pilaf, citrus parsley butter

Sole
SOUTH AFRICA
Lemon Pepper Sole
green mung beans, piri piri sauce

SCOTLAND
Amber Ale Sole Fingers
caraway potato chips, homemade mustard

UNITED STATES
Petrale Sole and Crab Pinwheel
sweet corn, butternut squash, vermouth

ENGLAND
Jersey Island Fillet of Sole Walnutine
golden raisin parsley butter

Pompano/Pomfret
FIJI
Fijian Pomfret Fish Balls
pineapple hoisin broth

LAOS
Rice Paper Wrapped Pompano
pickled green papaya, tangerine sauce

VIETNAM
Pompano Indochine
lemongrass caramel sauce

John Dory
FRANCE
John Dory en Papillotte
oyster mushrooms, fennel, tomatoes

JAPAN
Wasabi Green Pea Crusted John Dory
mochi gome, asian pear slaw

ROMANIA
Constanta Port John Dory Tochitura
toasted lemon rice

Snapper

Red snappers live offshore on the continental shelf, over deep reefs, banks, and muddy bottoms that provide a rich supply of shellfish for their daily diet.

Beware of "snapper" sold on the West Coast. "Pacific red snapper" is not true red snapper but red rockfish.

The only species that can be legally labeled red snapper is the American red snapper.

Red snapper have trademark red skin and red eyes. They are found in the Gulf of Mexico and the South Atlantic.

In the Wild

Snappers are a tropical fish abundant in the waters of Mexico, Venezuela, Brazil, Peru, the United States, the Caribbean, Thailand, Taiwan, and Philippines.

One hundred five species of snapper are known.

Their large mouths and sharp teeth facilitate their appetite for crustaceans and other fish.

Snappers travel in schools, at depths between 30 and 600 feet.

Other names include *vivaneau rouge, luciano-do-golfo, estrella,* and, in Mexico, the true red snapper is named *huachinango.*

In the Kitchen

Red snapper is lean and moist, with a sweetly mild, distinctive flavor. The semifirm meat is pinkish with yellow tones when raw, turning somewhat lighter when cooked.

The taste of this fish will differ from type to type of snapper, influenced by the environmental conditions of its location.

Always buy fillets with the skin on to make sure they're the real thing. When buying whole red snapper, look for clear, red eyes and bright red skin that fades toward the belly. Grilling with the skin on is easier as it holds the fish together.

Snapper is a great candidate both for crispy skin preparation and steaming whole in a wok.

Fresh snapper has a shellfish flavor that is awesome as ceviche.

Valuable Nutrients from Snapper

- Magnesium: maintains healthy blood pressure and strong bones, relaxes nerves

- Omega-3 fatty acids: prevent cardiovascular disease

- Phosphorus: builds healthy bones and strong teeth

- Potassium: for a healthy heart and kidneys, reduces stress

- Selenium: antioxidant, prevents arthritis

- Vitamin B_6: for a healthy metabolism and immune system

- Vitamin B_{12}: promotes healthy blood cells, prevents anemia, eases migraines

- Vitamin C: powerful antioxidant, prevents high blood pressure and cataracts

Fun Facts

Research shows that red snapper has been eaten in Japan since the Jomon Period, around 12,000 BC.

Red snapper is highly treasured in Japan and considered to be a good luck charm, a fish fit for celebrations, the New Year, and whenever well-wishes are made.

A snapper's age can be discovered by counting annual growth rings on their ear bone.

Cheena vala are fishing nets that are fixed land installations mostly found in the Indian state of Kerala. This seven-hundred-year-old tradition on Fort Kochi Beach is an unusual form of fishing. With only a few nets left, time is of the essence, as this old practice is disappearing. Huge mechanized wooden contrivances hold nets sixty feet across. Each structure is at least thirty feet high and comprises a cantilever with an outstretched net suspended over the sea. Operated by a team of up to six fishermen, the nets are lowered into the water and then lifted, catching everything in their paths. Fish and crustaceans are sold to passersby within minutes to be prepared as fish curry, the signature dish of Kerala. The taste varies dramatically according to the type of fish used, but the best is snapper. A fresh fish curry should have the essence of the sea. —BERNARD

Kerala Beach Snapper Curry

Cashew Date Basmati

SERVES 4

CURRY

2 pounds boneless red snapper fillets,
    skin on, cut into 1-inch cubes

1 teaspoon sea salt

2 tablespoons lemon juice

1 teaspoon lemon zest

6 cloves garlic, chopped

4 tablespoons curry powder, divided

3 tablespoons coconut oil

2 cups sliced white onions

3 anaheim chiles, stemmed, seeded, sliced

1 tablespoon grated ginger

2 cups diced, peeled eggplant

¾ cup cooked drained chickpeas

4 cups chopped red tomatoes

3 cups vegetable stock

to taste sea salt

to taste ground black pepper

Add snapper, salt, lemon zest, lemon juice, garlic, and 2 tablespoons curry powder to mixing bowl. Toss to coat. Cover. Refrigerate until needed. Add coconut oil to large saucepot over medium heat. Add onions, chiles, ginger, and remaining curry powder. Cook 3 minutes, stirring often. Add eggplant and chickpeas. Cook 3 minutes, stirring often. Add tomatoes and vegetable stock. Bring to simmer. Cover . Cook 5 minutes. Fold snapper and its marinade into tomato stew. Cover. Simmer 5 minutes or until snapper is cooked through. Season with salt and pepper if needed. Transfer to serving bowl.

CASHEW DATE BASMATI

1 tablespoon safflower oil

½ cup chopped white onion

3 whole cloves

2 cups water

1 teaspoon sea salt

1 bay leaf

1 cup basmati rice, rinsed, drained

⅓ cup chopped, toasted cashews

12 dates, sliced

2 teaspoons orange flower water

Add oil to small saucepan over medium heat. Add onion and cloves. Cook 2 minutes without browning, stirring often. Add water, salt, bay leaf, and rice. Cover. Bring to simmer. Reduce heat as low as possible. Cook 15 minutes or until water is fully absorbed. Remove from heat. Let sit covered 5 minutes. Fluff with fork. Fold in remaining ingredients.

1 teaspoon poppy seeds

3 tablespoons toasted, shaved coconut

1 tablespoon chopped cilantro leaves

1 tablespoon chopped mint leaves

Toss all ingredients in small mixing bowl. Sprinkle atop snapper curry.

Sweet, glutinous black jasmine rice populates the paddy fields of Thailand. Thousands of long straw-like green stems sway in synchronicity in the wind. Each is trimmed with a wreath of oblong black grains bending narcissistically toward the irrigated water that feeds them. Thai black rice is touted as a new super food. It is high in amino acids, fiber, iron, and vitamin B, to boot. In the absence of black rice, sushi rice can be used in this recipe. By salting the skin of the snapper to extract its moisture, you will be rewarded with an extra-crispy skin. —RON

Crispy Skin Red Snapper
Aromatic Sticky Black Rice
SERVES 4

AROMATIC STICKY BLACK RICE
1¼ cups Thai black rice
1 tablespoon sesame oil
1 small yellow onion, chopped
1 cup sliced celery
6 cloves garlic, smashed
¼ cup sliced ginger
1 cup chopped Thai basil leaves with stems
3 Kaffir lime leaves
1 tablespoon anchovy paste
3 cups vegetable broth
to taste sea salt
to taste ground black pepper

Rinse rice in colander under cold water until water runs clear. Drain. Set aside. Add sesame oil to saucepan over medium heat. Add onion, celery, garlic, and ginger. Cook 3 minutes, stirring often. Add basil and lime leaves. Cook 1 minute. Add anchovy paste and vegetable broth. Bring to low simmer. Cook 15 minutes. Strain through fine sieve. Transfer 2 cups broth to small saucepan over medium-low heat, reserving ½ cup for Sauce. Stir rice into saucepan. Bring to simmer. Cover. Reduce heat to low. Cook 15 minutes. Turn off heat. Fluff with fork. Season with salt and pepper.

SAUCE
½ cup reserved broth
½ cup toasted unsalted peanuts
2 tablespoons sesame oil
½ cup Thai basil leaves
1 tablespoon lime juice
1 teaspoon anchovy paste
¼ teaspoon minced, seeded red Thai chile pepper
to taste sea salt

Add all ingredients to blender, starting with broth. Puree until smooth. Transfer to serving dish.

SNAPPER
4 red snapper fillets, skin on, boneless (6 ounces each)
to taste sea salt
to taste ground white pepper
as needed canola oil spray
2 tablespoons canola oil

Season snapper on both sides with salt and pepper. Transfer fish skin side down to paper towel–lined side dish. Cover. Refrigerate 1 hour. Spray skin with canola oil. Add oil to skillet over medium heat until very hot but not smoking. Place snapper in skillet skin side down. Press fish with spatula to keep skin in contact with oil. Cook 3 minutes or until skin is golden brown and crisp. Turn snapper over. Cook 1 minute or until slightly underdone.

PRESENTATION

4 sprigs Thai basil
1 teaspoon chile oil

Place a 2-inch ring in center of warm serving plate. Spoon rice into ring, compacting to mold shape. Spread sauce onto plate around rice. Top with snapper. Garnish with basil sprig and chile oil.

Along Mexico's eastern coast, from Tampico to Cancún, whatever paved road or unmarked path leads to the beach will likely take you to at least one or up to a few hundred *enramadas*. *Enramada* literally translates to "lined with branches" and refers to the open-air, thatched-roof huts where seafood plucked just beyond the break surf is fire-grilled on skewers and eaten while your toes wiggle in the sand. Red snapper, called *huachinango* in Spanish, is the ubiquitous fare, along with octopus, shrimp, and lobster. Snapper's sweet tropical flavor always invites its chile, citrus, and garlic friends to come to the beach and have a grill party. —RON

Red Snapper Margarita
Charred Orange Tomatillo Salsa
SERVES 4

CHARRED ORANGE TOMATILLO SALSA

as needed canola oil spray
½ pound tomatillos, husked, halved
1 small red onion, peeled, cut into 4 slices
4 ears sweet corn, husked
2 oranges, peeled, cut into 4 slices each
1 red bell pepper, stemmed, seeded, quartered lengthwise
to taste sea salt
to taste ground black pepper
3 cloves garlic, minced
¼ cup chopped cilantro
2 tablespoons red wine vinegar
½ teaspoon hot chile powder

Preheat grill to medium high. Lightly coat grates with canola oil spray. Place tomatillos (cut side up), onion, corn, oranges, and red pepper on baking sheet. Spray with canola oil. Season with salt and pepper. Grill vegetables on all sides until lightly charred. Transfer back to baking sheet. Shave kernels from corn. Chop tomatillos, onion, oranges, and bell pepper. Transfer to mixing bowl. Combine with remaining ingredients.

SNAPPER

¼ cup lime juice
1 tablespoon agave nectar or honey
2 tablespoons gold tequila
1 teaspoon sea salt
2 cloves garlic, minced
1 tablespoon chopped, seeded jalapeño pepper
½ teaspoon ground cumin
2 tablespoons olive oil
4 red snapper fillets,
    1 inch thick, skin on, boneless (6 ounces each)
as needed canola oil spray

Combine all ingredients except snapper in nonreactive baking dish. Add snapper. Turn to coat. Cover. Refrigerate at least 2 hours. Remove from marinade. Spray both sides lightly with canola oil. Grill skin side up for 3 minutes or until caramelized. Using spatula, turn fish over. Cook until slightly underdone. Transfer to large serving platter. Spoon salsa atop.

The Pacific islanders all have their interpretation of *lomi lomi,* depending on their geography. *Oka i'a* means "raw fish" in Samoan; in Tahitian the term is *e'ia ota,* a traditional preparation of sliced raw fish, lime juice, coconut milk, onion, carrot, and tomatoes. The Hawaiian version, *lomi lomi* means "to massage," in this case to break the fish into small pieces and combine them with other ingredients. Opakapaka is a pink snapper that has a delicate flavor and good fat content, making it an interesting choice for sashimi and the perfect candidate for lomi lomi. The local pineapple brings a sweet and sour balance, giving it a delicious tangy taste. —BERNARD

Opakapaka Snapper Lomi Lomi
Papaya Seed Dressing
SERVES 4

SNAPPER

¼ **cup** kosher salt, divided

1½ **pounds** snapper fillet,
    boneless, skinless, at least 1 inch thick

½ **cup** Maui finely chopped onions

½ **cup** finely sliced scallions

1 **cup** finely diced pineapple

1 **cup** seeded, diced tomato

2 **tablespoons** canola oil

½ **teaspoon** Tabasco sauce

¼ **cup** chopped, toasted macadamia nuts

to taste kosher salt

to taste ground black pepper

Sprinkle 2 tablespoons kosher salt in bottom of nonreactive baking dish. Place snapper atop salt. Sprinkle with remaining salt. Cover. Refrigerate 45 minutes. Rinse under cold running water to remove salt. Pat dry with paper towels. Transfer to cutting board. Slice into ½-inch cubes. Transfer to mixing bowl. Combine with remaining ingredients, except macadamia nuts and salt and pepper. Refrigerate at least 2 hours. Fold in 3 tablespoons Papaya Seed Dressing and macadamias. Season with salt and pepper.

PAPAYA SEED DRESSING

2 Hawaiian papayas

6 **tablespoons** pineapple juice

3 **tablespoons** lime juice

¾ **cup** canola oil

to taste sea salt

to taste ground black pepper

1 **cup** watercress leaves

Cut papayas in half lengthwise. Slice off enough from bottom end of each papaya half to make a flat surface and prevent toppling when plated. Scoop out seeds. Transfer 1 tablespoon seeds to blender. Discard remaining seeds. Scoop 2 tablespoons flesh from center of each papaya half. Transfer to blender. Add pineapple juice and lime juice. Turn blender to medium speed. With motor running, slowly drizzle in oil to emulsify. Season with salt and pepper. Drizzle 1 tablespoon papaya seed dressing inside each papaya boat. Fill with snapper. Transfer to center of chilled serving platter. Garnish with watercress.

Once called Cannibal Isles, the island of Fiji now boasts beauty, peace, and serenity. Tropical vegetation, mangroves, hot springs, and old volcanic peaks surround the turquoise blue waters of Savusavu Bay. The local open-air market is full of big smiles and the Fijian greeting "*Bula*" as vendors sell exotic fruits, vegetables, and rainbow-colored fish. Glass jars of pickled mangoes of every size are set on makeshift wooden-box shelves. The pickles come in a variety of flavors, and everyone has their proprietary preparation. They say variety is the spice of life. This is reflected in the cuisine of this magical island! If you don't have a wok, use a lidded roasting pan—it will do the trick! —BERNARD

Wok-Steamed Whole Red Snapper

Mango Pickles

SERVES 4 FAMILY STYLE

RED SNAPPER

1 (3-pound) whole red snapper,
    scaled, gutted, washed, patted dry
2 tablespoons honey
¼ **cup** matchstick-cut ginger
¼ **cup** slivered green onions
2 teaspoons chopped garlic
2 tablespoons lime juice
1 teaspoon coarse sea salt
1 red Thai chile pepper, seeded, thinly sliced
1 stalk lemongrass,
    tender inner part only, thinly sliced crosswise
½ **cup** seasoned rice vinegar
2 cups coconut milk
2 (12-ounce) bottles ale beer
to taste sea salt
to taste ground black pepper

Using sharp knife make three ¼-inch-deep slashes crosswise, 2 inches apart, on both sides of fish. Place steaming rack in wok. Lay fish on rack. Combine honey, ginger, onion, garlic, lime, salt, chile, and lemongrass in mixing bowl. Cover surface of fish with mixture. Add vinegar, coconut milk, and beer to wok. Cover with lid. Place on stovetop over medium-high heat. Bring liquid to low simmer. Steam 20 minutes or until snapper is just cooked through. To test for doneness, make 1-inch slits behind gills with sharp knife. If the flesh does not stick to bone, it is done. Using large spatula, carefully transfer fish to serving platter. Reduce broth in wok by half. Season with salt and pepper. Transfer to sauce bowl.

MANGO PICKLES

2 under-ripe mangoes
1 tablespoon mustard oil
¼ **cup** thinly sliced shallots
1 teaspoon garam masala
1¼ **cups** rice vinegar
¾ **cup** water
1 teaspoon sea salt
2 tablespoons sugar

Peel mangoes and cut flesh into ¼-inch wide strips, discarding pit. Place in clean glass jar. Add mustard oil to sauté pan over medium heat. Add shallots. Cook 2 minutes. Add garam masala. Cook 30 seconds. Add vinegar, water, sea salt, and sugar. Bring to boil. Pour into jar to fill. Cool to room temperature. Cover. Refrigerate 24 hours. Strain. Transfer to serving bowl.

PRESENTATION

1 tablespoon toasted sesame seeds

1 red Thai chile pepper, seeded, thinly sliced

1 lime, halved

¼ **cup** cilantro sprigs

¼ **cups** sesame oil

Sprinkle fish with sesame seeds and chile. Squeeze lime atop. Garnish with cilantro sprigs. Add sesame oil to skillet over medium high heat. Heat until very hot but not smoking. Immediately spoon over surface of fish. Serve with Mango Pickles and broth.

Arctic Char

Arctic char are named for their native habitat, the Arctic Circle.

Char have silver skin with brushstrokes of pink and metallic green running along their backs.

A member of the Salmonidae family, some arctic char migrate the same way as salmon, swimming up streams or into lakes to breed, while others spend their entire lives landlocked in freshwater, a result of evolution from the glacial period.

Unlike most salmon, arctic char can migrate and breed multiple times during their lifetime, which can span up to twenty-five years.

Whole arctic char average 5 pounds, but some can grow to triple that size.

In the Wild
This species is also called alpine trout.

Besides the arctic waters of Canada, Alaska, Europe, and Russia, char are found in the cold lakes of Scotland, Ireland, Iceland, the Alps, and Siberia. Arctic char also inhabit cold freshwater northern lakes, as well as high altitude alpine lakes.

Pale peach to deep red in color and rich in flavor. Its delicate flaky flesh is milder than salmon's.

In the Kitchen
Char is interchangeable with salmon, but it is usually smaller so you will need to adjust cooking times accordingly.

A light brine and pan roasting heightens the richness.

Baking char with a crust locks in the moisture.

Pickled char evokes memories of Scandanavia.

Use as a substitute in our salmon recipes—especially Cedar Plank Smoked Salmon (p. 196).

Valuable Nutrients from Arctic Char
- Omega-3 fatty acids: prevents cardiovascular disease
- Potassium: for a healthy heart and kidneys, reduces stress
- Selenium: antioxidant, prevents arthritis
- Vitamin B_{12}: promotes healthy blood cells, prevents anemia, eases migraines

Fun Facts
Eskimos, also known as Inuits, have enjoyed arctic char as one of their main sources of protein for thousands of years. They show respect for the fish, and the waters that supply them, by continuing a long tradition of sustainable fishery: A hole is made in the ice. At the edge of the hole, the Eskimo waits patiently and silently for a char to appear. The fish is then speared with quick precision under the watchful eyes of sled dogs hoping for a snack. It is as much an art as a survival technique.

Lake Windermere was created thirteen thousand years ago during the last major ice age. It is still inhabited by the majestic arctic char, which became landlocked at that time. To catch a char on Lake Windermere, long poles are placed in the front of a wooden fishing boat outfitted with a string of tiny multiple spinners set at different depths. The poles have brass bells that serve as bite alarms. As the arctic char takes the lure, you are in for a battle of skill against pure instinct, but the reward is priceless! —BERNARD

Horseradish Baked Arctic Char

Parsnip Puree, Apple, Asparagus

SERVES 4

PARSNIP PUREE

2 pounds chopped, peeled parsnips
1 cup peeled, diced russet potato
3 shallots, sliced
3 cloves garlic
4 cups vegetable stock
¼ cup double (or heavy) cream
3 sprigs fresh thyme
1 lemon, zested
2 tablespoons walnut oil
to taste sea salt and ground white pepper

Add parsnips to large sauce pot with potatoes, shallots, garlic, stock, cream, and thyme. Simmer 20 minutes or until parsnips are very soft. Strain, reserving liquid. Add parsnip mixture to blender along with lemon zest, walnut oil, and 1 cup of reserved liquid. Puree until smooth, adding more liquid if necessary to facilitate blending. Season with salt and pepper.

APPLES AND ASPARAGUS

2 tablespoons honey
2 tablespoons walnut oil
1 teaspoon anise seeds
1 tablespoon lemon juice
1 green apple, cored
12 large green asparagus, stems peeled, trimmed
to taste sea salt and ground black pepper
¼ cup chopped walnuts.

Preheat broiler to high. Whisk honey, walnut oil, anise seeds, and lemon juice in baking dish. Slice apple crosswise into four ¼-inch rings. Transfer to baking dish along with asparagus. Toss gently to coat. Season with salt and pepper. Place under broiler. Cook 3 minutes or until apples are lightly caramelized and asparagus are al dente. Sprinkle with walnuts.

CHAR

1 egg white
3 tablespoons finely grated horseradish
2 tablespoons chopped parsley
¼ cup finely chopped red onion
¾ cup toasted bread crumbs
1 lemon, peeled, seeded, diced
3 tablespoons unsalted butter, melted
4 arctic char fillets, center-cut,
   skin on, boneless (6 ounces each)
to taste sea salt and ground black pepper
2 tablespoons olive oil, divided

Preheat oven to 350°F. Whisk egg white in large mixing bowl to soft peaks. Fold in horseradish, parsley, and onions. Stir in bread crumbs, diced lemon, and melted butter. Season char with salt and pepper. Brush baking dish with 1 tablespoon oil. Place fish in baking dish. Brush fish with remaining oil. Spread horseradish mixture evenly over surface of char. Transfer to oven. Bake 8 minutes or until char is slightly underdone.

2 teaspoons walnut oil

Place apple ring in center of warm serving plate. Place fish atop. Spoon Parsnip Puree onto plate. Garnish with asparagus. Drizzle with walnut oil.

The Finnish food culture is deeply rooted in tradition. Inhabitants devote a great deal of energy to pickling, drying, or preserving the short summer's bounty for the brisk winters ahead. Arctic wild berries and mushrooms are distinctively featured in Finnish cuisine for their flavor profile and high nutrient content. A popular outdoor activity among Finns is to forage for mushrooms and wild berries and pickle them, straight from the forest, in spirit vinegars and spices like white pepper, cloves, allspice, nutmeg, cinnamon, and ginger. —BERNARD

Orange Peel Pickled Arctic Char

Beet Root Jam, Cucumber Salad

SERVES 4

CHAR

1½ **pounds** arctic char fillets, center-cut, boneless, skinless

1 **tablespoon** kosher salt

1 orange

1 **cup** white wine

½ **cup** white wine vinegar

2 **cloves** garlic, thinly sliced

1 **teaspoon** caraway seeds

2 **tablespoons** chopped dill

2 **tablespoons** sugar

¼ **teaspoon** red chile flakes

1-inch piece peeled ginger, chopped

Cut arctic char into 2-inch-long by ½-inch-wide slices. Transfer to mixing bowl. Sprinkle salt over fish. Toss gently to coat. Cover. Refrigerate 1 hour. Peel orange with vegetable peeler to remove pure orange-colored outer layer. Add to sauce pot. Cut orange in half. Squeeze into pot. Add white wine, vinegar, garlic, caraway seeds, dill, sugar, chile flakes, and ginger. Bring to simmer. Transfer to casserole dish. Refrigerate until chilled. Add arctic char to vinegar mixture. Cover. Refrigerate overnight. Transfer to resealable glass jar.

BEET ROOT JAM

½ **cup** blackberry jam

½ **cup** grated red onion

¼ **teaspoon** dried thyme

1 **teaspoon** sea salt

¼ **teaspoon** black pepper

2 **cups** grated peeled red beets

Add jam, onions, thyme, salt, and pepper to saucepan over medium heat. Bring to simmer. Cook to marmalade consistency. Fold in beets. Cook 20 minutes or until liquid evaporates. Refrigerate until well chilled. Transfer to resealable glass jar.

CUCUMBER SALAD

⅔ **cup** thinly sliced English cucumber

2 **cups** frisée lettuce leaves, washed, patted dry

4 **teaspoons** lemon juice

2 **tablespoons** olive oil

16 **sprigs** dill

2 **teaspoons** brown mustard seeds

to taste sea salt

to taste ground black pepper

Combine all ingredients in serving bowl.

The Inuits who live near the town of Cambridge Bay on Victoria Island, British Columbia, call their home *Ikaluktutiak*—"Place of Good Fishing." In part this is due to the arctic char that swim from the sea to the freshwater lakes near Cambridge Bay in the fall and stay over winter. Prime fishing season runs from midsummer to late fall, when the rivers and lakes start to freeze. One ancient method of fishing is still practiced today. A V-shaped underwater fence called a "weir" acts like a funnel, directing the fish toward traps or nets, with minimal stress. This method has been passed down through hundreds of generations of native Inuit people, who continue to catch these fish by hand to feed their families. —BERNARD

Pan-Roasted Arctic Char

Black-Eyed Pea Succotash

SERVES 4

SUCCOTASH

1 tablespoon olive oil
1 cup red onion, thinly sliced on bias
½ cup diced red bell pepper
½ cup diced celery
1 small red jalapeño,
    halved lengthwise
1 tablespoon paprika
¼ pound thick bacon,
    sliced into ¼-inch pieces
¼ cup white wine
3 cups chicken stock
4 sprigs thyme
to taste sea salt
to taste ground black pepper
1 cup dried black-eyed peas,
    soaked in water overnight

CHAR

1 cup white grape juice
3 tablespoons kosher salt
½ teaspoon ground black pepper
4 arctic char fillets, skin on, boneless,
    at least ¾ inch thick (6 ounces each)
2 tablespoons grapeseed oil
as needed canola oil spray
to taste sea salt
to taste ground black pepper
3 tablespoons unsalted butter
1 cup sliced shallots
1 teaspoon chopped sage
½ cup dried cherries
2 tablespoons apple cider vinegar
4 leaves sage
2 teaspoons extra-virgin olive oil

Add oil to large pot over medium heat. Add onions, bell pepper, celery, jalapeño, and paprika. Cook 3 minutes, stirring often. Add bacon, white wine, chicken stock, and thyme. Season with salt and pepper. Bring to simmer. Drain peas. Add to pot. Simmer 20 minutes or until peas are tender. Keep warm.

Combine grape juice, salt, and pepper in casserole dish. Stir to dissolve salt. Add char to brine, skin side down. Cover. Refrigerate 15 minutes. Turn fillets over. Refrigerate additional 15 minutes. Remove char from brine. Pat dry with paper towels. Add oil to large skillet over medium-high heat. Add fish to skillet, flesh side down. Cook 2 minutes or until char is lightly caramelized. Spray skin lightly with canola oil. Turn fish over. Cook 3 minutes or until skin is crisped and fish is slightly underdone. Adjust seasoning if needed. Transfer char to side dish. Tent with foil to keep warm. Discard excess oil from skillet. Return to medium-high heat. Add butter until lightly golden and foamy. Add shallots, chopped sage, and cherries. Cook 3 minutes, stirring often. Add vinegar. Bring to boil. Season with salt and pepper. Divide Succotash between four warm serving bowls. Top with char, skin side down. Spoon cherry mixture over char. Garnish with sage leaves. Drizzle with olive oil.

Naknek Lake emerges in the splendor of the Valley of Ten Thousand Smokes on the Alaska Peninsula. The lake is known for its sockeye salmon, which migrate to streams where they will lay millions of eggs. The opportunistic arctic char have a great life feasting on these delicacies. As a kid my father told me tales of his fishing exploits in Canada catching the *omble chevalier,* aka arctic char. While exploring the rocky Alaskan islands, living a dream with fly-fishing rod in hand, I landed the most beautiful fish with its amazing blue, green, orange, and olive hues. Roasted kasha buckwheat has a rich nutty flavor that lends itself perfectly to the sweet delicate favor of the char. —BERNARD

Blue Corn and Sunflower Crusted Arctic Char

Apricot Kasha Pilaf, Citrus Parsley Butter

SERVES 4

CITRUS PARSLEY BUTTER

⅔ **cup** unsalted butter, cut into small pieces
1 tablespoon lemon zest
¼ **cup** sliced flat-leaf parsley leaves
to taste sea salt and ground black pepper

Combine all ingredients in mixing bowl. Use tines of fork to mash into a paste. Roll into cylinder shape, 1 inch in diameter, and wrap in plastic. Freeze. Slice into ½-inch-thick medallions. Remove and discard plastic wrap.

APRICOT KASHA PILAF

1 egg white
1 cup whole grain kasha (buckwheat groats)
2½ **cups** vegetable broth
1 bay leaf
3 sprigs thyme
3 tablespoons olive oil, divided
1 small head cauliflower, cut into florets (about 2 cups)
½ **cup** diced onion
to taste sea salt and pepper
½ **cup** pecan halves
½ **cup** diced dried apricots

Beat egg white in mixing bowl until frothy. Stir in kasha. Refrigerate 1 hour. Bring broth, bay leaf, and thyme to simmer in sauce pot. Keep hot. Add 2 tablespoons oil to large nonstick, ovenproof saucepan over medium heat. Add kasha. Cook 3 minutes, stirring constantly.

Add cauliflower and onions. Cook 4 minutes, stirring constantly. Pour in broth. Season with salt and pepper. Cover. Place in oven. Bake 20 minutes or until liquid is absorbed. Fluff with fork. Fold in remaining olive oil, pecans, and apricots. Transfer to serving dish.

ARCTIC CHAR

½ **cup** crumbled blue corn tortilla chips
½ **cup** toasted sunflower seeds
½ **teaspoon** anise seeds
1 teaspoon chopped oregano
4 arctic char fillets, center-cut, skin on, boneless
  (6 ounces each)
to taste sea salt and ground black pepper
as needed canola oil spray

Preheat oven to 350°F. Add tortilla chips, sunflower seeds, anise seeds, and oregano to food processor. Process to a coarse meal. Transfer to large plate. Pat char dry with paper towels. Season with salt and pepper. Spray lightly with canola oil. Place flesh side of fish down into blue corn mixture. Press and roll the fish with your fingers so that flesh becomes thoroughly coated. Transfer fish, crust side up, to oiled baking sheet. Sprinkle with more crust if needed to cover the flesh. Spray crust side lightly with canola oil. Bake 10 minutes or until char is slightly underdone. Transfer to serving platter. Place Citrus Parsley Butter atop char. Serve with Apricot Kasha Pilaf.

Sole

Sole are flatfish whose name comes from the Latin word for "sandal."

The king of sole is the Dover sole, but don't confuse the European Dover sole with America's West Coast "Dover" sole; they maybe in the same family, but they are not the same fish.

True Dover sole, a mainstay of the European seafood scene for generations, is considered one of the foundations of continental cuisine.

Pacific Dover sole have been harvested off the West Coast since World War II.

Petrale sole, lemon sole, and Pacific Dover sole are all actually right-eyed flounders, a group of flatfish that lie on the ocean floor on their left side with both eyes on their right side.

The oddest name is the lemon sole: It is not a true sole, nor does it taste like lemon.

In the Wild

In England Dover sole is fished from the Mediterranean to the North Sea and was named after the fishing port that landed the most sole in the nineteenth century. The port supplied fish for London's Billingsgate market, the country's largest inland fish market.

Most Pacific Dover sole are caught off the coasts of Oregon, California, and Washington State.

The native habitat of petrale sole stretches from the Bering Sea to Baja California.

Sole live near the ocean floor and prefer a soft-bottom habitat in waters 7 to 4,500 feet deep. They migrate in step with the seasons, moving from the deep waters of the outer continental shelf to shallower waters in the summer to feed.

Like halibut, sole lie on the ocean floor with their dark side up. This helps them to camouflage from predators while they look up in anticipation of their next meal.

In the Kitchen

Few fish command more respect in culinary circles than the true Dover sole, which yields thin yet firm fillets that hold together well in many preparations.

The raw meat is dense and glistening white; it remains snow white when cooked.

The flavor of the Dover sole is mild and sweet. Cooked fillets are very thin and delicate.

Stuffing petrale sole with crabmeat will turn an everyday type of fish into an elegant pinwheel presentation.

Sole is delicious deep-fried and served with homemade mustard. While you have the oil on, why not make some chips!

Valuable Nutrients from Sole

- Omega-3 fatty acids: prevents cardiovascular disease

- Phosphorus: builds healthy bones and strong teeth

- Selenium: antioxidant, prevents arthritis

- Vitamin B_5: prevents acne and loss of hair, reduces cholesterol

- Vitamin B_6: for a healthy metabolism and immune system

- Vitamin B_{12}: promotes healthy blood cells, prevents anemia, eases migraines

- Vitamin E: powerful antioxidant that battles free radicals in your body

- Zinc: controls acne, boosts immune system

Fun Facts

Most sole are dark on one side and white on the other, but the North Sea's albino sole is white on both sides. This creates a challenge for survival as the sole loses its camouflage from predators swimming above them. As a result, they often become the dinner of gourmet seals.

Female Dover sole grow faster and larger than males, but males live longer.

Females can produce hundreds of thousands of eggs at a time, several times per season. This may be the reason why they have a shorter life.

In Africa, *pili pili* in Swahili and *peri peri* in Malawi are the general words for "pepper." People in the Portuguese colonies of Mozambique and Angola used the name *piri piri* to describe the African bird's-eye chile. A treasured bushy, super-hot chile pepper plant, bearing bright red to purple pods, it captures the hot sun side by side with its cousin the peppadew, which has a sweet piquant bite. Piri piri is often used in preparing sauces and marinades for roasts and grilled dishes, especially chicken and various fish. The Victoria & Albert Waterfront is set in the working harbor of Cape Town, South Africa, against the breathtaking backdrop of Table Mountain and surrounded by its historical waterfront heritage. Cape Town cuisine is brimming with fish. Sole caught between Cape Agulhas and the Great Kei River in South Africa is one of the most prized species at the local fish market. Fillet of sole served with homemade lemon pepper and piri piri is a simple culinary gift from the land and the sea. —BERNARD

Lemon Pepper Sole
Green Mung Beans, Piri Piri Sauce
SERVES 4

SOLE

1 large lemon
2 tablespoons coriander seeds
½ teaspoon white peppercorns
1 teaspoon cumin seeds
1 tablespoon lemon thyme leaves
2 tablespoons chopped
 lemon verbena leaves
¼ cup parsley leaves
2 teaspoons sea salt flakes
4 sole fillets,
 boneless, skinless (6 ounces each)
2 tablespoons unsalted butter

Preheat oven to 200°F. Using a vegetable peeler, cut thin strips of lemon zest from top to bottom, with no white pith on peel. Cut into fine strips. Transfer to mixing bowl. Combine with coriander, peppercorns, cumin, lemon thyme, lemon verbena, parsley, and sea salt. Transfer to parchment-lined baking sheet, spreading in thin layer. Transfer to oven. Bake for 1 hour or until ingredients are dry and brittle. Transfer to mortar and pestle or spice grinder. Process to coarse powder. Season sole on both sides with lemon-spice mixture. Add butter to skillet over medium heat. Cook until lightly brown and foamy. Place sole in skillet. Cook 2 minutes on each side or until fish is slightly underdone. Divide mung bean mixture between four warm serving bowls. Place sole atop. Spoon Piri Piri Sauce into bowl.

PIRI PIRI SAUCE

5 African bird's-eye chiles
 or red Thai chiles
½ cup olive oil
5 cloves garlic, minced
¼ cup chopped parsley
2 tablespoons finely chopped cilantro
½ cup lemon juice
to taste sea salt

Cut chiles in half lengthwise. Discard seeds and stems. Add chiles, oil, and garlic to small skillet. Place over medium heat. Cook until chiles sizzle. Remove from heat. Add parsley, cilantro, and lemon juice. Transfer to blender. Puree until smooth. Season with sea salt.

GREEN MUNG BEANS

1 cup dried green mung beans, rinsed, drained

3 tablespoons olive oil

½ cup sliced shallots

1 cup quartered button mushrooms

1 cup diced peeled carrots

1 bay leaf

to taste sea salt

to taste ground black pepper

3½ cups vegetable stock

¼ cup chopped basil

2 tablespoons cider vinegar

Toast mung beans in deep skillet over medium heat until lightly golden. Add oil, shallots, mushrooms, carrots, and bay leaf to skillet. Season with salt and pepper. Cook 3 minutes, stirring often. Add vegetable stock. Bring to simmer. Skim top. Cover. Cook for 35 minutes until mung beans are tender. Remove from heat. Fold in basil and cider vinegar. Season to taste with salt and pepper.

When Jewish refugees from Portugal landed in the United Kingdom in the seventeenth century, they carried little more than a scant hope for the future and a strong sentiment for the flavors of their homeland. From this humble yet turbulent beginning evolved the United Kingdom's most highly recognized dish: fish-and-chips. Lagers and ales became a popular addition to the batter for their ability to leaven and create a light, crispy texture. Traditionally the fish was deep-fried in lard, but healthier oils are more commonly used today. Another tradition is to serve the dish in yesterday's newspaper, giving the dish a symbolic link to the past. —RON

Amber Ale Sole Fingers
Caraway Potato Chips, Homemade Mustard
SERVES 4

SOLE

1 quart grapeseed oil

4 sole fillets, boneless, skinless (6 ounces each)

2 large eggs

1 tablespoon chopped parsley leaves

1 tablespoon orange zest

⅔ cup amber ale, chilled

½ cup all-purpose flour

½ cup cornstarch

1 teaspoon baking soda

1 teaspoon baking powder

1 teaspoon sugar

½ teaspoon flaky sea salt

¼ teaspoon ground black pepper

to taste sea salt and pepper

2 lemons, cut into wedges

4 sprigs parsley

Heat oil in heavy sauce pot to 365°F. Cut sole into 12 strips of equal size. Whisk eggs in large mixing bowl with parsley and orange zest. Stir in ale. Combine dry ingredients in small bowl. Sift over egg mixture. Mix gently, just to incorporate. Dip sole into batter. Fry 1 minute or until golden, crisp, and slightly underdone. Transfer to paper towel–lined platter. Season with salt and pepper. Serve with Caraway Potato Chips, Homemade Mustard, and lemon wedges. Garnish with parsley sprigs.

HOMEMADE MUSTARD

¼ cup yellow mustard powder

½ cup white wine vinegar

¼ cup honey

2 teaspoons canola oil

2 tablespoons brown mustard seeds

1 egg

1 teaspoon sea salt

2½ teaspoons arrowroot

Combine 2 tablespoons water, mustard powder, vinegar, and honey in stainless steel mixing bowl. Cover. Refrigerate overnight. Add oil and mustard seeds to small skillet over medium heat. Cook gently for 2 minutes or until mustard seeds start to pop. Remove from heat. Cool to room temperature. Add to mustard powder mixture along with egg, salt, and arrowroot. Whisk to combine. Place bowl over pot of simmering water. Whisk constantly 3 minutes or until mustard thickens. Remove from heat. Cool to room temperature, whisking occasionally. Transfer to glass jar. Cover. Refrigerate up to 10 days.

CARAWAY POTATO CHIPS

2 quarts canola oil, for frying
1 pound russet potatoes
to taste flaky sea salt
1 teaspoon caraway seeds

Heat oil in deep fryer or large heavy-bottomed pot to 300°F. Using mandoline or vegetable slicer, cut potatoes crosswise into ⅛-inch-thick slices. Rinse under cold running water to remove excess starch. Pat dry. Add to oil in small batches. Use slotted spoon to constantly move potato slices in the oil. Fry 5 minutes or until golden crisp. Transfer to paper towel–lined plate. Sprinkle with sea salt and caraway seeds.

The Historic Old Bayfront District and marina of coastal Newport, Oregon, are dotted with piles of colorful crab pots as floats line up on the wide, wooden boardwalk. Fish, salt, and ocean smells fill the air as working fishing vessels come and go, and groups of barking sea lions chase the boats in hope of a big fat meal. At the docks, fishermen unload their morning catch of halibut, lingcod, rockfish, salmon, and petrale sole. Birds flap busily, screeching as they launch into the air and eyeball a crate of pink shrimp and Dungeness crab. The sweet, mild, and slightly nutty flavor of Dungeness crab meat wrapped in petrale sole creates the perfect combination of flavors. In a bind, you can substitute one crabmeat for another or replace it with local pink shrimp. You can also substitute another type of sole for petrale. —BERNARD

Petrale Sole and Crab Pinwheel
Sweet Corn, Butternut Squash, Vermouth
SERVES 4

SOLE

2 tablespoons unsalted butter

1 cup sliced leeks, white part only

½ cup finely diced, peeled carrots

½ cup finely diced celery

1 cup sliced button mushrooms

2 tablespoons chopped parsley

¼ teaspoon paprika

½ pound crabmeat, shelled

½ cup cottage cheese

to taste sea salt

to taste ground black pepper

8 petrale sole fillets, boneless, skinless (4 ounces each)

Preheat oven to 375°F. Add butter to saucepan over medium heat. Add leeks, carrots, celery, and mushrooms. Cook 5 minutes or until all liquid is evaporated, stirring often. Transfer to mixing bowl. Combine with parsley, paprika, crab, and cottage cheese. Season with salt and pepper. Lay petrale sole fillet on flat surface, skin side up. Spoon crabmeat mixture onto thickest edge of sole. Roll up fillet. Set aside. Repeat with remaining fillets.

FOR BRAISING

1 cup vermouth wine

1 tablespoon tarragon leaves

6 cloves garlic, smashed

1 cup corn kernels

as needed canola oil spray

to taste sea salt, ground black pepper, and paprika

Combine wine, tarragon, and garlic in roasting pan. Place stuffed sole fillets, seam side down, into pan. Sprinkle corn in between sole. Spray sole with canola oil. Season with salt, pepper, and paprika. Tent with foil. Transfer to oven. Braise 18 minutes or until stuffing in center of sole is hot. Remove sole and squash from oven. Turn off oven. Divide squash between four warm serving plates. Place sole atop squash. Place in oven to keep warm. Transfer liquid, corn, and all contents of braising pan to blender. Puree until smooth. Strain through colander. Season with salt and pepper if necessary. Spoon sauce onto plates.

BUTTERNUT SQUASH

4 cups diced butternut squash

2 cups packed, stemmed kale, small inner leaves only

½ cup dried cranberries

¼ cup chopped, toasted pecans

2 tablespoons butter

2 tablespoons honey

to taste sea salt

to taste cayenne pepper

Combine all ingredients in mixing bowl. Transfer to casserole dish. Cover. Bake in oven 25 minutes or until squash is tender.

The public markets of Jersey in the English Channel were established in the late sixteenth century, and they remain a central part of the island's life and culture. The splendid high-domed roof of the Victorian Central Market is the heart of the island. At the fish market across the street, Beresford Market, the overflowing fish stalls provide a spectacle for the eyes as well as the table. A cast of individual characters—including the thick-lipped gray mullet, shiny striped mackerel, jersey skate, and Dover sole—are the stars of the show. Gastropubs in the neighborhood list the fish special. One caught my eye: Sole Walnutine, a genius twist on a culinary classic! —BERNARD

Jersey Island Fillet of Sole Walnutine
Golden Raisin Parsley Butter
SERVES 4

SOLE
8 sole fillets, boneless, skinless (3 ounces each)
to taste sea salt and ground black pepper
1 cup all-purpose flour
4 large eggs, beaten
1 cup toasted bread crumbs
1 cup chopped walnuts
1 tablespoon dried parsley flakes
4 tablespoons olive oil, divided
2 tablespoons unsalted butter, divided

Season sole with salt and pepper. Place flour and beaten eggs into two separate shallow bowls. Combine bread crumbs, walnuts, and dried parsley in third shallow bowl. Dredge sole lightly in flour, shaking off excess. Dip into beaten egg. Transfer to bread crumbs, turning to coat all sides. Transfer to baking sheet. Repeat process with remaining sole. Add 2 tablespoons oil and 1 tablespoon butter to large skillet over medium heat. When butter is foamy, place 4 breaded sole in skillet. Cook 2 minutes or until breading is golden brown and crisp. Turn fish over. Cook until breading is golden brown and sole is slightly underdone. Transfer to serving platter. Repeat process with remaining oil, butter, and sole.

VEGETABLES
8 baby turnips, trimmed, peeled
8 baby yellow beets, trimmed, peeled
8 baby carrots, trimmed, peeled
12 small green asparagus
2 tablespoons chopped chives
1 tablespoon walnut oil
1 tablespoon honey
1 tablespoon malt vinegar
¼ teaspoon mustard seeds
to taste sea salt and ground black pepper

Bring 4 quarts salted water to boil. Add turnips and beets. Cook 1 minute. Add carrots. Cook 1 minute. Add asparagus. Cook 1 minute or until vegetables are al dente. Toss with remaining ingredients.

SAUCE
3 tablespoons unsalted butter
½ cup golden raisins
4 gherkins or cornichons, sliced
1 tablespoon lemon juice
1 tablespoon chopped parsley
1 tablespoon Worcestershire sauce
to taste sea salt and ground black pepper

Add butter to skillet over medium heat. When butter is foamy, add raisins and gherkins. Cook 1 minute. Add remaining ingredients. Season with salt and pepper. Spoon atop sole.

Pompano/Pomfret

The pompano is a saltwater fish that enjoys warm water temperatures, between 70°F and 88°F.

They have bluish-green silver skin and forked tails that steer them swiftly through the water, often with their dorsal fin above the surface.

Pompano feed on small crustaceans and mollusks, especially shrimp, crab, and clams.

A warm-water fish, pompano migrate to avoid cold temperatures, which can be fatal. They swim in schools along sandy beaches, oyster bars, and estuaries.

Most of the two hundred species are valuable in the kitchen.

In the Wild

Florida Pompano
Found in abundance off the Atlantic and Gulf coasts of the southern United States, especially around Florida. They migrate north in the spring and south in the winter, reaching between Massachusetts and Brazil.

Most weigh less than three pounds, though they can grow to be nine pounds.

Florida pompano is most highly acclaimed for cooking.

Black Pomfret
This is actually a pompano, not a pomfret as its name suggests.

They swim in large schools in the coastal areas of the West Pacific and Indian Ocean, from Africa to Japan and Australia.

The meat has light color and holds together when cooked.

The skin shrinks minimally when cooked, making it a great fish to serve whole.

Black pomfret is very popular and often seen in large supply in the wet markets (which serve meats, fish, and produce) of Asia. They breed very rapidly, so overfishing is not a concern.

Permit

Also called great pompano, this is the largest of the pompano family, weighing thirty pounds on average.

Permit are blue on top and silver on the side with hints of gold on their chest.

A game fish found in shallow tropical waters of the western Atlantic Ocean.

In the Kitchen

Pompano's rich, oily flesh takes well to the caramelized sugars that result from grilling or searing with a tropical marinade, or you can make a caramel sauce (see Pompano Indochine, p. 178). Favorite preparation methods include these:

- In a "pocket," when rice paper or papillote locks in the richness
- Seared with tropical fruit marinade for nice caramelization
- Spiced up—substitute it in our Jerk Spiced Shark Loin (p. 289)

Valuable Nutrients from Pompano

- Niacin: increases good cholesterol levels
- Omega-3 fatty acids: prevent cardiovascular disease
- Phosphorus: builds healthy bones and strong teeth
- Selenium: antioxidant, prevents arthritis
- Thiamin: maintains regular heartbeat, good for healthy eyes
- Vitamin B_6: for a healthy metabolism and immune system
- Vitamin B_{12}: promotes healthy blood cells, prevents anemia, eases migraines

Fun Facts

Four species of pompano exist in the world, and they all belong to the jack family.

The city of Pompano Beach, Florida, was named after the fish.

Young permit fish have teeth on their tongue.

Two submarines of the United States Navy were named USS *Permit* in honor of the fish.

The permit was one of the fish featured by Swedish scientist Carolus Linnaeus in his famous 1758 work *Systema Naturae*, a book that categorized classifications of plants and animals.

On the island of Vatulele, in the tidal pools at Korolamalama Cave near the north coast, sacred red prawns are known as *ura-buta*. They can be seen in the shallow waters being chased by schools of pomfret. At a local home, I attended the ancient custom of drinking kava, a tea made from pepper-tree root powder and fresh water, served in a coconut shell before dinner. In the kitchen I watched five ladies make a delicious meal without measuring the ingredients; it is always done by taste and years of practice. For the fish balls there are two important rules: Too little slapping gives you mushy balls, and too much slapping gives you toothy ones. Fijians don't believe in time or watches, but their cuisine is always spot on! If you don't have pomfret, don't fret—John Dory, pompano, or sea bass will do. —BERNARD

Fijian Pomfret Fish Balls

Pineapple Hoisin Broth

SERVES 6

FISH BALLS

½ **pound** shrimp, size 16/20
2 **tablespoons** sesame oil
½ **cup** chopped onion
8 **cloves** garlic, crushed
¼ **cup** chopped ginger
1 **teaspoon** black peppercorns
2 **quarts** vegetable stock
½ **cup** chopped Thai basil
4 **stalks** lemongrass, crushed
1½ **teaspoons** sea salt, divided
½ **pound** pomfret fillet,
   skinless, boneless
¼ **cup** cold water
¼ **teaspoon** ground white pepper

Peel shrimp. Set aside, reserving shells. Add oil to large stockpot over medium high heat. Add shrimp shells. Roast 1 minute. Add onion, garlic, ginger, and peppercorns. Cook 2 minutes without browning, stirring often. Add stock, basil, lemongrass, and 1 teaspoon sea salt. Bring to simmer. Cook 10 minutes.

Strain through fine sieve into large saucepan. Return to stovetop. Bring to low simmer. Using sharp knife, slice pomfret fillet and reserved shrimp into small pieces then mince to a coarse, sticky paste. Transfer to mixing bowl. Fold in cold water, remaining sea salt, and white pepper. Moisten hands. Pick up ball of paste and slap down into bowl. Repeat fifty times or until paste develops firm, springy texture. Refrigerate 15 minutes. Remoisten hands. Roll paste into walnut-size balls, transferring to plastic-wrap-lined baking sheet as you go. Working in batches of 12, transfer fish balls to simmering stock. Raise heat to high. Return to simmer. Cook 5 minutes or until fish balls float to the top. Transfer to large serving bowl. Repeat process with remaining balls. Reserve stock.

PINEAPPLE HOISIN BROTH

2 **cups** chopped napa cabbage
2 **cups** chopped pineapple
2 **tablespoons** hoisin sauce
1 red chile pepper, stemmed, seeded,
   thinly sliced

Add cabbage and pineapple to reserved shrimp stock. Cook 1 minute. Whisk in hoisin sauce. Bring to boil. Ladle over fish balls. Garnish with chile pepper.

The core concept of Laotian cuisine is balance. It has to be since most Lao dishes rely on the perfect combination of sweet, spicy, savory, salty, and sour. With that many elements, balance on your palate can mean the difference between blissfully addictive and painfully unexpected. Like a tightrope walker, the Laotian cook calculates each step, guided only by feel and familiarity. Each action brings the final result closer, until at last the perfect blend is achieved. This recipe provides all the flavor elements of traditional Lao cuisine, but with a modern approach. We use green (under-ripe) papaya, the most popular food item in Lao culture, but carrots can be used just as well. —RON

Rice Paper Wrapped Pompano
Pickled Green Papaya, Tangerine Sauce
SERVES 4

POMPANO

1½ pounds pompano fillets, boneless, skinless, trimmed
to taste sea salt
1 tablespoon chili oil
4 (9-inch) rice paper wrappers
1 tablespoon toasted sesame seeds
16 large Thai basil leaves
2 tablespoons grapeseed oil

Cut pompano fillets into 6-ounce portions. Season lightly on all sides with sea salt. Toss with chili oil. Add 1 quart hot water to shallow baking dish. Soak one rice paper wrapper in water for 30 seconds, or until softened. Transfer to plastic-wrap-lined cutting board. Pat dry. Sprinkle with sesame seeds. Top with 4 basil leaves. Place pompano atop basil. Fold edges of wrapper over fillet. Wrap tightly. Press seams to seal. Cover with light, damp towel to prevent fish packet from drying out. Repeat process with remaining ingredients. Add grapeseed oil to large nonstick skillet over medium heat. Place fish packets into skillet, seam side up. Cook 6 minutes, turning occasionally or until rice paper is crispy and fish is slightly underdone. Spoon Tangerine Sauce onto warm serving plate. Top with pompano, basil side up. Serve with a side dish of Pickled Green Papaya.

PICKLED GREEN PAPAYA

1 small green papaya
1¼ cups rice vinegar
¼ cup honey
¾ cup water
½ cup rice wine or sake
½ teaspoon ground turmeric
1 tablespoon chopped ginger
1 teaspoon kosher salt
1 teaspoon chile powder

Peel green papaya. Using potato peeler, slice long, thin strips from top to bottom, turning papaya as you go; yield will be about 3 cups. Place papaya strips in large nonreactive resealable container. Combine remaining ingredients in large sauce pot over medium heat. Simmer 5 minutes. Pour over papaya. Cool. Seal. Refrigerate.

TANGERINE SAUCE

2 cups tangerine juice

1¼ cups chopped, peeled carrots

½ teaspoon sambal chile paste

1 tablespoon miso paste

1 tablespoon brown sugar

2 cloves garlic, chopped

⅓ cup chopped green onion

1 tablespoon sesame oil

Add tangerine juice, carrots, sambal, miso, sugar, and garlic to saucepan over medium heat. Bring to simmer. Reduce heat to low. Cook 10 minutes or until carrots are soft. Transfer to blender. Add green onion and sesame oil. Puree until smooth. Set aside.

Dessert is not common in Vietnam. A treat after a meal usually consists of sweet beans and chewy strands of gelatin. But a Vietnamese kitchen is often filled with the alluring aroma of nearly burnt sugar. You may ask, "If there's no dessert, then what's the caramel for?" Well, it's for dinner. Caramel can be thought of as a Vietnamese "mother sauce" in which many types of fish are simmered to bittersweet perfection. The sauce starts off in the traditional way of melting sugar until nicely browned, but fish sauce is added instead of cream or butter. The pungent scent of the fish sauce erupts upon contact, leaving in its wake a salty umami accent in the caramel. —RON

Pompano Indochine
Lemongrass Caramel Sauce
SERVES 4

RICE

1 tablespoon light sesame oil
1 cup brown rice
2 cups vegetable stock
¼ **cup** finely chopped scallions
¼ **cup** chopped, toasted peanuts
⅓ **cup** thinly sliced basil leaves

Add sesame oil to saucepan over medium heat. Add rice. Cook 2 minutes, stirring often. Add vegetable stock. Cover. Bring to simmer. Reduce heat to low. Cook 20 minutes or until liquid is absorbed. Fluff with fork. Fold in scallions, toasted peanuts, and basil.

POMPANO

2 tablespoons fish sauce, nam pla or nuoc nam
¼ **cup** orange juice
¼ **cup** matchstick-cut peeled ginger
¼ **cup** thinly sliced lemongrass, inner tender part only
⅓ **cup** water
1 tablespoon light sesame oil
¾ **cup** thinly sliced shallots
1 red hot chile pepper, stemmed, seeded, sliced
6 cloves garlic, sliced
½ **cup** granulated sugar
4 pompano fillets, boneless (6 ounces each)
2 limes, halved
to taste ground black pepper

Combine nam pla, orange juice, ginger, lemongrass, and water in small mixing bowl. Set aside. Add oil to large skillet over medium high heat. Add shallots, chile pepper, and garlic. Cook 4 minutes or until golden brown. Transfer to side dish. Rinse pan. Wipe clean with paper towel. Return skillet to stovetop over medium heat. Add sugar and 2 tablespoons water. Stir once to mix. Cook until sugar liquefies and turns amber brown, swirling pan occasionally to ensure even cooking. Remove from heat. Ladle fish sauce mixture into caramel, being careful as it may splatter. Return pan to medium heat. Bring to simmer, stirring to ensure caramel dissolves. Add pompano and reserved shallot mixture to sauce. Simmer 5 minutes or until pompano is slightly underdone. Mound cooked rice in center of warm large serving platter. Place Pompano atop. Spoon sauce onto fish. Squeeze lime atop. Season with pepper.

John Dory

Some say the name "John Dory" comes the French words *jaune* and *dorée,* which mean "yellow" and "gilded." Others think it comes from the hero of an ancient ballad's name. But the fish is also called Saint Peter's fish, so who knows?

John Dory is also known as butterfish because it melts in your mouth.

In New Zealand, the indigenous Māori people know it as *kuparu,* and they gave some to Captain Cook on his first voyage to New Zealand in 1769.

In the Wild
John Dory is largely associated with New Zealand but is also caught in Australia, Russia, South Africa, and along South America's southern coast.

The John Dory is a predator and captures its prey by shooting a tube out of its mouth.

The John Dory commonly feeds on schooling fish, such as sardines, but sometimes dines on squid and cuttlefish.

In the Kitchen
John Dory has a dense and creamy flesh and fine flakes similar to Dover sole. It holds up well when cooked. John Dory has a small number of bones, which are easy to remove. The skin has no scales. These are our favorite cooking methods:

- **Pan-seared**—especially good with Mediterranean flavors
- **Steamed**—substitute it in our Black Bass in Bamboo Steamer (p. 227) recipe
- **Piccata**—buttery flesh is luscious with lemony piccata sauce
- **En papillote**—locks in the fish's natural goodness

Valuable Nutrients from John Dory
- Calcium: maintains strong bones, prevents colon cancer
- Omega-3 fatty acids: for a healthy heart, prevents cardiovascular disease
- Omega-6 fatty acids: for healthy brain function, healthy skin, and hair growth
- Phosphorus: builds healthy bones and strong teeth
- Potassium: for a healthy heart and kidneys, reduces stress
- Tryptophan: an amino acid used to make serotonin, promotes good mood

Fun Facts

Legend has it that the dark spot on the side of a John Dory is Saint Peter's thumbprint, which was left behind when Saint Peter removed a coin from the fish's mouth. However the spot got there, it has an important function of scaring off potential threats. The fish will flash the spot at predators like an evil eye.

The John Dory's real eyes have binocular vision and impressive depth perception, allowing the fish to spot predators early.

To find out what the latest gossip is in Australia, ask "What's the John Dory, mate?"

The concept of cooking *en papillote* is a healthy and flavorful French cooking method in which fish, herbs, and vegetables are cooked in a folded pouch of parchment paper that is tightly sealed before baking. The ingredients retain moisture and juices as they cook quickly, trapped in aromatic steam. A successful papillote should be prepared ahead of time with the freshest ingredients and cooked at the last minute. Your friends will inhale the small cloud of steam and pungent rush of aroma that escapes when opening the John Dory en Papillote. Papillote can also be made using aluminum foil in lieu of parchment paper, which adds the option of cooking on the grill. —RON

John Dory en Papillote
Oyster Mushrooms, Fennel, Tomatoes
SERVES 4

JOHN DORY

1 **small bulb** fennel, trimmed

¼ **pound** oyster mushrooms, stems trimmed

½ **cup** sliced shallots

3 **cloves** garlic, thinly sliced

1 **small** zucchini, sliced crosswise ⅛ inch thick

2 **tablespoons** lemon juice

⅓ **cup** sherry wine

2 **tablespoons** olive oil

to taste sea salt

to taste ground black pepper

pinch cayenne pepper

4 **sheets** parchment paper, 12 inches wide

4 John Dory fillets, boneless, skinless (4 ounces each)

6 **each** red and yellow teardrop tomatoes,
    halved lengthwise

8 **sprigs** fresh thyme

¼ **cup** butter, cut into 4 cubes

as needed canola oil spray

Using vegetable slicer, shave fennel bulb crosswise into thin slices to make 1 cup. Transfer to mixing bowl. Tear mushrooms into ½-inch pieces. Add to fennel along with shallots, garlic, zucchini, lemon juice, sherry wine, and olive oil. Season with salt, pepper and cayenne. Refrigerate 30 minutes. Preheat oven to 400°F. Using kitchen scissors, cut parchment paper into four 12-inch circles. Fold in half and crease the edge. Unfold. Lay ⅛ of the vegetable mixture onto one side of the fold. Season John Dory fillets with salt and pepper. Lay atop vegetables. Place another ⅛ of the vegetable mixture atop sole. Drizzle juices from bowl over vegetables. Place 2 thyme sprigs, a butter cube, 3 red tomato halves, and 3 yellow tomato halves atop vegetables. Fold other half of parchment over top of fish until edges meet. Seal edges by making small, tight, overlapping folds at ½-inch intervals along outside edge until package is completely sealed. Repeat with remaining ingredients to make 3 more packets. Transfer packets to oiled baking sheet. Spray thoroughly with canola oil. Bake 15 minutes. Packets will puff and brown as they bake. Transfer to serving plate. Serve with sharp knife so diners can slice open their own papillote.

Shizuoka Prefecture is home to Mount Fuji (the tallest mountain in Japan), green-tea fields, stone-wall strawberries, citrus groves, lotus roots, and Mochimune, which is known throughout Japan for its fishing harbor. In early morning at Mochimune's famous Shizuoka Fish Market, one of the largest fish auctions in the country takes place. The highest quality of regional catch, including tuna, marlin, mackerel, sardines, seabreams, red alfonsino, and octopus is feverishly bid on. The subtle heat from the Japanese horseradish (wasabi) and the crispy texture of wasabi peas make the ideal crust for our matodai; If you don't have John Dory, this recipe is also delicious with salmon, halibut, and sea bass. —BERNARD

Wasabi Green Pea Crusted John Dory
Mochi Gome, Asian Pear Slaw
SERVES 4

ASIAN PEAR SLAW

¼ **cup** sour cream

2 **teaspoons** honey

4 **teaspoons** lime juice

to taste sea salt

to taste ground black pepper

1 **cup** matchstick-cut Asian pear

2 **cups** finely chopped napa cabbage

2 **tablespoons** chopped scallions

2 **tablespoons** chopped mint

2 **teaspoons** sesame oil

Whisk sour cream, honey, and lime juice in large serving bowl. Season with salt and pepper. Add remaining ingredients. Toss gently to coat. Transfer to serving dish.

MOCHI GOME

4 kumquats

2 **tablespoons** sesame oil

½ **cup** chopped sweet onion

1 **cup** mochi gome (sticky brown rice)

1 **cup** vegetable stock

1 **cup** soy milk

¼ **cup** chopped cilantro

¼ **cup** chopped walnuts

to taste sea salt

to taste cayenne pepper

Peel kumquats, discarding flesh. Finely chop peel. Add sesame oil to saucepan over medium heat. Add onion. Cook 2 minutes without browning, stirring often. Add rice and kumquat peel. Stir to coat. Add stock and soy milk. Bring to simmer. Cover. Cook 25 minutes or until liquid is absorbed. Fold in cilantro and walnuts. Season with sea salt and cayenne pepper. Cover pan 2 minutes. Transfer to lidded serving dish. Cover to keep warm.

JOHN DORY

¼ **cup** soy sauce

¼ **cup** orange juice

⅛ **teaspoon** shichimi togarashi pepper

½ **cup** Japanese wasabi peas

1 **tablespoon** white sesame seeds

¼ **cup** panko bread crumbs

2 **tablespoons** nori flakes

3 **tablespoons** sesame oil, divided

4 John Dory fillets,
    skinless, boneless (6 ounces each)

4 **sprigs** mizuna or mint

Preheat oven to 350°F. Combine soy sauce, orange juice, and togarashi in small mixing bowl. Set aside. Add wasabi peas, sesame seeds, bread crumbs, and nori flakes to food processor. Process to coarse meal. Transfer to mixing bowl. Stir in 1 tablespoon sesame oil. Brush fish with remaining sesame oil. Transfer to oiled baking sheet. Coat with wasabi pea mixture. Bake 7 minutes or until fish is slightly underdone. Divide soy sauce mixture between four warm serving plates. Place fish atop. Garnish with mizuna. Serve with Mochi Gome and Asian Pear Slaw.

Romanian cuisine is steeped in the country's ever-changing history. Positioned at the crossroads of land and sea routes, many cultures came, traded, or conquered, and left their own culinary influences behind like souvenirs. Today Romanian cooking is layered with the flavors of Greeks, Romans, Turks, Saxons, and Slavs. Not to be outdone by the others, the Romans also gave the country her name. The port of Constanta, located where the Danube river spills into the Black Sea, was originally created to facilitate trade between Romanians and Greeks. Today the port provides a passageway to the landlocked countries of Europe. *Tochitura* is a traditional Romanian dish made by braising meats and sausages in a spicy sauce often containing tomatoes. This recipe is a seafood version that showcases John Dory, an esteemed catch in the Black Sea. —RON

Constanta Port John Dory Tochitura

Toasted Lemon Rice

SERVES 4

SAUCE

1 pound vine-ripened tomatoes
¼ cup extra-virgin olive oil
½ cup sliced white onion
2 medium green bell peppers,
    stemmed, seeded, sliced
2 jalapeño chiles,
    quartered lengthwise
6 cloves garlic, thinly sliced
2 bay leaves
to taste sea salt and pepper
¼ cup raisins
½ teaspoon dried oregano
¼ cup pitted green olives, quartered
2 tablespoons drained capers

Core and chop tomatoes. Transfer to colander set over mixing bowl. Drain 20 minutes. Add oil to large saucepan over medium high heat. Add onion, bell pepper, jalapeños, garlic, and bay leaves. Season with salt and pepper. Cook 3 minutes, stirring often. Add raisins and liquid from drained tomatoes. Cook until tomato liquid evaporates. Add chopped tomatoes and oregano. Cook 5 minutes. Fold in olives and capers. Adjust seasoning.

JOHN DORY TOCHITURA

¼ cup extra-virgin olive oil, divided
1½ pounds large John Dory fillet,
    skinless, boneless
to taste sea salt and pepper

Preheat oven to 400°F. Drizzle 2 tablespoons oil into baking dish large enough to hold fish and sauce. Spread 2 cups Sauce evenly in dish. Season John Dory with salt and pepper. Lay fish atop sauce. Cover with remaining sauce. Place in oven. Bake 12 minutes or until John Dory is slightly underdone.

TOASTED LEMON RICE

1½ cups uncooked
    long-grain white rice
2 tablespoons unsalted butter
1 teaspoon lemon peel
2-inch piece vanilla bean, chopped
3 cups chicken broth
2 tablespoons lemon juice
to taste sea salt and pepper

Place rice in strainer. Rinse under cold water until water runs clear. Drain well. Spread onto baking sheet 30 minutes, uncovered, to dry. Add butter to large saucepan over medium heat. Cook until lightly brown and foamy. Add rice, lemon peel, and vanilla. Cook 1 minute, stirring constantly. Add chicken broth and lemon juice. Season with salt and pepper. Stir once. Cover. Bring to low simmer. Cook 15 minutes or until liquid is absorbed and rice is tender. Fluff with fork. Serve with John Dory Tochitura.

CHAPTER 5

Big Swimmers
SALMON, MAHI MAHI, BASS, COD, MONKFISH

Salmon

ITALY
Tarragon Pesto Crusted Salmon
butternut leek farro

FRANCE
Olive Oil Poached Salmon
crushed fennel potatoes

CANADA
Cedar Plank Smoked Salmon
green apple grape slaw

ISRAEL
Falafel Crusted Salmon
wilted greens, tahini sauce

SCOTLAND
Apple Cider Braised Salmon
warm green bean salad

JAPAN
Black and White Sesame Coated Salmon
orange miso sauce, soba noodles

TURKEY
Salmon "Balik Pilaki"
root vegetables, feta cheese

UNITED STATES
SoCal Salmon Burger
ancho chile aioli

Mahi Mahi

CUBA
Mahi Mahi Mojo de Habanero
vanilla boniato

COSTA RICA
Mahi Mahi Pescador
almond cilantro rice

CAMBODIA
Khmer Mahi Mahi Amok
jasmine tea rice, curry broth

PERU
Layered Mahi Mahi Causa
organic egg, avocado, pepitas

BRAZIL
Tempero Baiano Mahi Mahi
hearts of palm, mango,
brazil nuts

Bass

CHILE
Sea Bass a la Plancha
queso fresco bread (cuñapes),
pebre verde

FRANCE
Loup de Mer in Sea Salt Crust
absinthe fennel cream

TAIWAN
Black Bass in Bamboo Steamer
sesame eggplant noodles

TANZANIA
Zanzibar Black Sea Bass
goat cheese ugali

UNITED STATES
Maryland Wild Striped Bass
broad bean casserole

Cod

PORTUGAL
Porto Moniz Bacalhau
crispy goat cheese potatoes, anise
infused raisins

KOREA
Chungcheong Province Kalbi Glazed Cod
vegetable bibimbap

HUNGARY
Cod in Paprika Cream
poppy seed pinched noodles

CANADA
New Brunswick Codfish Cake
endive salad, canuck ketchup

Monkfish

ITALY
Marsala Braised Monkfish Osso Buco
cremini polenta, almond
gremolata

INDIA
Tandoori Monkfish Skewers
banana mint raita

MOROCCO
Monkfish Eggplant Tagine
apricot harissa sauce

FRANCE
Bacon Wrapped Monkfish Tail
fennel coulis, rosemary peaches

Salmon

Seven types of salmon are found in the Atlantic and Pacific Oceans. All migrate and breed in a similar pattern, but Atlantic salmon can spawn multiple times, while Pacific salmon breed only once and then die.

Salmon can swim hundreds or thousands of miles, migrating from their birthplace in a freshwater stream to the ocean. After living in the sea and stocking up on food, they return to their spawning grounds. It is a long, difficult journey as they swim against the current, navigating strong rapids and dodging natural predators, all the while getting energy only from their stored body fat. Finally, when they reach their destination, they breed, and the cycle begins again.

Each type of salmon has its unique characteristics. Pink salmon live around two years and max out at 6 pounds, while the noble king salmon can live seven years and weigh up to 120 pounds.

Salmon's distinct orange, pink, or red flesh comes from carotenoid pigments in their diet of plankton, shellfish, and sometimes small fish.

Salmon caught at the mouth of a river on their way upstream have a bountiful store of oil in their flesh.

In the Wild

Atlantic Salmon
Found along both American and European Atlantic coasts. Some subspecies live in lakes, having evolved into nonmigratory fish that don't enter the ocean even though they have access.

Cherry Salmon
Also called masu salmon.

Found in the western Pacific Ocean near Japan, Korea, and Russia.

King Salmon
Also called chinook salmon, this is the largest of all Pacific salmon. Rich flavor, firm flesh, and orange-red color.

Swims the Pacific coast from Alaska to Northern California. It is the official state fish of Alaska.

Chum Salmon
Also called dog, keta, or calico salmon. Light red color, low fat content, and delicate flavor.

Found from the Sea of Japan to California's Sacramento River and the Mackenzie River in Canada.

Coho Salmon
Also called silver salmon and found in coastal waters from Alaska to central California's Monterey Bay.

High fat content. Firm-textured pink to red-orange flesh retains its color during cooking.

Pink Salmon
The smallest of the Pacific salmon, these are found in short streams from Northern California to Korea, Canada, and Siberia.

It is low fat with a delicate flavor.

The majority of harvested pinks go to the canning industry.

Sockeye Salmon
Also called red salmon, this species is found in California, Japan's Hokkaido Island, and Canada's Arctic Sea.

Sockeye salmon has exquisite flavor; its flesh is deep red in color both before and after cooking.

Black Sea Salmon
Also called black sea trout. Pale-colored flesh with a mild flavor.

Small salmon that lives in the Black Sea and Danube river. Available in Turkey, Republic of Georgia, Romania, and Bulgaria.

In the Kitchen
Sweet, acidic, and aromatic flavors of marinades do a great job to balance the rich oiliness of salmon. Our favorite cooking methods include these:

- On the grill with a marinade, which balances the richness
- Oil poached, which highlights the true flavor
- Seared with skin on—crispy outside, rich, creamy texture inside
- Cured with aromatic herbs and spices—so silky
- Raw as sashimi and tartare with a rich, buttery texture

Valuable Nutrients from Salmon
- Chloride: aids in digestion, helps to maintain healthy pH level in the body
- Niacin: increases good cholesterol levels
- Omega-3 fatty acids: for a healthy heart, prevent cardiovascular disease
- Phosphorus: builds healthy bones and strong teeth
- Selenium: antioxidant, prevents arthritis
- Vitamin B_6: for a healthy metabolism and immune system
- Vitamin B_{12}: promotes healthy blood cells, prevents anemia, eases migraines
- Vitamin D: helps the body to absorb calcium and phosphorus, promotes healthy cell function

Fun Facts
Salmon brought food and prosperity to the Native Americans of the Pacific Northwest, who paid tribute by returning the bones of the season's first-caught salmon to the river it came from.

The Tsimshian, Native Americans of the Pacific Northwest, have a legend that salmon were originally people living in five different villages. Each village represented one of the five types of Pacific salmon known to them. According to the legend, every spring the people of each village would transform into salmon and swim downstream to the ocean.

The ancient Romans ate a paste called *moretum,* a precursor to pesto, made by crushing cheese, garlic, and herbs together. In the modern Ligurian adaptation, basil, pine nuts, and olive oil, all grown in abundance in the region, are added to the paste. The ingredients are ground by hand in a mortar and pestle, using a circular motion. This fragrant green treasure will make your salmon a superstar. The pesto can be refrigerated for up to two days. Pour a thin film of olive oil over the surface to prevent discoloration, then cover tightly. Experimenting with your favorite nuts and garden herbs will expand your pesto repertoire. —RON

Tarragon Pesto Crusted Salmon
Butternut Leek Farro
SERVES 4

SALMON
¼ **cup** blanched hazelnuts

1 **cup** tightly packed whole basil leaves

¼ **cup** fresh tarragon

¼ **cup** plus **2 tablespoons** olive oil, divided

2 **cloves** garlic

6 **tablespoons** grated Parmesan cheese

1 **tablespoon** orange juice

¼ **teaspoon** orange zest

to taste sea salt

to taste ground black pepper

1½ **pounds** center-cut salmon fillet, boneless

Preheat oven to 375°F. Add hazelnuts, basil, tarragon, ¼ cup olive oil, garlic, Parmesan, orange juice, and orange zest to blender. Pulse to coarse paste. Transfer to small mixing bowl. Season with salt and pepper. Set aside. Place salmon on cutting board. Slice crosswise into eight 1-inch thick medallions. Season on both sides with salt and pepper. Add 1 tablespoon oil to large heavy-bottomed skillet over medium-high heat. Sear 4 salmon medallions, 30 seconds on each side. Transfer to baking sheet. Repeat process. Place a heaping teaspoonful of pesto onto each medallion. Transfer to oven. Bake 5 minutes or until salmon is slightly underdone.

BUTTERNUT LEEK FARRO
1 **cup** farro or wheat berries

3 **tablespoons** olive oil

1 **cup** quartered brown button mushrooms

1 **cup** butternut squash, diced ¼ inch

1 **cup** sliced leeks, white part only

2 **tablespoons** vermouth wine

2 **tablespoons** balsamic vinegar

to taste sea salt

to taste ground black pepper

Soak farro in 2 cups water for 4 hours. Drain. Bring 1 quart water to boil. Add farro. Bring back to simmer. Turn down heat. Cover. Simmer 20 minutes. Transfer to colander. Rinse under cold water. Drain thoroughly. Add oil to skillet over medium heat. Add mushrooms and squash. Cook 4 minutes, stirring occasionally. Add leeks. Cook 2 minutes without browning, stirring often. Add vermouth and balsamic. Bring to simmer. Fold in farro. Cook until hot, stirring often. Season with salt and pepper.

PRESENTATION
4 **teaspoons** extra-virgin olive oil

4 **sprigs** tarragon

Spoon Butternut Leek Farro in center of warm serving plate. Drizzle with extra-virgin olive oil. Top with salmon medallions. Garnish with tarragon sprig.

While we more often think of poaching salmon in water or stock, using oil as the cooking liquid gives new meaning to the method, enhancing the richness of the flesh. This cooking technique is a favorite in the South of France, where the olive groves produce the finest oil, the fish are abundant, and the fields are covered with fragrant herbs. We all know that fat carries flavors. Adding aromatics to the olive oil enhances and intensifies the flavor of the fish. For this technique, tuna, halibut, sea bass, and scallops are fantastic substitutes! Infusing the olive oil with your own favorite aromatics makes it fun. —RON

Olive Oil Poached Salmon
Crushed Fennel Potatoes
SERVES 4

CRUSHED FENNEL POTATOES
2 pounds small gold potatoes, washed
¼ cup extra-virgin olive oil, divided
1 large fennel bulb, thinly sliced
to taste sea salt
to taste ground black pepper
1 bunch watercress leaves

Add potatoes to lightly salted cold water in large stockpot. Place over medium heat. Bring to simmer. Cook 15 minutes or until tender. Meanwhile add 2 tablespoons olive oil to skillet over medium heat. Add fennel. Cook 3 minutes or until tender, stirring often. Season with salt and pepper. Set aside. Drain potatoes in colander. Add to fennel. Gently crush each potato using the back of a fork. Add watercress and remaining olive oil. Stir to combine. Season again with salt and pepper if needed.

VINAIGRETTE
¼ cup hazelnut oil
1 tablespoon chopped chives
2 tablespoons Champagne vinegar
1 tangerine, zested, juiced
2 tablespoons chopped, toasted hazelnuts
¼ cup pitted, quartered kalamata olives
½ cup quartered teardrop tomatoes
to taste sea salt
to taste ground black pepper

In small mixing bowl, combine hazelnut oil, chives, Champagne vinegar, and tangerine juice and zest. Whisk together until well mixed. Add hazelnuts, olives, and tomatoes. Season with salt and pepper.

SALMON
8 sprigs lemon thyme
4 sage leaves
½ teaspoon cracked black peppercorns
1 teaspoon sea salt
4 cloves garlic, peeled, sliced
1 tangerine, zested
4 cups olive oil
4 salmon fillets, boneless (6 ounces each)

Combine thyme, sage, peppercorns, salt, garlic, tangerine zest, and olive oil in wide heavy-bottomed saucepan over low heat to infuse oil. When garlic starts to sizzle slightly, turn off heat. Use tongs to immerse salmon into oil. Steep salmon in oil 10 minutes or until slightly underdone. If necessary, return briefly to low heat to finish cooking process. Salmon should be translucent and bright orange in the middle but flake easily. Transfer salmon to serving plate atop crushed potatoes. Spoon Vinaigrette onto plate. Garnish with thyme sprig and sage leaf.

Rooted in fishing tradition, aboriginals of the Canadian West Coast have always worshipped salmon. The first caught salmon is shared ceremonially, and its bones returned to the sea to ensure an abundant salmon run. Chinook salmon return from their long voyage at sea to spawn in the river of their birth. West Coast natives invented salmon jerky by brining fillets and hot smoking the flesh with alder and cherry woods. Smoking salmon on cedar planks is an old tradition in North America's Pacific Northwest; it gives wild salmon a unique, rich flavor that evokes the surrounding deep woods. —RON

Cedar Plank Smoked Salmon
Green Apple Grape Slaw
SERVES 4

MARINADE
1½ cups amber beer
1 tablespoon sea salt
½ teaspoon cracked black pepper
¼ cup grade-B maple syrup
1 tablespoon rosemary leaves
1 teaspoon crushed fennel seeds
4 salmon fillets, skin on, scaled,
    boneless (6 ounces each)

Whisk all ingredients except salmon in mixing bowl to dissolve salt. Pour mixture into large resealable bag. Add salmon. Seal. Refrigerate at least 4 hours. Drain marinade.

SALMON
4 cedar planks, 8 x 5 x ½ inch,
    soaked in water overnight
2 small oranges,
    cut into ⅛-inch-thick slices
⅛ teaspoon crushed red pepper flakes
1 medium red onion,
    cut into ⅛-inch-thick rings
8 sprigs rosemary
as needed canola oil spray

Preheat grill to medium high. Place planks on grill. Close lid 10 minutes or until planks start to smoke and char. Line planks with orange slices. Carefully place salmon atop oranges. Sprinkle with red pepper flakes. Place onion rings and rosemary sprigs atop salmon. Spray lightly with canola oil. Reduce heat to medium. Close lid. Cook 12 minutes or until salmon is slightly underdone. Slide heatproof spatula under oranges. Transfer salmon along with onions and rosemary to serving dish.

GREEN APPLE GRAPE SLAW
2 cups matchstick-cut green apples
1 cup quartered seedless red grapes
2 cups finely sliced napa cabbage
¼ cup chopped mint leaves
¼ cup olive oil
1 tablespoon grade-B maple syrup
2 tablespoons cider vinegar
½ teaspoon celery seeds
to taste sea salt
to taste ground black pepper

Combine all ingredients, including salt and pepper, in mixing bowl. Refrigerate 30 minutes before serving.

Falafel are tasty herb-laden vegetarian fritters made from ground fava beans or chickpeas. They are thought to have originated in Egypt, where they replaced meat dishes during Lent, but as with many foods around the globe, several countries adamantly stake claim to their invention. There is no debate about their importance to the street-food scene in Israel, where they are fried to order then dressed with tahini sauce or served inside flatbread bursting with your customized selection of pickles, fresh vegetables, and sauces. It is the ultimate convenience food—healthy, tasty, cheap, and quick. In this recipe we bake the falafel batter atop salmon fillets, giving a unique modern twist to a historical dish. —RON

Falafel Crusted Salmon

Wilted Greens, Tahini Sauce

SERVES 4

WILTED GREENS

2 tablespoons olive oil

1 cup sliced shallots

2 cups packed arugula leaves

2 cups packed, chopped, stemless kale leaves

2 cups packed, chopped, stemless swiss chard leaves

¼ cup sun-dried currants

to taste sea salt

to taste ground black pepper

½ cup apple juice

Add oil to large skillet over medium-high heat. Add shallots. Cook 2 minutes or until lightly caramelized, stirring often. Add arugula, kale, swiss chard, and currants. Season with salt and pepper. Cook 2 minutes or until the greens are wilted and tender, stirring often. Add apple juice. Toss well. Adjust seasoning if needed.

FALAFEL

1 cup cooked drained chickpeas

½ cup finely chopped white onion

2 teaspoons minced garlic

2 tablespoons finely chopped parsley

1 teaspoon finely chopped cilantro

½ teaspoon ground cumin

¼ teaspoon ground turmeric

⅛ teaspoon red chile flakes

1 tablespoon extra-virgin olive oil

to taste sea salt

Add all ingredients except salt to food processor. Process to coarse paste. Season with salt. Set aside.

SALMON

1 tablespoon grapeseed oil

4 salmon fillets, skin on, scaled, boneless (6 ounces each)

to taste sea salt

to taste ground black pepper

as needed canola oil spray

Preheat oven to 375F°. Add grapeseed oil to large ovenproof skillet over medium-high heat. Season salmon on both sides with salt and pepper. Sear, flesh side down, 1 minute. Spray skin with canola oil. Flip over. Use spoon to spread falafel evenly over top of salmon. Transfer to oven. Cook 4 minutes or until salmon is slightly underdone. Spread 2 tablespoons Tahini Sauce in center of warm serving plate. Place Wilted Greens over Tahini Sauce. Top with salmon.

TAHINI SAUCE

4 cloves garlic, chopped fine
2 teaspoons grated ginger
1 teaspoon lemon zest

½ teaspoon sea salt
6 tablespoons tahini (sesame paste)
¼ cup Greek yogurt

2 tablespoons lemon juice
pinch cayenne pepper

Mash garlic, ginger, lemon zest, and salt to a paste with back of a wooden spoon in mixing bowl. Whisk in remaining ingredients. Add more salt or cayenne if desired. Set aside.

SCOTLAND

The Oykel is a river in the solitary northern part of Scotland. Her water rises near the town of Ullapool on the western coast and splits the solemn green landscape on a journey to the North Sea. Wild salmon take the opposite route. They enter the river in January on their way to their birthplace, baited by the rising water temperature as spring turns to summer. This is the best time to land your catch while the salmon flesh is still rich with stored oils. Braising salmon is a great way to spotlight its luscious texture. —RON

Apple Cider Braised Salmon
Warm Green Bean Salad
SERVES 4

SALMON

32 ounces hard apple cider

1 green apple, cored, sliced

3 small ribs celery, cut into 2-inch-long pieces

1 lemon, sliced

6 sprigs fresh thyme

2 bay leaves

1 2-inch stick cinnamon

1 tablespoon mustard seeds

1 teaspoon sea salt

½ teaspoon whole black peppercorns

4 salmon fillets, center-cut, boneless, skinless
(6 ounces each)

to taste sea salt and ground black pepper

Add apple cider, apples, celery, lemon, thyme, bay leaves, cinnamon, mustard seeds, salt, and peppercorns into wide heavy-bottomed saucepan over medium heat. Bring liquid to low simmer. Do not boil. Cook 10 minutes. Season fish with sea salt and ground black pepper. Carefully immerse salmon into liquid. Cook 8 minutes or until salmon is slightly underdone.

WARM GREEN BEAN SALAD

½ pound red new potatoes, quartered

½ pound fresh green beans, trimmed

2 tablespoons olive oil

1 cup sliced red onions

½ cup diced red bell pepper

2 teaspoons honey

1 teaspoon fresh thyme leaves

to taste sea salt

to taste ground black pepper

¼ cup chopped smoked almonds

Bring 2 quarts lightly salted water to boil in large pot. Add potatoes. Cook 5 minutes or until tender. Transfer to ice bath. Return water to boil. Add beans. Cook 3 minutes or until beans are tender. Drain. Transfer to ice bath. Drain potatoes and beans in colander. Pat dry. Set aside. Add oil to skillet over medium heat. Add onions, peppers, and potatoes. Cook 3 minutes or until caramelized, stirring often. Add honey, thyme, and beans. Cook 2 minutes, tossing often. Season with salt and pepper. Sprinkle with almonds. Transfer to large serving platter. Arrange salmon atop.

Hokkaido, the northernmost island of Japan, is home to an aboriginal people called the Ainu. Like most indigenous peoples of the world, the Ainu live in harmony with the land, respecting the fate of nature and bowing down to the rites of the seasons. The annual salmon run is one of those rites, and it brings a celebration of singing and dancing in autumnal "welcome back salmon" festivals. As the fish return from the sea in scores of plenty, the Ainu people release their dogs that they've trained to catch the salmon with better efficiency than a fisherman. Salmon is highly regarded throughout Japan, where it is often cooked with traditional ingredients like miso and the seven-spice mixture *shichimi togarashi*. —RON

Black and White Sesame Coated Salmon
Orange Miso Sauce, Soba Noodles
SERVES 4

SALMON
3 tablespoons white sesame seeds
3 tablespoons black sesame seeds
4 (6-ounce) salmon fillets,
    skin on, scaled, boneless
to taste sea salt
to taste ground black pepper
2 tablespoons grapeseed oil
as needed canola oil spray

Mix sesame seeds together. Spread onto shallow bowl. Season salmon with salt and pepper on both sides. Press flesh side onto sesame seeds. Add oil to large skillet over medium heat. Place salmon, sesame side down, in pan. Cook 3 minutes or until seeds are toasted. Spray skin with canola oil. Flip over. Cook on skin side 4 minutes or until slightly underdone.

SOBA NOODLES
4 ounces uncooked soba
    buckwheat noodles
2 tablespoons light sesame oil
½ cup shelled edamame
1 cup sliced shiitake mushrooms
3 cloves garlic, thinly sliced
1 tablespoon seeded, chopped red chile pepper
2 tablespoons teriyaki sauce
to taste sea salt
to taste ground black pepper
¼ cup sliced scallions

Bring 2 quarts of lightly salted water to boil in large pot over high heat. Add noodles. Stir. Cook 5 minutes or until tender but firm to the bite. Transfer noodles to colander. Rinse thoroughly under cold running water. Drain. Add 1 tablespoon sesame oil to large skillet over medium high heat. Add edamame, shiitake, garlic, and chile pepper. Cook 3 minutes, tossing often. Add teriyaki sauce. Cook 1 minute. Add noodles and remaining oil. Stir-fry 1 minute. Season with salt and pepper. Toss in scallions. Transfer to serving bowl. Place salmon atop. Serve with Orange Miso Sauce.

ORANGE MISO SAUCE

½ cup mayonnaise
2 tablespoons orange juice
1 teaspoon orange zest
1 tablespoon lime juice
1 tablespoon sesame oil
1½ tablespoons miso paste

1 teaspoon wasabi paste
1 teaspoon grated ginger
2 tablespoons minced chives
to taste sea salt
to taste ground black pepper

Whisk first 9 ingredients in large mixing bowl. Season with salt and pepper. Transfer to serving bowl. Cover. Refrigerate.

The double-deck Galata Bridge spans the Golden Horn, a portion of the Bosporus waterway that separates Turkey into its Asian and European parts. The Bosporus is fed by the Black Sea on one end and the Sea of Marmara on the other, creating a "fish highway." Back on the upper level of the Galata, while the setting sun turns the towering mosques of Istanbul into silhouettes, fishermen stand shoulder to shoulder across the entire length of the bridge, filling their buckets with whatever fish is running that day. The bridge is full of life. Locals cross to and fro, flowing as steadily as the water beneath their feet. Street hawkers peddle bait and baked goods. Fishermen bond, sharing smokes and stories in between tending their lines. From the lower deck of the bridge, the scents of the tobacco cafes and the warm, aromatic air from the wall-to-wall restaurants rise amid the sounds of constant chatter. The energy of people and moving water and cooking and commerce and conversation all converge here. While most bridges are intended as a means of transport, this one is also a destination. Many of the fish caught here will be prepared *pilaki* style, meaning cooked with tomatoes, potatoes, garlic, carrots, parsley, lemon, and olive oil. —RON

Salmon "Balik Pilaki"
Root Vegetables, Feta Cheese
SERVES 4

1½ **pounds** salmon, center-cut, skinless, boneless
2 **tablespoons** olive oil
1 **cup** chopped onions
½ **pound** small new potatoes, washed, cut into eighths
1 **cup** diced, peeled carrots
1 **cup** diced, peeled celery root
1 **tablespoon** all-purpose flour
2 **cups** chopped tomatoes
2 **cloves** garlic, chopped
½ **cup** red wine
1½ **cups** vegetable stock
2 bay leaves
⅛ **teaspoon** crushed red pepper flakes
1 **teaspoon** lemon zest
6 **sprigs** thyme
to taste sea salt and pepper
2 **tablespoons** chopped parsley
½ **cup** diced feta cheese
½ lemon

Place salmon on cutting board. Slice crosswise into 1-inch-thick strips. Add oil to large skillet over medium-high heat. Add onions, potatoes, carrots, and celery root. Cook 6 minutes, stirring often. Stir in flour to coat vegetables. Cook 2 minutes, stirring constantly. Add tomatoes, garlic, wine, stock, bay leaves, red pepper flakes, lemon zest, and thyme. Bring to simmer. Season with salt and pepper. Add salmon, nestling pieces into the vegetables until barely covered with liquid. Return to very low simmer. Cover. Cook 15 minutes or until salmon is slightly underdone. Remove from heat. Sprinkle with parsley and feta cheese. Squeeze lemon atop.

Every salmon has a story, and the wild salmon story is a long one thankfully. In early June the Alaskan salmon migration is in full swing on the Kenai Peninsula, where I am fly fishing. Watching from a distance, my competition is a massive brown bear standing on a stretch of low waterfalls, catching a generous diet of fatty spawning salmon with its claws. Salmon belly is the best part of the fish, often used for salmon tartare, but it's ideal for burgers because it is the fattiest part of the fish. It's incredibly flavorful and will stay juicy when cooked. For a lighter flavor, use snapper, sea bass, or tuna. —BERNARD

SoCal Salmon Burger
Ancho Chile Aioli
SERVES 6

SALMON
1 pound salmon fillet,
    boneless, skinless, cut into ½-inch cubes
2 tablespoons finely chopped parsley
¼ cup minced scallions
1 lemon, zested, juiced
¾ teaspoon Tabasco sauce
1 tablespoon Dijon mustard
½ teaspoon sea salt
½ teaspoon ground black pepper
2 egg whites, beaten
1 whole egg
1 cup bread crumbs
as needed canola oil spray
2 tablespoons olive oil
6 multigrain rolls, split

Place salmon in food processor. Pulse until roughly chopped. Transfer to large mixing bowl. Fold in parsley, scallions, lemon zest, lemon juice, Tabasco sauce, mustard, salt, pepper, egg whites, and whole egg. Fold in bread crumbs. Form into 6 patties, 4 inches wide and 1 inch thick. Transfer to plate. Cover. Refrigerate at least 2 hours. Preheat grill to medium high. Lightly coat grates with canola oil spray. Brush olive oil onto cut sides of rolls and surface of salmon patties. Grill patties 2 minutes on each side for medium rare, or to desired doneness. Grill rolls.

ANCHO CHILE AIOLI
1 cup mayonnaise
1 teaspoon lemon juice
½ teaspoon sugar
1 teaspoon ancho chile powder
2 teaspoons paprika
to taste sea salt

Whisk all ingredients together in mixing bowl. Cover. Refrigerate

PRESENTATION
1 head butter lettuce, leaves separated, washed, patted dry
1 mango, peeled, seeded, thinly sliced
1 avocado, peeled, seeded, sliced
4 red radishes, thinly sliced
¼ cup daikon sprouts
6 lemon wedges

Spread 1 tablespoon aioli evenly over toasted buns. Transfer remaining aioli to serving dish. Top buns with salmon burger, lettuce, mango, avocado, radish, and daikon sprouts. Serve with a lemon wedge.

Mahi Mahi

Mahi mahi (or as we say in the kitchen, just "mahi"), is a saltwater fish found in warm coastal waters around the world.

In Spanish the fish is known as *dorado*, which means "golden," referring to the gold coloring on its skin.

In English it is called dolphin fish, but it is not related to the dolphin mammal.

Mahimahi is a Hawaiian name meaning "strong, strong," referring to the fish's powerful grace in the ocean.

Hawaiian mahi mahi reaching more than 15 pounds are the most highly regarded of all the mahis.

In the Wild

Mahi mahi are native to tropical and subtropical oceans.

They feed near the surface, eating a varied diet of fish and crustaceans.

They are caught in Hawaii, Florida, Taiwan, Ecuador, Brazil, Costa Rica, Fiji, and northern Australia.

Mahi mahi can reach 7 feet in length and weigh 90 pounds. Despite reaching that size and strength, mahi mahi only live three to four years.

In the Kitchen

Mahi mahi is a delicious combination of firm texture and sweet tropical flavor. It needs to be slightly undercooked or else it can get dry. Our favorite preparation methods include these:

- Raw as sashimi—rich mouthfeel

- Spice rubbed or blackened

- Seared and served with fruit salsa, which complements the natural tropical flavor

- Grilled like a burger, topped with guacamole and papaya salsa

- In ceviche—tender texture with a pleasant bite

Valuable Nutrients from Mahi Mahi

- Niacin: increases good cholesterol levels

- Omega-3 fatty acids: for a healthy heart, prevent cardiovascular disease

- Phosphorus: builds healthy bones and strong teeth

- Potassium: for a healthy heart and kidneys, reduces stress

- Selenium: antioxidant, prevents arthritis

- Vitamin B_5: prevents acne and loss of hair, reduces cholesterol

- Vitamin B_6: for a healthy metabolism and immune system

- Vitamin B_{12}: promotes healthy blood cells, prevents anemia, eases migraines

Fun Facts

Mahi mahi are fast swimmers, reaching speeds up to 60 miles per hour to elude their predators.

The Japanese are prolific fishers of mahi mahi, landing more than half of the world's catch.

Most fish are juveniles at four months, but mahi mahi are considered adults.

By pure coincidence the word *mahi* means "fish" in Persian.

Mahi mahi travel in pairs; a pair would be a mahi mahi mahi mahi.

Mojo is a sauce that originated in the Canary Islands as a pureed combination of sweet and spicy red or green peppers, olive oil, and bread. Along with its Canarian inventors, the sauce later migrated to Cuba. In this new environment, the sauce was transformed into a blend of garlic, olive oil, and sour orange juice. Now considered a cornerstone of the Cuban kitchen, mojo is used as both a sauce and a marinade. Its ability to provide a captivatingly sweet-salty-sour-garlicky flavor makes mojo essential to good Cuban cooking. In this recipe, the taste of sour orange is mimicked by combining regular orange juice with lime juice. Boniato is a tropical gold-fleshed sweet potato popular in the Caribbean, especially Cuba. —RON

Mahi Mahi Mojo de Habanero
Vanilla Boniato
SERVES 4

MOJO
8 cloves garlic, peeled
1 habanero chile, seeded
2 teaspoons sea salt
⅓ **cup** lime juice
¼ **cup** orange juice
2 tablespoons olive oil

Add garlic, habanero chile, and salt to mortar. Use pestle to process to a paste. Stir in citrus juices. Add oil to small skillet over medium heat. Add garlic mixture. Cook 1 minute, stirring constantly. Keep warm on side of grill while cooking fish.

MAHI MAHI
2 tablespoons vegetable oil
4 mahi mahi fillets, center-cut, skinless, boneless, 1 inch thick (6 ounces each)
1 teaspoon ground cumin
1 teaspoon dried oregano, crushed
to taste sea salt and ground black pepper

Brush oil onto mahi mahi, coating all sides. Season with cumin, oregano, salt, and pepper. Transfer to side dish. Cover. Refrigerate at least 1 hour.

VANILLA BONIATO
2 pounds boniato sweet potatoes
⅓ **cup** sour cream
¼ **cup** dark rum
¼ **teaspoon** vanilla extract
2 tablespoons maple syrup
pinch cayenne pepper
to taste sea salt

Preheat oven to 450°F. Wrap potatoes individually in foil. Bake until soft in center. Peel. Place pulp in mixing bowl. Mash until smooth. Fold in sour cream, rum, vanilla, and maple syrup. Season with cayenne and salt. Keep warm.

PRESENTATION
as needed canola oil spray
2 tablespoons finely sliced mint leaves
4 sprigs basil

Preheat grill to high. Lightly coat grill grates with canola oil spray. Place mahi mahi on grill grates at 45-degree angle and cook 1 minute or until grill marks form. Using tongs, lift and rotate mahi mahi quarter turn with the same side down. Cook 1 minute. Turn fish over. Repeat process, cooking until fish is slightly underdone. Spoon Vanilla Boniato onto center of warm serving plate. Lean fish against boniato. Stir mint into Mojo. Spoon generously atop mahi mahi. Garnish with basil sprig.

The Golfo Dulce ("Sweet Gulf") of Costa Rica is bordered on three sides by virgin rain forest and secluded Caribbean beaches, and on the fourth by the Pacific Ocean. This is the only body of water on earth that hosts migrating whales from both hemispheres. The gulf's gentle surface stares unblinkingly day and night at the Osa Peninsulsa, whose canopy of trees creeps up to the water's edge. Considering the 400 species of birds and 250 mammals on land, one can just imagine the marine life teeming below the surface. Snapper, barracuda, needlefish, snook, bonito, mackerel, and blackfin tuna are all tenants of the deep, awaiting their untimely date with a fisherman. Leaving these beautiful confines for the Pacific Ocean, one may enter into battle with a yellowfin tuna or a golden mahi mahi. It's a *pescador*'s paradise. —RON

Mahi Mahi Pescador

Almond Cilantro Rice

SERVES 4

MAHI MAHI

4 large vine-ripened tomatoes

4 lemons

4 mahi mahi fillets, center-cut, skinless, boneless
(6 ounces each)

to taste sea salt

to taste ground black pepper

16 leaves basil

3 tablespoons extra-virgin olive oil

½ cup tequila

Preheat oven to 375°F. Cut tomatoes into sixteen ⅛-inch-thick slices. Peel and cut lemons into sixteen ⅛-inch-thick slices, discarding seeds. Season mahi mahi with salt and black pepper. Transfer to oiled baking dish. Shingle tomato, lemon, and basil atop fish, overlapping to cover fish from one edge to the other. Drizzle with olive oil. Season again with salt and black pepper. Pour tequila into dish around mahi mahi. Place in oven. Cook 15 minutes or until fish is slightly underdone.

ALMOND CILANTRO RICE

1 cup long-grain white rice

½ cup packed cilantro leaves

3 cloves garlic

½ cup chopped scallions

¼ cup sliced almonds, toasted

2 cups cold vegetable stock

1½ teaspoons sea salt

½ teaspoon ground black pepper

1 tablespoon olive oil

Add rice to large bowl. Cover with hot water. Soak 15 minutes. Drain. Spread onto cookie sheet in thin layer for 15 minutes or until dry. Add cilantro, garlic, scallions, almonds, vegetable stock, salt, and pepper to blender. Puree until smooth. Add oil to sauce pot over medium heat. Add rice. Cook 5 minutes or until lightly browned, stirring often. Add vegetable mixture. Bring to simmer. Cover. Simmer 15 minutes. Remove from heat. Let stand, covered, 5 minutes. Fluff with fork. Season with more salt and pepper if needed.

PRESENTATION

Place mahi mahi in center of large serving plate. Spoon pan juices atop. Serve with Almond Cilantro Rice.

Sitting atop Bokor Mountain, which overlooks the Cambodian seaside town of Kep, you can see the cobalt-blue ocean on one side and cows grazing in rolling green fields on the other. Every morning a fleet of long, narrow wooden boats filled with colorful fish and crabs arrives from fishing expeditions, offloading at the market within hours of their catch. Seafood vendors line the road along the beach. The people of the region are very friendly, and love talking about their food culture. I joined a group of local villagers feasting on fish *amok,* a classic Khmer dish made of fish simmering in a large clay pot with curry paste, coconut, lemongrass, and other aromatics. Always use firm-fleshed fish like mahi mahi, salmon, ono, or swordfish to make this dish, or it will break down while cooking. —BERNARD

Khmer Mahi Mahi Amok

Jasmine Tea Rice, Curry Broth

SERVES 4

MAHI MAHI

- **1 pound** mahi mahi fillet, center-cut, boneless, skinless
- **2 cups** broccoli florets
- **4 cloves** garlic, crushed
- **1 cup** chopped white onion
- **½ cup** thinly sliced lemongrass, tender inner stalk only
- **½-inch piece** ginger, peeled and finely chopped
- **1 teaspoon** lime zest
- **1 teaspoon** turmeric
- **1 teaspoon** sea salt
- **1** red Thai chile pepper, seeded, sliced
- **2 tablespoons** honey
- **1 tablespoon** anchovy paste
- **3 tablespoons** coconut oil
- **2 cups** coconut milk
- **2 tablespoons** lime juice
- **to taste** sea salt
- **to taste** ground black pepper

Slice mahi mahi into pieces 3 x ½-inch. Refrigerate until needed. Add broccoli to pot of boiling salted water. Cook 1 minute. Transfer to colander. Rinse under cold water to cool. Set aside. Add garlic, onion, lemongrass, ginger, lime zest, turmeric, salt, chile pepper, honey, and anchovy paste to food processor. Process 2 minutes to form a curry paste. Add coconut oil to skillet over medium heat. Add ½ cup curry paste. Cook 1 minute or until fragrant, stirring constantly, being careful as it may splatter. Stir in coconut milk and lime juice. Bring to low simmer. Gently fold in mahi mahi. Simmer 3 minutes. Add broccoli. Cover. Cook additional 2 minutes or until mahi mahi is slightly underdone. Serve with Jasmine Tea Rice.

JASMINE TEA RICE

- **½ teaspoon** sea salt
- **1 bag** mint tea
- **2 bags** jasmine tea
- **1½ cups** jasmine rice
- **2 tablespoons** coconut oil

Add 2⅓ cups water, salt, mint tea, and jasmine tea to saucepan over medium heat. Bring to low simmer. Turn off heat. Steep 5 minutes. Discard tea bags. Rinse jasmine rice in colander under cold running water until water runs clear. Drain thoroughly. Stir rice into tea. Return to medium heat. Cover. Bring to simmer. Reduce heat to low. Cook 15 minutes or until liquid is absorbed and rice is tender. Drizzle coconut oil atop. Fluff with fork.

When Spaniards arrived in Peru during their colonization of South America, a great hybridization of European and Native American culture began. Spaniards adapted native Incan foods and language, and vice versa, creating many uniquely Peruvian dishes that are still loved today. The Incan word *kausaq,* which means "that which gives life," was pronounced "causa" by the Spaniards and used to describe a stuffed potato puree. The most traditional version of the dish combines Peru's indigenous potato, avocado and *aji* amarillo chiles with the limes, garlic, and chicken brought from across the ocean. Today all kinds of variations exist, but tuna salad, chicken salad, and ceviche are the most common accompaniment. Some *causas* are stuffed and others layered. The potato puree is moistened with olive oil and lime juice instead of dairy, a purely Peruvian technique. —RON

Layered Mahi Mahi Causa
Organic Egg, Avocado, Pepitas
SERVES 4 FAMILY STYLE

POTATO PUREE
1½ pounds (about 8 medium-size) golden Idaho potatoes
1 ear corn, husked
4 cloves garlic
2 large eggs
1 tablespoon aji amarillo paste or hot chile paste
3 tablespoons lime juice
2 tablespoons extra-virgin olive oil
to taste sea salt

Place potatoes in large pot. Cover with cold water. Bring to simmer over medium heat. Add corn, garlic, and eggs (in their shells). Cook 12 minutes. Transfer corn, garlic, and eggs to side dish. Cook potatoes additional 10 minutes, or until fork tender. Peel. Process potatoes and reserved garlic through ricer set over large pot. In absence of ricer, use potato masher. Fold in *aji* amarillo paste, lime juice, olive oil, and sea salt. Peel eggs and shave kernels from corn. Set aside.

AVOCADO
2 cups diced avocado (about 2 large)
2 teaspoons lime juice
to taste sea salt

Add all ingredients to mixing bowl. Mash coarsely.

MAHI MAHI
½ cup lime juice
½ teaspoon sea salt
1 small clove garlic, sliced paper-thin
¾ pound mahi mahi, sashimi-quality, boneless, skinless

Add lime juice, sea salt, and garlic to nonreactive mixing bowl. Stir to dissolve salt. Dice mahi mahi into ⅜-inch cubes. Add to marinade. Cover. Refrigerate 2 hours.

PRESENTATION
3 tablespoons finely diced red onion
¼ cup cilantro leaves
2 tablespoons extra-virgin olive oil
to taste sea salt
to taste ground black pepper
2 tablespoons pepitas (hulled pumpkin seeds)
¼ cup pitted, halved kalamata olives

Drain mahi mahi in colander. Transfer to mixing bowl. Add red onion, cilantro, corn kernels, olive oil, salt, and pepper. Set 6-inch ring mold in center of chilled serving platter. Fill bottom with ½-inch layer of Potato Puree. Spread Avocado evenly atop. Top with another ½-inch layer of Potato Puree. Top with mahi mahi mixture. Sprinkle with pepitas. Remove ring. Slice eggs into 6 wedges each. Decorate platter with eggs and olives. Season with sea salt and pepper.

Bahian seasoning (*tempero baiano*) originated in the northeastern state of Bahia in Brazil, the largest country in South America and home to one of the most celebrated cuisines in the world. Popular in every Brazilian kitchen, each family has their own interpretation of the fabulous spice mixture. Some like it hot, while others keep it on the mild side. This spice mixture is distinctive, aromatic, versatile, and herbaceous. When cooking your favorite fish, adding a healthy dose of tempero baiano will energize an ordinary preparation into a dynamic and flavorful masterpiece, making your taste buds do the samba. —BERNARD

Tempero Baiano Mahi Mahi
Hearts of Palm, Mango, Brazil Nuts
SERVES 4

TEMPERO BAIANO MAHI MAHI

½ **tablespoon** roasted whole coffee beans

1 **teaspoon** fennel seeds

½ **teaspoon** white peppercorns

1-inch piece vanilla bean, chopped

½ **teaspoon** sea salt

⅛ **teaspoon** red pepper flakes

2 **tablespoons** dried parsley flakes

¼ **teaspoon** turmeric

1½ **pounds** mahi mahi fillet, center-cut, boneless, skinless, trimmed

2 **tablespoons** canola oil

½ lemon

HEARTS OF PALM

½ **pound** green string beans, string removed

½ **pound** fingerling potatoes, sliced crosswise ¼-inch thick

3 **tablespoons** extra-virgin olive oil

2 **tablespoons** red wine vinegar

1 **clove** garlic, minced

1 **tablespoon** whole grain mustard

to taste sea salt

to taste ground black pepper

½ **cup** sliced red onion

1 mango, peeled, seeded, diced

2 **large** hearts of palm, sliced thinly crosswise

¼ **cup** chopped Brazil nuts

Add coffee beans, fennel seeds, peppercorns, vanilla bean, sea salt, and red pepper flakes to skillet over medium-low heat. Toast 2 minutes or until fragrant, stirring constantly. Transfer to spice grinder. Add parsley and turmeric. Process to powder. Slice mahi mahi into 3-ounce portions. Season on all sides with spice blend. Add oil to large skillet over medium heat. Place mahi mahi in skillet. Pan-roast 2 minutes or until lightly browned. Turn fish over. Roast 1 more minute or until mahi mahi is slightly underdone. Squeeze lemon over mahi mahi. Transfer mahi mahi to platter of Hearts of Palm salad.

Bring pot of lightly salted water to boil over medium high heat. Add beans and potatoes. Cook 4 minutes or until green beans are al dente. Drain in colander. Rinse under cold water. Drain thoroughly. Whisk olive oil, vinegar, garlic, and mustard in large serving bowl. Season with salt and pepper. Add beans, potatoes, and remaining ingredients. Toss gently to coat. Adjust seasoning. Transfer to serving platter.

Bass

Bass is a very general name used for many different species of fish in the perch family.

Bass are found all over the world in both fresh and saltwater, but they prefer the temperate waters of Latin America, Namibia, Taiwan, North America, and Europe.

Some bass, such as the revered North American striped bass, enter rivers to spawn.

Saltwater bass, appropriately called sea bass, feed on fish, crustaceans, mollusks, and other critters. Their bodies are long and round, giving them a nice yield of fillet.

Bass typically have small scales, a large mouth, and either a straight-edged or rounded tail.

In the Wild
These are our five favorites:

Black Sea Bass
Also called black perch, rock bass, chub, and tallywag

Caught in the western Atlantic Ocean

Blue Nose
Also called Antarctic butterfish, blue bream, blue-eye trevalla

Caught in the southern Pacific Ocean

White Sea Bass
Also called king croaker, weakfish, sea trout

Caught along the Pacific coast of the United States

Branzino
Also called European sea bass, branzini, *loup de mer*

Caught in the waters of the Mediterranean

Striped Bass
Also called striper, rockfish, linesides, greenhead

Caught in the Atlantic Ocean and rivers on the East Coast of the United States

In the Kitchen

Sea bass has firm, lean flesh with a mild flavor, making it a very versatile fish. For that reason, sea bass are often called the "chicken of the sea."

The meaty but delicate flesh can stand alone in simple preparations like baking and grilling, lightly seasoned and finished with a squeeze of lemon.

It can also benefit from the more assertive flavors of sauces and marinades like in Sea Bass a la Plancha (p. 223).

Bass is a great candidate for wrapping in salt crust.

Sea bass ceviche is a classic from Latin America.

In Taipei steamed bass is wrapped in lotus leaf.

Valuable Nutrients from Bass

- Magnesium: maintains healthy blood pressure and strong bones, relaxes nerves
- Niacin: increases good cholesterol levels
- Phosphorus: builds healthy bones and strong teeth
- Riboflavin: for healthy skin and healing
- Selenium: antioxidant, prevents arthritis
- Thiamin: maintains regular heartbeat, good for healthy eyes
- Vitamin B_5: prevents acne and loss of hair, reduces cholesterol
- Vitamin B_6: for a healthy metabolism and immune system

Fun Facts

Black sea bass are the Tiresias of the sea. They start life functioning as a female, then later switch to functioning as a male! (In Greek mythology, Tiresias was a blind prophet who was transformed into a woman.)

Bass have a sixth sense! They can pick up water vibrations from a sensor that runs down their back, enabling them to capture prey that they can't see.

In 1639, colonists of Massachusetts Bay enacted the very first conservation law in the New World, forbidding the use of bass (and cod) in the production of fertilizer.

CHILE

Famous in Santa Cruz, Bolivia, *cuñapes* are cheese rolls made from yucca flour. Their interesting name comes from the local Guarani words *cuña* and *pe,* which translate to "woman's breast," probably an homage to the bread's provocative shape. They are gluten-free when made with yucca flour, which is commonly found in Asian and Spanish grocers and sometimes labeled as tapioca flour or cassava flour. Using cherry tomatoes in place of green tomatoes and red chiles for the serranos will transform Chile's famous *pebre verde* sauce into *pebre rojo.* —RON

Sea Bass a la Plancha

Queso Fresco Bread (Cuñapes), Pebre Verde

SERVES 4

QUESO FRESCO BREAD (CUÑAPES)

1 cup tapioca flour or all-purpose flour
1½ teaspoons baking powder
2½ cups grated queso fresco
2 eggs, beaten separately
¼ cup milk
1 teaspoon cocoa powder
to taste sea salt
to taste ground black pepper

Preheat oven to 350°F. Sift tapioca flour and baking powder together into large mixing bowl. Add queso fresco. Rub mixture between your hands to break cheese into pebble-size pieces. Add 1 beaten egg. Combine well. If necessary, add some or all of the milk until dough can be formed into balls that hold their shape; it usually takes about 2 tablespoons milk. Divide dough into 8 portions. Form each portion into a ball. Place 3 inches apart on buttered baking sheet. Using fingertips, flatten slightly. Brush lightly with reserved beaten egg. Sift cocoa powder atop. Sprinkle with sea salt and ground black pepper. Bake 20 minutes, or until lightly browned on top.

PEBRE VERDE

3 cloves garlic
½ cup diced onion
1½ teaspoons sea salt
¼ teaspoon ground pepper
¼ cup olive oil
2 tablespoons red wine vinegar
1 tablespoon lemon juice
1 cup diced green tomatoes
6 green onions, finely chopped
1 serrano chili, seeded, finely chopped
1 cup packed fresh cilantro leaves

Add all ingredients to blender. Process to coarse salsa consistency.

SEA BASS

4 sea bass fillets,
     skinless, boneless (6 ounces each)
2 tablespoons olive oil
¼ cup chopped salted corn nuts

Reserve ½ cup Pebre Verde for presentation. Add remainder to casserole dish. Add sea bass, turning to coat fish in marinade. Cover. Refrigerate at least 2 hours. Add 2 tablespoons oil to cast-iron skillet over medium heat. Remove fish from marinade. Place in skillet. Cook 2 minutes on both sides or until lightly charred and fish is slightly underdone. Spoon 2 tablespoons reserved Pebre Verde onto each of four warm serving plates. Top with sea bass. Garnish with corn nuts. Serve with Queso Fresco Bread.

Loup de mer en crôute is Brittany's amazing and clever way of marrying locally harvested salt and dayboat line-caught sea bass. It is a dish that celebrates the sea and all its brilliance, showcasing the coastal region. This cooking method is simple but absolutely dramatic. The whole fish is encased in a vault of salt, flavored with fragrant herbs and spices. The cool part comes after the baking, when the brittle salt crust is cracked open, revealing the delicate, moist, and succulent fish within. It is the perfect preparation, as you can enjoy a nice aperitif with your friends while your fish is baking. —BERNARD

Loup de Mer in Sea Salt Crust
Absinthe Fennel Cream
SERVES 4

SEA BASS
2 oranges
2 tablespoons cracked black peppercorns
3 tablespoons anise seeds
2 tablespoons mustard seeds
3 pounds Brittany gray salt, coarse sea salt, or kosher salt
2 pounds rock salt
12 large egg whites, lightly beaten
1 red chile pepper, sliced
2 bay leaves
8 sprigs sage
1 onion, chopped
1 (3-pound) whole sea bass, gutted, cleaned, scaled

Preheat oven to 400°F. Zest both oranges into mixing bowl, reserving 1 for further instructions. Combine zest with peppercorns, anise seeds, mustard seeds, and salt. Fold in egg whites. Cut 1 of the zested oranges into ½-inch pieces. Transfer to separate mixing bowl. Combine with chile pepper, bay leaves, sage, and onion. Stuff mixture into fish cavity. Using a baking sheet large enough to hold the fish, line baking sheet with waxed paper. Spread one-third of the salt mixture onto waxed paper, making sure it is the same length as the fish measuring from the gills to just before the tail. Place fish atop, standing it up so it is positioned as if it were swimming. Mound and pack remaining salt evenly over the fish. The fish will be fully wrapped in salt mixture, with only head and tail showing. Place in oven. Bake 30

minutes or until 140°F in center. (To accurately check temperature, stick thermometer behind head into center of fish.) Remove from oven. Let fish stand 5 minutes. Crack salt crust with back of chef's knife and remove. Peel off and discard skin. Use spatula or serving fork to remove top fillet from bones. Peel bones in one piece up and away from bottom fillet. Serve with Absinthe Fennel Cream.

ABSINTHE FENNEL CREAM
2 tablespoons olive oil
½ **cup** minced shallots
1 cup thinly sliced fennel
½ **cup** Sauvignon Blanc wine
¼ **cup** orange juice
¾ **cup** crème fraîche
¼ **cup** minced chives
2 tablespoons absinthe liqueur
to taste sea salt
to taste ground white pepper

Add oil to saucepan over medium heat. Add shallots and fennel. Cook 3 minutes or until lightly browned. Add Sauvignon Blanc and orange juice. Bring to simmer. Reduce by half. Stir in crème fraîche. Return to simmer. Reduce to sauce consistency. Add chives and absinthe. Season with salt and pepper. Transfer to sauce boat and serve with fish.

The Fuji Fishing Harbor in the village of Shimen is a hidden jewel located between Linshan Bi and Fugui Jiao, and known for its landmark stone gate on the beach which gives the little village its name. The good thing about living in an island country is the constant supply of fresh seafood brought by the sea currents. At the harbors you can pick out live shrimp, clams, fish, and crabs just unloaded from the fishing boats. Or you can enjoy your seafood purchase at local restaurants, prepared at the cook's whim. I handed the cook a two-pound black bass and received it back twenty minutes later in a bamboo steamer topped with leafy vegetables and spicy XO sauce. A cooking tip I learned in Tawain from an elderly street food vendor: To cut fresh ginger into fine matchsticks, slice the ginger into thin planks, stack several pieces at a time, and then cut them into fine slivers. —BERNARD

Black Bass in Bamboo Steamer

Sesame Eggplant Noodles

SERVES 4

SEA BASS

2 tablespoons Chinese XO sauce

½ teaspoon chili oil

¼ cup matchstick-cut, peeled ginger

¼ cup thinly sliced shallots

1 orange, zested

8 large spinach leaves

4 sea bass fillets, center-cut,
   skin on, boneless, trimmed (6 ounces each)

8 sprigs cilantro

1 green onion, finely sliced

SESAME EGGPLANT NOODLES

¼ cup sesame paste or tahini

2½ tablespoons soy sauce

2 tablespoons rice vinegar

2 tablespoons mirin

½ teaspoon ground black pepper

4 ounces large udon noodles

3 tablespoons sesame oil, divided

3 cups diced Japanese eggplant

1 tablespoon toasted sesame seeds

2 tablespoons scallions finely sliced on bias

Combine XO sauce, chili oil, ginger, shallots, and orange zest in small bowl. Line bottom of bamboo steamer with spinach leaves. Place bass atop. You may use 2 steamer racks. Spread XO mixture onto flesh side of fish. Cover. Bring water to simmer in wok. Set steamer atop. Cover. Steam 8 minutes or until bass is slightly underdone. Transfer bass to serving platter. Garnish with cilantro sprigs and green onions.

Add sesame paste, soy sauce, rice vinegar, mirin, and black pepper to mixing bowl. Whisk until smooth. Set aside. Bring a pot of water to boil. Add noodles. Cook 5 minutes or until al dente. Transfer to colander. Rinse thoroughly under cold running water to remove excess starch. Toss with 1 tablespoon sesame oil to coat. Set aside. Add remaining sesame oil to seasoned wok or large nonstick skillet over high heat. Add eggplant. Stir-fry 5 minutes or until golden brown and caramelized. Add noodles. Cook until heated. Turn off heat. Fold in sesame paste. Transfer to serving bowl. Sprinkle with sesame seeds and scallions.

The archipelago of Zanzibar, with its eclectic mix of nationalities, cultures, and religions, lies off the coast of East Africa. Home to many spice plantations, the tiny islands brought the sultans of Oman across the Indian Ocean in long thin-hulled sailboats called dhow. Fish curry, also called *mchuzi wa samaki,* is a traditional Swahili dish from the island. *Samaki* is the Swahili word for "fish," and *mchuzi* means "curry." Various samaki, including bass, snapper, and shrimp, are simmered in coconut milk, fragrant herbs, and spices. This dish is the preferred staple for those living in coastal communities. *Ugali* is a traditional Tanzanian white corn gruel similar to polenta. —BERNARD

Zanzibar Black Sea Bass

Goat Cheese Ugali

SERVES 4

GOAT CHEESE UGALI

2½ **cups** vegetable stock
½ **teaspoon** sea salt
¼ **teaspoon** ground black pepper
1 **cup** finely ground white cornmeal
    or grits
3 **leaves** swiss chard, stemmed,
    chopped
¼ **cup** goat cheese

Add stock, salt, and pepper to saucepan over medium heat. Bring to simmer. Slowly stir in cornmeal. Reduce heat to low. Cook 5 minutes, stirring often. Add swiss chard. Cook 1 minute. Fold in goat cheese. Transfer to serving dish.

BASS

8 sea bass fillets, thick-cut, skin on,
    boneless (3 ounces each)
to taste sea salt
to taste ground black pepper
3 **tablespoons** peanut oil
as needed canola oil spray
1 **teaspoon** garam masala

Preheat oven to 350°F. Season bass on all sides with salt and pepper. Add oil to large skillet over high heat. Spray skin of bass with canola oil. Place in skillet, skin side down. Press on fish with spatula to keep skin in contact with oil. Cook 2 minutes or until skin is golden brown and crisp. Turn bass over. Cook 30 seconds. Transfer to side dish. Sprinkle with garam masala. Discard excess oil. Return skillet to medium high heat to make Sauce.

SAUCE

2 **tablespoons** canola oil
1 **cup** sliced onion
¾ **cup** chopped Anaheim peppers
1 **cup** sliced celery
6 **cloves** garlic, minced
1 **teaspoon** ground turmeric
1 **cup** chopped tomatoes
1 **cup** vegetable stock
½ **cup** coconut milk
2 **tablespoons** smooth peanut butter
2 **tablespoons** lime juice
¼ **cup** chopped cilantro
to taste sea salt
to taste ground black pepper
2 **sprigs** thyme

Add oil to skillet over medium-high heat. Add onion, peppers, celery, garlic, and turmeric to hot skillet. Cook 5 minutes, stirring often. Add tomatoes, vegetable stock, and coconut milk. Bring to simmer. Cook 5 minutes. Whisk in peanut butter, lime juice, and cilantro. Season with salt and pepper. Transfer to casserole dish. Place fish in sauce. Bake 8 minutes or until fish is slightly underdone. Garnish with thyme sprigs.

Spring is here, and for many of us that means it's time to go fishing! In Easton, Maryland, the weatherman is calling for temperatures hovering around the eighties. The Chesapeake Bay region is packed with anglers chasing the elusive iconic striped bass, better known as rockfish. As the fog lifts over the calm water by the creek at Locust Grove, from the corner of my eyes, by the lily pads, I see a big fish rolling on the surface. Instinctively I cast a crab peeler lure, landing right in the spot. As I am free-spooling, the striper takes the hook, and the fight is on! —BERNARD

Maryland Wild Striped Bass
Broad Bean Casserole
SERVES 4

BROAD BEAN CASSEROLE
½ **cup** olive oil

2 cups red pearl onions, peeled

1 cup diced, peeled yellow beets

1 cup diced, peeled rutabaga

1 cup sliced, peeled carrots

½ **pound** new red potatoes, quartered

6 cloves garlic, halved

¾ **cup** white wine

2 sprigs oregano

1 cup dried broad beans, soaked overnight, drained

3 cups chicken stock

¼ **cup** cider vinegar

to taste sea salt

to taste cayenne pepper

1 cup stemmed, chopped kale leaves

2 tablespoons maple syrup

½ **cup** sun-dried blueberries or sun-dried cherries

Add oil to sauce pot over medium-high heat. Add onions, beets, rutabaga, carrots, potatoes, and garlic. Cook 5 minutes, stirring often. Add wine, oregano, and broad beans. Return to simmer. Add chicken stock and cider vinegar. Season with sea salt and cayenne pepper. Bring to simmer. Cover. Cook 1 hour. Add kale, maple syrup, and sundried blueberries or cherries. Cook 5 minutes. Season with sea salt and cayenne pepper.

BASS
4 striped bass fillets, skin on, pin bone removed (6 ounces each)

to taste sea salt

to taste ground black pepper

1 tablespoon olive oil

as needed canola oil spray

4 sprigs thyme

1 tablespoon thyme leaves

1 tablespoon chopped oregano leaves

1 tablespoon unsalted butter

1 tablespoon lemon juice

Season bass with salt and pepper. Transfer skin side down to paper towel–lined plate. Refrigerate 30 minutes. Add olive oil to large skillet over medium heat. Spray skin of bass lightly with canola oil. Add bass skin side down onto skillet. Cook 2 minutes or until skin is crispy and lightly brown. Turn fish over. Cook 2 minutes, or until slightly underdone. Transfer to warm serving dish. Garnish with thyme sprigs. Return skillet to medium-high heat. Add oregano, butter, and thyme leaves. Cook until foamy and lightly brown. Add lemon juice. Spoon onto bass.

Cod

Cod makes up 10 percent of the worldwide fish catch.

Cod has been an important fish to local and global economies ever since the Viking period (around AD 800). Norwegians dried cod in order to preserve it for travel. This product, today known by the Portuguese word *bacalhau*, became very popular, and soon a market for dried cod developed in Europe. In the New World, in the seventeenth century, cod became a major commodity, creating trade networks and cross-cultural exchanges.

Cod are migratory and feed on other fish. They can weigh 200 pounds and reach 6 feet in length. Cod have ear stones, which develop annual growth rings that tell the cod's age. They live an average of fifteen years.

In the Wild

Cod are found on both sides of the North Atlantic, in Alaska, Antarctic, New England, Iceland, Canada, Norway, Russia, and China. They have also been fished off the Great Australian Bight, Chile, and around the Falkland Islands on rocky reefs.

Cod is a cold-water fish, which attributes to its richness in fat. They prefer to stay near the ocean floor, and range from coastal to deep, frigid waters.

Tara

Also known as snow fish and, in Japan, as *ibodara, maidara,* and *ara*

Caught on the east and west coasts of Japan

Lingcod

Also known as blue cod, bluefish, buffalo cod, green cod, and white cod

Unique to the West Coast of North America

Sablefish

Also called Alaskan cod, black cod, butterfish, and (in Japan) *gindara*

Caught in the cold waters of Alaska and the Canadian Pacific

Rich and buttery taste and texture

In the Kitchen

Cod is rich and very flaky. It is a great candidate for any method except grilling; it will fall apart. Cod is widely popular throughout the world, perhaps best known through these preparations:

- **Fish-and-chips** crispy on the outside, moist and flaky in the middle
- **Baked** with lemon, white wine, and bread crumbs
- **Poached** infused by the aroma of the poaching liquid
- **Bacalhau** great for hors d'oeuvres

Valuable Nutrients from Cod

- Cod liver oil: great source of vitamins A and D
- Niacin: increases good cholesterol levels
- Phosphorus: builds healthy bones and strong teeth
- Potassium: for a healthy heart and kidneys, reduces stress
- Selenium: antioxidant, prevents arthritis
- Vitamin B_6: for a healthy metabolism and immune system
- Vitamin B_{12}: promotes healthy blood cells, prevents anemia, eases migraines

Fun Facts

Norwegian scientists have a very unique way of luring cod to feeding sites: They serenade them with underwater tuba music—not rock 'n' roll.

The Alaskan sablefish (or black cod) has antifreeze proteins in its blood.

The Portuguese proudly proclaim that they can eat salt cod (*bacalhau*) every day of the year and never prepare it the same way twice.

Scientists believe codfish today resemble their ancestors from 120 million years ago.

Cod swim with their mouths open and eat anything that happens to be in their way—even other cod.

In the fifteenth century, "the age of discovery," the Portuguese had a monopoly on the spice trade from the Malabar Coast of India to the region of Ceylon (present-day Sri Lanka). During the long journey they mapped the globe and collected rare spices, including the famous black peppercorns that were as valuable as gold. The discovery of the New World brought a culinary revolution in Portugal, adding tomatoes, potatoes, and chiles to its repertoire. *Bacalhau* (dried, salted cod), nicknamed *fiel amigo* ("faithful friend"), is the national dish, reflecting Portugal's seafaring history. The ancient technique was to dry and salt the rich cod fillets, preserving its nutritional value. —RON

Porto Moniz Bacalhau

Crispy Goat Cheese Potatoes, Anise Infused Raisins

SERVES 4

SALTED COD

1 pound salted cod
1 lemon
6 cups milk
2 bay leaves
6 sprigs oregano
1 teaspoon black peppercorns

Add cod to 1 gallon cold water. Refrigerate 24 hours, changing water after 12 hours. Transfer to colander. Rinse cod under cold running water. Peel lemon with vegetable peeler to remove pure yellow outer layer. Add peel to saucepan with milk, bay leaves, oregano, and peppercorns. Bring to simmer over medium heat. Turn off heat. Steep 15 minutes. Add cod. Return to stovetop over medium heat. Simmer 10 minutes. Transfer cod to side dish. When cool enough to handle, shred cod, discarding bones. Cover. Refrigerate until chilled.

ANISE-INFUSED RAISINS

1 cup anisette, preferably Anis Escarchado Primavera from Portugal
1 teaspoon cumin seeds
3 tablespoons honey
2 cups sultana or golden raisins

Add anisette, cumin, and honey to 24-ounce resealable glass jar. Stir to dissolve honey. Fill with raisins. Seal. Let sit 3 days. Refrigerate. Use as needed.

CRISPY GOAT CHEESE POTATOES

2 large russet potatoes, peeled
1 tablespoon chopped chives
1 large egg, beaten
¼ cup bread crumbs
⅓ cup goat cheese
1 tablespoon chopped parsley
to taste sea salt
to taste ground black pepper
2 tablespoons olive oil
4 sprigs oregano

Coarsely grate potatoes to yield 1¼ cups. Transfer to colander. Rinse and drain, squeezing out as much liquid as possible. Transfer to mixing bowl. Fold in chives, egg, bread crumbs, cheese, and parsley. Season with salt and pepper. Form into eight ¼-inch-thick patties. Add oil to large nonstick skillet over medium heat. Fry patties 2 minutes on each side or until golden brown and cooked through. Transfer to paper towel–lined plate to drain. Transfer to warm serving plate. Mound bacalhau atop. Garnish with oregano sprig. Spoon raisin mixture onto plate.

BACALHAU

1 large egg yolk

1 teaspoon minced garlic

1 tablespoon lemon juice

1 teaspoon lemon zest

1 teaspoon coriander seeds, crushed

¼ teaspoon chile powder

½ cup olive oil

¼ cup Greek yogurt

2 tablespoons chopped parsley

pinch freshly grated nutmeg

to taste sea salt

to taste ground black pepper

Whisk egg yolk, garlic, lemon juice, lemon zest, coriander, and chile powder in mixing bowl. Add oil in a slow, steady stream, whisking vigorously to emulsify. Stir in yogurt, parsley, and nutmeg. Fold in cod. Adjust seasoning if necessary. Cover. Refrigerate.

It would be difficult to find a more luscious, buttery textured fish than black cod, also called butterfish and, more correctly, sablefish. Marinated in *kalbi,* Korea's kicked-up version of teriyaki, then broiled until it glistens, it is a literal melt-in-your-mouth experience. From AD 57 to 668, Korea was divided into three kingdoms, each one's diet dominated by a grain. The Silla Kingdom revered barley, the Goguryeo Kingdom loved millet, and the Baekje Kingdom (in Chungcheong Province) ate rice. Bibimbap is one of Korea's signature dishes. Its name means "mixed rice," and it's served as a sizzling deconstructed casserole mixed up by the diner just before eating. —RON

Chungcheong Province Kalbi Glazed Cod
Vegetable Bibimbap
SERVES 4

KALBI GLAZE
½ cup tangerine juice

½ cup soy sauce

½ teaspoon sambal chile sauce

2 teaspoons grated ginger

2 tablespoons seasoned rice vinegar

2 teaspoons sesame oil

¼ cup brown sugar

2 teaspoons finely chopped garlic

¼ cup finely sliced scallions

3 tablespoons chopped cilantro leaves

Combine all ingredients in mixing bowl. Whisk well.

COD
8 black cod fillets, boneless, 1 inch thick (3 ounces each)

Preheat broiler to high. Reserve ½ cup Kalbi Glaze for Bibimbap. Transfer remaining Kalbi Glaze to casserole dish. Add cod, coat with Kalbi Glaze, then position skin side up. Cover. Refrigerate 3 hours. Remove cod from marinade. Transfer to ovenproof nonstick skillet, skin side down. Broil 4 minutes or until slightly underdone. Transfer to serving platter. Note: For timing, place cod in broiler during the last 4 minutes of cooking the Bibimbap.

VEGETABLE BIBIMBAP
1 cup cooked short-grain brown rice

1 cup matchstick-cut green zucchini

5 teaspoons toasted sesame oil, divided

2 cups sliced napa cabbage leaves

1 cup thinly sliced, peeled carrots

1 cup whole honshimeji or sliced shiitake mushrooms

½ cup bamboo shoots

1 cup snow peas, trimmed, halved on bias

1 tablespoon toasted sesame seeds

Add rice and 2 cups cold water to small saucepan over medium heat. Cover. Bring to simmer. Reduce heat to low. Cook 18 minutes or until water is absorbed. Transfer to colander. Rinse under cold running water to remove excess starch. Drain thoroughly. Set aside. Toss zucchini with 1 tablespoon reserved Kalbi Glaze. Set aside. Add 2 teaspoons sesame oil to Bibimbap pot or cast iron skillet over medium heat. Add cabbage. Stir-fry 1 minute or until wilted. Transfer to side dish. Return pot or skillet to medium heat. Add remaining sesame oil. Add rice. Drain zucchini. Arrange zucchini, carrots, mushrooms, bamboo shoots, snow peas, and stir-fried cabbage atop of rice in wagon-wheel design. Cover. As rice fries in the oil, steam will form and cook the vegetables. Cook 4 minutes or until carrots al dente and bottom of rice crispy. Uncover. Sprinkle with toasted sesame seeds. Pour remaining reserved Kalbi Glaze into skillet. Place cod atop Bibimbap. Serve family style while sizzling.

Three famous stews, all kindled from the same heady red powder, make up the culinary identity of Hungary. They are distinct in preparation but all spice relatives by way of paprika. One of them, appropriately called *paprikas,* is the creamy version, usually made by simmering chicken or codfish in paprika-laced cream and serving it with noodles that are formed by pinching dime-size pieces of egg dough with your fingertips. The name of this noodle, *csipetke,* comes from the Hungarian word *csip* meaning "to pinch." Turks introduced paprika to Hungary during their 150-year rule, where it quickly replaced pepper and, adding a rose-colored hue to all things stewed, became the national emblem of Hungarian cuisine. —RON

Cod in Paprika Cream
Poppy Seed Pinched Noodles
SERVES 4

COD

1½ pounds cod fillet, skinless, boneless
1 tablespoon Hungarian paprika, divided
to taste sea salt
to taste ground black pepper
3 tablespoons olive oil
½ cup all-purpose flour
1 cup chopped onions
4 cloves garlic, smashed
2 tablespoons unsalted butter
pinch cayenne pepper
2 teaspoons caraway seeds, divided
2 cups chopped, seeded tomatoes
¾ cup red wine
¾ cup vegetable stock
4 sprigs marjoram
⅓ cup sour cream

Cut cod into eight 3-ounce pieces. Season all sides with 1 teaspoon paprika, salt, and pepper. Add oil to deep cast-iron skillet over medium high heat. Dredge cod lightly in flour, shaking off excess. Place in skillet. Sear 1 minute on each side or until slightly underdone. Transfer to side dish, leaving skillet on the heat. Add remaining oil, onions, garlic, butter, remaining paprika, cayenne, and 1 teaspoon caraway seeds to skillet. Cook 1 minute, stirring often. Add tomatoes. Cook 3 minutes, stirring often. Add wine, vegetable stock, and marjoram. Bring to simmer. Reduce by half. Adjust seasoning. Transfer to blender.

Add sour cream. Puree until smooth. Strain sauce through coarse sieve into skillet over medium heat. Add cod and pinched noodles to sauce. Sprinkle with remaining caraway seeds. Bring to simmer. Serve immediately.

POPPY-SEED PINCHED NOODLES

2 large eggs
1½ teaspoons poppy seeds
½ teaspoon dried marjoram
½ teaspoon sea salt
1 cup sifted all-purpose flour
2 tablespoons olive oil

Add eggs, poppy seeds, marjoram, and salt to mini food processor. Blend until smooth. Add flour to mixing bowl. Make well in center. Pour egg mixture into well. Stir with wooden spoon to combine. If necessary, add ½ teaspoon water at a time to form stiff dough. Knead until smooth. Rub surface of dough lightly with ½ teaspoon olive oil. Wrap in plastic wrap. Let rest 30 minutes in refrigerator, then 30 minutes at room temperature. Divide dough into 6 pieces. Flour palms of hands. Flatten dough to ⅛-inch thickness. Using thumb and side of index finger, pinch dough into ½-inch pieces. Bring large pot of salted water to boil. Add noodles. Cook 5 minutes or until noodles rise to surface of water and are tender. Drain in colander. Rinse under cold water. Transfer to baking sheet. Toss with remaining oil to coat.

Riding a ferry from Nova Scotia to Port aux Basques, Newfoundland, in a storm is an adventure that can scar your soul! The town sits in the lowlands along the coastline, with the Long Range Mountains towering as a backdrop. I journeyed for one week to reach the astounding ancient Viking village of L'Anse aux Meadows. Silver-dollar-size snowflakes blanketed the streets and weighed heavily on top of my hat. I took refuge in an old tavern, packed with locals enjoying the warmth of a roaring fire. Behind the rustic oak bar, a blackboard listed the only special of the day: Norseman codfish cake, molasses pork belly, and fiddlehead fern. I savored the two crispy, plump fish cakes with their supporting cast and a nice pint of local Storm Island Gold Pale Ale. —BERNARD

New Brunswick Codfish Cake

Endive Salad, Canuck Ketchup
SERVES 4

COD

1½ pounds cod fillet, skinless, boneless, cut into 8 pieces
to taste sea salt
to taste ground white pepper
6 tablespoons olive oil, divided
2 teaspoons thyme leaves
1 pound peeled russet potatoes
2 tablespoons unsalted butter
½ cup buttermilk
8 cloves garlic, sliced
1 tablespoon onion powder
pinch grated nutmeg
½ teaspoon baking powder
1 cup all-purpose flour

Preheat oven to 350°F. Season cod with salt and pepper. Transfer to casserole dish. Add 1 tablespoon olive oil and thyme leaves. Cover. Set aside. Cut potatoes into ½-inch cubes. Transfer to separate casserole dish. Add butter, buttermilk, garlic, onion powder, and nutmeg. Season with salt and pepper. Cover. Place cod and potatoes in oven. Remove cod after 15 minutes or when slightly underdone. Bake potatoes additional 30 minutes or until tender. Transfer potatoes and content of their dish to mixing bowl. Mash until smooth. Set aside. Break cod into large flakes, discarding pan juices. Fold baking powder, 3 tablespoons olive oil, and flaked cod into potatoes. Adjust seasoning. Form mixture into 8 balls. Dredge in flour, shaking off excess. Press into 3-inch cookie-cutter ring to form patties. Working in two batches Add remaining oil to large nonstick skillet. Place patties in skillet. Fry 1 minute on each side or until golden brown.

CANUCK KETCHUP

¼ cup olive oil
2 cups thinly sliced red onion
6 cloves garlic, smashed
2 teaspoons anise seeds
3 pounds vine-ripened tomatoes, cored, cut into wedges
1 teaspoon ground ginger
2 tablespoons molasses
¼ cup apple cider vinegar
1 tablespoon thyme leaves
1 hot chile pepper, stemmed, seeded, halved
to taste sea salt
to taste ground black pepper

Add oil to sauce pot over medium heat. Add onion, garlic, and anise seeds. Cook 4 minutes or until translucent. Add remaining ingredients. Turn heat to medium high. Bring to simmer. Cook 45 minutes or to thick jam consistency. Transfer to food processor. Puree until smooth. Strain through colander. Cool completely. Store in resealable glass jar.

ENDIVE SALAD

1 tablespoon maple syrup

2 tablespoons apple cider vinegar

2 tablespoons olive oil

to taste sea salt

to taste ground black pepper

2 Belgian endive

1 cup packed watercress leaves

¼ cup shaved red onion

Whisk maple syrup, vinegar, and oil together in mixing bowl. Season with salt and pepper. Cut 1 inch from bottom of endive. Discard. Cut endive lengthwise into quarters. Separate leaves. Transfer to mixing bowl. Add watercress and onion. Toss gently to coat.

Monkfish

Monkfish is also known as allmouth, angler, anglerfish, fishing frog, goosefish molligut, frogfish, and sea devil.

The only edible portions of a monkfish are the liver and the flesh of the tail.

Monkfish liver is a delicacy often referred to as the "foie gras of the sea." The liver is also prepared as sushi in Japan and called *ankimo*.

Monkfish are the undisputed ugliest fish in the ocean. They have an enormous flat head that makes up 75 percent of their body, with a large mouth and razor-sharp teeth. Their smooth, scaleless skin is gray in color with blotches of purple that look like bruises.

Beneath their appearance you will find a flesh that is dense, sweet, and tender like a crustacean, which is why monkfish is called "poor man's lobster."

In the Wild

Monkfish have a wide range of habitat, from the waters of the North American Atlantic to the Barents Sea of northern Scandinavia, Europe's Strait of Gibraltar, and the Mediterranean and Black Seas.

They live from shallow offshore waters to depths of 3,000 feet.

Monkfish can grow 4 feet long and weigh 50 pounds.

As members of the anglerfish family, monkfish have a long piece of skin projecting from the top of their head like a fishing pole that lures in prey.

In the Kitchen

A great substitute for lobster or scallops in most any recipe.

The dense and firm fish is awesome when grilled.

Wrap in bacon for a delicious combination.

Monkfish osso buco is a great recipe for non-meat eaters (see Marsala Braised Monkfish Osso Buco, p. 244).

Monkfish bones are high in gelatin and make a great fish broth.

Valuable Nutrients from Monkfish

- Niacin: increases good cholesterol levels
- Phosphorus: builds healthy bones and strong teeth
- Potassium: for a healthy heart and kidneys, reduces stress
- Selenium: antioxidant, prevents arthritis
- Vitamin B_6: for a healthy metabolism and immune system
- Vitamin B_{12}: promotes healthy blood cells, prevents anemia, eases migraines

Fun Facts

The monkfish is nicknamed "all mouth" by fishermen because its body is mostly head, and its head is mostly mouth.

"Monkfish" was an entry in Conrad Gesner's *Historiae Animalium,* a famous animal reference guide published in the fifteenth century.

Monkfish have been known to attack and eat waterbirds that are swimming on the surface.

Monkfish are the ugliest fish known to man. That is not a fact, just our opinion.

Osso buco is a specialty from Milan, Italy. An Italian-style veal shank pot roast, *osso buco* literally means "bone with hole," referring to the marrow bone at the center of the shank. Originally a peasant farmhouse dish, osso buco has grown into a staple of fashionable haute cuisine. Perhaps it is taking this Milan thing too seriously. To adorn its image even more, here is a coastal version of the dish using bone-in monkfish steaks. You can easily cut a whole monkfish tail into steaks yourself, or ask your fishmonger to do it. —RON

Marsala Braised Monkfish Osso Buco

Cremini Polenta, Almond Gremolata

SERVES 4

MONKFISH

2 tablespoons grapeseed oil
4 monkfish steaks, bone-in, trimmed (10 ounces each)
to taste sea salt
to taste ground black pepper
½ **cup** all-purpose flour
½ **cup** diced pancetta
2 cups diced, peeled carrots
1 cup diced, peeled celery root
1 cup sliced, peeled parsnips
½ **cup** chopped red onions
4 leaves sage
8 sprigs thyme
3 bay leaves
6 cloves garlic, crushed
2 cups Marsala wine
2 tablespoons balsamic vinegar
1½ **cups** beef stock

Preheat oven to 350°F. Add oil to large dutch oven over high heat. Season monkfish with salt and pepper. Dredge in flour, shaking off excess. Place monkfish in dutch oven. Sear on all sides until golden brown. Transfer to side dish. Reduce heat to medium. Add pancetta. Cook until fat is rendered. Add carrots, celery root, parsnips, onions, sage, thyme, bay leaves, and garlic. Cook 5 minutes, stirring occasionally. Add Marsala, balsamic vinegar, and beef stock. Bring to simmer. Cook 15 minutes or until vegetables are soft.

Return monkfish to pot, nestled into vegetables and broth until covered with liquid. Cover. Bring to simmer. Cook 10 minutes or until slightly underdone. Adjust seasoning if necessary.

CREMINI POLENTA

2 tablespoons olive oil
½ **cup** finely chopped red onion
½ **pound** cremini mushrooms, brushed, trimmed, thinly sliced
2 teaspoons sea salt
½ **teaspoon** white pepper
1 cup Marsala
3½ **cups** vegetable stock
1 cup yellow cornmeal
1 cup grated Parmesan
¼ **cup** mascarpone

Add oil to saucepan over medium-low heat. Add onions and mushrooms. Season with salt and pepper. Cook 4 minutes, stirring often or until liquid evaporates. Add Marsala and vegetable stock. Bring to simmer. Whisk in cornmeal slowly so that the polenta is smooth and free of lumps. Cook for 5 minutes or until thickened, stirring constantly. Fold in remaining ingredients. Remove from heat. Season with additional salt and pepper if needed.

ALMOND GREMOLATA

2 tablespoons olive oil

½ cup almond meal

¼ cup minced parsley leaves

2 cloves garlic, minced

1 lemon, zested

Combine all ingredients in small mixing bowl. Set aside.

PRESENTATION

1 tablespoon truffle oil

6 sprigs flowering fresh herbs

Scoop polenta in center of warm shallow pasta plate. Place monkfish steak beside polenta. Arrange vegetables around fish. Spoon sauce onto plate. Drizzle with truffle oil. Garnish with Almond Gremolata and flowering herbs.

Punjabi cuisine originates from the Punjab region of northern India. Mughal rulers brought tandoori cooking to India from the nomadic tribes of the steppes in Central Asia. Tandoor ovens are multipurpose ovens often used for baking bread. Its distinctive quality is retaining high levels of moisture during the cooking of meat and fish. Tandoori food is a Punjabi specialty, an exotic cuisine prepared with artful and exquisite combinations of spices and a variety of different curries where the level of spice varies from minimal to quite prevalent. Allow fish to marinate for several hours to absorb the flavors of herbs and spices. As you may not have a tandoor oven at home, your broiler or grill will do the job if you keep it closed and at the highest temperature possible to attain a perfect caramelized flavor. —BERNARD

Tandoori Monkfish Skewers

Banana Mint Raita

SERVES 4

MONKFISH

1½ pounds monkfish tails,
    boneless, skinless, membrane removed
1 large red onion
½ teaspoon ground cardamom
1 teaspoon ground ginger
1 teaspoon ground turmeric
1 teaspoon ground cumin
⅛ teaspoon cayenne pepper
1 teaspoon paprika
1 teaspoon sea salt
1 tablespoon chopped garlic
¼ cup chopped cilantro
1 tablespoon lemon juice
1 teaspoon lemon zest
¾ cup plain yogurt
4 metal skewers
as needed canola oil spray

Preheat broiler to high. Cut monkfish into 1½-inch pieces. Peel and quarter red onion, separating layers. Combine cardamom, ginger, turmeric, cumin, cayenne, paprika, and sea salt in large mixing bowl. Add garlic, cilantro, lemon juice, lemon zest, and yogurt. Add monkfish and onions. Toss to coat. Cover. Refrigerate at least 3 hours. Thread monkfish and onions onto 4 skewers. Lightly coat baking sheet with canola oil spray. Broil skewers 4 minutes. Turn fish over. Broil an additional 4 minutes or until golden brown and slightly underdone.

BANANA MINT RAITA

2 slightly under-ripe bananas
1 tablespoon lemon juice
½ cup plain yogurt
1 teaspoon grated ginger
1 teaspoon mustard seeds
1 teaspoon cumin seeds
to taste sea salt and ground black pepper
1 cup thinly sliced napa cabbage
3 tablespoons chopped mint
3 tablespoons toasted unsweetened coconut flakes

Peel bananas. Cut crosswise into ¼-inch slices. Transfer to side dish. Toss gently with lemon juice. Combine yogurt, ginger, mustard seeds, cumin seeds, salt, and pepper in mixing bowl. Whisk to combine. Fold in remaining ingredients. Transfer to serving dish. Refrigerate at least 1 hour.

A *tagine* is a one-pot meal created by the Berber people of North Africa. The name refers both to the preparation—a slowly braised stew of meats, vegetables, and fruits—and to the unique dish in which it is served. Traditionally molded from clay, the dish has a shallow round base that holds the stew, topped with a tall cone-shaped lid, designed to trap condensation and deliver it back to the base. This was historically significant during times when available water was scarce. Tagines designed for cooking are traditionally placed above hot coals. Today many tagine pots are created as masterfully decorated pieces of art, while others are intended for serving only, so be informed when purchasing. The meaty texture of monkfish makes for a perfect seafood tagine. —RON

Monkfish Eggplant Tagine

Apricot Harissa Sauce

SERVES 4

TAGINE

1½ pounds monkfish tail, boneless, skinless, outer membrane removed

to taste sea salt

to taste ground black pepper

4 tablespoons olive oil, divided

1 cup diced red onion

4 cups diced, peeled eggplant

½ teaspoon sea salt

¼ teaspoon ground black pepper

4 cloves garlic, minced

2 teaspoons paprika

1 tablespoon grated ginger

1 teaspoon cumin seeds

1 large pinch saffron threads

2 cups tomato juice

¼ cup lemon juice

1 cup cooked chickpeas

¼ cup dark raisins

⅓ cup pitted, quartered green olives

1 tablespoon extra-virgin olive oil

Cut monkfish into eight 3-ounce pieces. Season with salt and pepper. Add 2 tablespoons olive oil to large, deep skillet over medium-high heat. Working in batches of 4, place monkfish in skillet. Roast 1 minute on each side, transferring to side dish. Return skillet to medium-high heat. Add remaining 2 tablespoons olive oil, onions, eggplant, salt, pepper, garlic, paprika, ginger, cumin, and saffron. Cook 3 minutes, stirring often. Add tomato juice and lemon juice. Add monkfish, chickpeas, raisins, and olives. Cover. Simmer 20 minutes or until monkfish is slightly underdone. Transfer to tagine dish. Drizzle extra-virgin olive oil atop. Cover with tagine lid to keep warm.

APRICOT HARISSA SAUCE

1 bag mint tea

1 teaspoon honey

1 tablespoon red wine vinegar

¼ teaspoon coriander seeds

4 cloves garlic, crushed

¼ cup finely chopped sun-dried apricots

½ teaspoon sea salt

1 cayenne pepper, stemmed, seeded

2 guajillo chiles, stemmed, seeded

½ cup extra-virgin olive oil

Add 1 cup water, mint tea, honey, vinegar, coriander, and garlic to small saucepan. Bring to simmer. Add apricots, sea salt, cayenne pepper, and guajillos. Turn off heat. Cover. Steep 30 minutes. Remove tea bag and discard. Transfer mixture to blender. Puree until smooth. Add olive oil in slow stream while blender is running. Strain through medium sieve.

On the rugged coast of Brittany, indented by coves and creeks, lies the regional harbor of Port Navalo where fishermen unload their catch into baskets on the pier chatting in their local tongue. Lobster, *loup de mer,* langoustine, scallops, and monkfish are available to the locals at the crisp, early hour of 5 a.m. My friend Didier spoke the Breton language and was eager to strike a bargain. He quickly scored a kilo (2.2-pound) monkfish tail with its cheeks and liver, aka sea foie gras, for a Sunday family feast. At the house, my uncle Bernard, a retired butcher, wrapped the monkfish tail in oak-smoked heirloom bacon, a tasty and speedy way to prepare the fish. Roasting in the fireplace brings aromatherapy to the kitchen and gets everyone in a festive mood! The combination of fragrant herbs and salty bacon works equally well with scallops, salmon, and tuna. —BERNARD

Bacon Wrapped Monkfish Tail

Fennel Coulis, Rosemary Peaches

SERVES 4

ROSEMARY PEACHES

1 tablespoon unsalted butter
2 teaspoons honey
1 teaspoon chopped rosemary leaves
2 slightly under-ripe peaches, halved, pitted
to taste sea salt
to taste ground black pepper
¼ cup apple juice

Add butter, honey, and rosemary to ovenproof skillet over medium heat. Cook until foamy. Add peaches, cut side down. Cook 2 minutes or until caramelized, swirling pan occasionally. Turn peaches over. Season with salt and pepper. Add apple juice to skillet. Transfer to oven. Cook 3 minutes or until warm in center.

FENNEL COULIS

1 tablespoon unsalted butter
3 cups thinly sliced (crosswise) fennel
1 cup sherry wine
¼ teaspoon saffron threads
½ teaspoon flaky sea salt
pinch cayenne pepper

Add butter to large saucepan over medium heat. Add fennel, sherry, saffron, salt, and cayenne. Bring to simmer. Cover. Reduce heat to low. Cook 20 minutes or until fennel is very soft. Uncover. Cook until remaining liquid evaporates.

MONKFISH

1½ pounds monkfish tails, boneless, skinless
2 tablespoons lemon thyme leaves, divided
to taste sea salt
to taste ground black pepper
16 thin slices applewood-smoked bacon
2 tablespoon unsalted butter
1 tablespoon grapeseed oil

Preheat oven at 375°F. Cut monkfish into eight 3-ounce pieces. Season with 1 tablespoon lemon thyme, sea salt, and black pepper. Wrap each piece evenly with 2 slices of bacon. Refrigerate 1 hour. Add butter and oil to large ovenproof skillet over medium-high heat. Place monkfish in skillet with seam side of bacon down. Cook 6 minutes, turning fish occasionally to brown on all sides. Transfer skillet to oven. Cook 5 minutes or until slightly underdone. Remove from oven. Sprinkle with remaining thyme. Allow the fish to rest for 2 minutes. Serve with Fennel Coulis and Rosemary Peaches.

CHAPTER 6

Kings of the Ocean
TUNA, SWORDFISH, SHARK, HALIBUT

Tuna
SPAIN
Basque Albacore Crudo
serrano ham, apricot,
shaved manchego

MARTINIQUE
Thon Roti de Martinique
rum tomato marmalade

INDONESIA
Bali Tuna Spears
javanese peanut sauce

ITALY
Sicilian Tuna Pot Roast
marsala caponata

TRINIDAD
Island Spiced Albacore Tuna
fried plantain, mango callaloo

JAPAN
Spicy Tuna Hand Roll
meyer lemon ponzu

Swordfish
TURKEY
**Swordfish Wrapped in
Vine Leaves**
zaatar yogurt sauce

TURKS AND CAICOS ISLANDS
**Turks and Caicos
Barbecued Swordfish**
ginger beer hush puppies

ITALY
Swordfish Piccata
parmesan gnocchi, pancetta, sage

LEBANON
Pomegranate Infused Swordfish
green lentil mujadara

MOROCCO
Swordfish Chermoula Casserole
preserved lemons

Shark
MEXICO
Cabo Shark Tacos
jicama orange salad,
avocado crema

ARGENTINA
Chimichurri Shark Steak
chorizo batata

CANARY ISLANDS
Shark Bites
wrinkled potatoes, mojo picon

JAMAICA
Jerk Spiced Shark Loin
red pepper papaya chutney

Halibut
PORTUGAL
**Aromatic Madeira
Scented Halibut**
new potatoes, kumquats,
dry-cured olives

UNITED STATES
**Peach Bourbon Basted
Halibut Steak**
sweet potatoes, romaine,
grapefruit dressing

NORWAY
Leek Parsley Coated Halibut
oven-roasted tomatoes

ITALY
Savelletri Baked Halibut
limoncello orzo, roasted figs,
prosciutto

CHINA
**Hong Kong–Style
Steamed Halibut**
shiitake, bok choy, five-spice

JAPAN
Halibut Sashimi
watermelon, watercress,
wasabi oil

Tuna

Ahi is the Hawaiian word for yellowfin tuna. The word literally translates to "fire," referring to the tuna's bright yellow fin that flashes through the water like sparks of fire. Tuna are shaped like torpedos—with a plump round midsection that tapers toward the tail.

Tuna have been fished from the temperate parts of the Mediterranean Sea since ancient Greek and Roman times. They are also found in the Pacific, Atlantic, and Indian Oceans.

Tuna are in perpetual motion and cruise effortlessly at speeds of 55 miles per hour.

They eat 10 percent of their body weight in fish, squid, shellfish, and plankton daily. Depending on the variety, their weight averages from 10 to 600 pounds.

Tuna is called *maguro* in Japanese.

In the Wild

Line-caught tuna is better for the environment than net-caught tuna because there is much less bycatch.

There are seven different tuna species with different characteristics:

Albacore
Marked with a shining blue stripe on each side

Bigeye
Metallic blue on the back, white undersides, large eyes

Blackfin Tuna
Black backs, yellow on the fins and on the side

Yellowfin
Yellow fins and a golden stripe on each side

Northern Bluefin Tuna
Despite the name, has yellow fins with silvery spots or bars

Longtail Tuna
Dark blue, black, or silvery-white color with yellow fins

Southern Bluefin Tuna
Dusky yellow-bluish hue, silvery white color

In the Kitchen

Fresh tuna should be firm and have a vibrant color. Bluefin and yellowfin should have a rich red, dense, meaty texture and a sweet, mild flavor. Albacore tuna has a very pale color. Favorite methods for eating tuna include these:

- **In the raw** sushi style, *crudo,* or just flame-kissed

- **Barbecued on the grill** healthy alternative to traditional beef

- **Bluefin or yellowfin roast** carved into rare thin slices

- **Island spiced** tuna calls out for tropical heat

Valuable Nutrients from Tuna

- Niacin: increases good cholesterol levels

- Phosphorus: builds healthy bones and strong teeth

- Riboflavin: for healthy skin and healing

- Selenium: antioxidant, prevents arthritis

- Thiamin: maintains regular heartbeat, good for healthy eyes

- Vitamin A: for healthy eyes and vision

- Vitamin B_6: for a healthy metabolism and immune system

- Vitamin B_{12}: promotes healthy blood cells, prevents anemia, eases migraines

Warning: Some tuna may contain high levels of the pollutant methylmercury.

Fun Facts

The American canned tuna industry started in 1903 and was an overnight success, coming on the heels of the 1902 sardine shortage.

Albacore tuna travel in schools up to 19 miles wide. Each school is made up entirely of same-size fish.

In the Maldives in the Indian Ocean, tuna are fished exclusively by the pole-and-line method, making the Maldives tuna-fishing industry the most environmentally sustainable and dolphin friendly in the world.

Tuna have a built-in thermostat, a network of blood vessels below the skin that acts as a temperature-regulating system.

For over a century, from July to September, fishermen in the Bay of Biscay in Spain's Basque region have caught *bonito del norte,* otherwise known as albacore tuna, with hooks and lines— an ecologically friendly method! Beneath the vaulted ceiling of San Sebastián's central market, stalls are filled with seafood, vegetables, and cheeses. Hanging from the rafters, the cured, tender, sweet, and lightly smoked Bayonne ham is a specialty of the area. Combining the bright flavors of the albacore, ham, Manchego, and local market vegetables is a hallmark of Basque cuisine. —BERNARD

Basque Albacore Crudo
Serrano Ham, Apricot, Shaved Manchego
SERVES 4

VEGETABLES

2 tablespoons olive oil
½ cup finely diced carrot
½ cup finely diced red onion
½ cup finely diced yellow beets
2 cloves garlic, thinly sliced
2 tablespoons sherry vinegar
1 teaspoon honey
⅛ teaspoon dried oregano
to taste sea salt
to taste ground black pepper
¼ cup quartered, pitted green olives

Add oil to skillet over medium heat. Add carrot, onion, and beets. Cook 2 minutes, stirring constantly. Add garlic, vinegar, honey, and oregano. Cook until liquid evaporates. Season with salt and pepper. Toss in green olives. Transfer to large platter, spreading to cool quickly.

PRESENTATION

4 apricots, halved, pitted
as needed canola oil spray
1 teaspoon granulated sugar
¾ pound albacore tuna loin, center-cut
to taste sea salt
to taste ground black pepper
¼ cup toasted, shelled pistachios
8 slices serrano ham
12 leaves basil
1 ounce Manchego cheese
1 tablespoon extra-virgin olive oil

Preheat broiler to high. Line apricots, cut side up, on baking sheet. Spray lightly with canola oil. Sprinkle top of apricots evenly with sugar. Broil 3 minutes or until caramelized. Set aside to cool. Place tuna in freezer 1 hour before plating. Using sharp knife, cut tuna into ¼-inch slices. Arrange on serving platter. Season with salt and pepper. Spoon Vegetables in center of tuna. Garnish with apricots, pistachios, serrano ham, and basil leaves. Shave Manchego atop. Drizzle with olive oil.

Cultivating my love of travel and culture, I feast my way through the picturesque and colorful food markets in Fort-de-France, the capital of the French overseas region of Martinique. At the fish market, an old man prepared a tuna steak, explaining that he just caught it off San Miguel Island. It tasted zesty, tangy, exotic, vibrant, and fresh. Fort-de-France's spice market—with its fragrant ginger, cinnamon, cardamom, coriander, cumin seeds, anise, and chiles—is one of the city's culinary gems. The fusion of these spices adds color and flavor not only to the Creole cuisine but also to the local market stalls. Traditional Creole cuisine is a delicious mélange of French, African, and Indian flavors. —BERNARD

Thon Roti de Martinique

Rum Tomato Marmalade

SERVES 4

TUNA

1½ pounds tuna loin, center-cut
½ teaspoon ground cumin
⅛ teaspoon ground cardamom
¼ teaspoon ground star anise
¼ cup extra-virgin olive oil
1 cup thinly sliced onion
2 teaspoons hot red chile pepper, seeded, minced
1 tablespoon minced garlic
¼ cup matchstick-cut, peeled ginger

Cut tuna into 4 steaks at least 1 inch thick. Combine remaining ingredients in deep dish. Add tuna and toss to coat. Cover. Refrigerate overnight. Remove tuna, reserving the entire marinade for marmalade.

RUM TOMATO MARMALADE

3 tablespoons brown sugar
3 cups diced tomatoes
½ cup spiced dark rum
3 tablespoons red wine vinegar
¼ cup unsweetened coconut flakes
to taste sea salt flakes
to taste ground black pepper

Transfer reserved marinade to saucepan over medium heat. Add brown sugar. Cook until onion in the marinade is lightly caramelized, stirring constantly. Add tomatoes. Bring to simmer. Cook 3 minutes. Add rum, vinegar, and coconut. Cook 10 minutes or to jam consistency, stirring occasionally. Remove from heat. Season with salt and pepper.

PRESENTATION

1 tablespoon grapeseed oil
to taste sea salt flakes
to taste ground black pepper
4 reserved marinated tuna steaks
1 tablespoon extra-virgin olive oil
½ cup sunflower sprouts

Add oil to skillet over medium-high heat. Sear tuna 30 seconds on each side for rare or longer until desired doneness. Transfer to warm serving plate. Top tuna with Rum Tomato Marmalade. Spoon extra-virgin olive oil onto plate around tuna. Garnish with sea salt and sunflower sprouts.

The Balinese have the most beautiful smiles on earth. Roadside food stands on Kuta Beach remind you that the island of Bali is a quilt of ethnicities, a melting pot of cultures offering their own rich culinary traditions. Satay is the quintessence of fast food in Southeast Asia. You'll find it sizzling on small grills over hot coals in hawker stalls all over the island. An amazing variety of seafood satays are cooked to order by vendors. On the island of Bali, tuna is used in *satay lilit*. It is seasoned with freshly pounded spices and shaped around the skewers before grilling. Cashews, almonds, hazelnuts, or macadamias can be used in place of peanuts in the sauce. —BERNARD

Bali Tuna Spears
Javanese Peanut Sauce
SERVES 4

TUNA

1 tablespoon finely chopped lemongrass, inner tender part only
1 tablespoon brown sugar
1 tablespoon finely chopped ginger
½ teaspoon ground turmeric
¼ teaspoon ground cumin
2 tablespoons cilantro leaves
½ tablespoon chopped garlic
½ teaspoon lime zest
½ red Thai chile, seeded
2 tablespoons sliced scallions, white part only
2 tablespoons coconut milk
1½ pounds tuna fillet, trimmed, cut into small cubes
to taste sea salt
to taste ground black pepper
24 bamboo skewers, soaked in water overnight
as needed canola oil spray

Add lemongrass, sugar, ginger, turmeric, cumin, cilantro, garlic, lime zest, chile, and scallions to mortar or food processor. Puree to coarse paste. Transfer to mixing bowl. Stir in coconut milk. Add tuna to food processor. Pulse until finely chopped. Add to lemongrass mixture. Combine well. Season with salt and pepper. Moisten hands. Pick up whole ball of paste and slap down into bowl. Repeat thirty times or until paste develops firm, springy texture. Divide into 24 portions. Place each portion in palm of hand. Squeeze into ball shape. Insert skewer in center. Squeeze firmly to adhere to skewer. Transfer to oiled side dish. Cover. Refrigerate at least 3 hours. Preheat barbecue grill to high. Lightly coat grates with canola oil spray. Spray skewers lightly with canola oil. Grill 3 minutes or until lightly charred, turning occasionally to cook evenly.

JAVANESE PEANUT SAUCE

5 ounces roasted unsalted peanuts
2 tablespoons dark brown sugar
1 tablespoon chopped ginger
2 cloves garlic, chopped
½ teaspoon chile paste
6 tablespoons coconut milk
2 tablespoons rice vinegar
2 tablespoons soy sauce
2 tablespoons cilantro leaves

Add all ingredients to blender. Puree until smooth. Transfer to serving dish.

Every year in the early spring, Mediterranean tuna are caught off the western coast of Sicily. Using dense nets, fishermen herd the tuna into ever smaller, shallower net chambers that are lifted onto the boats. This ancient fishing technique is called *mattanza*. While the tuna are being caught, *tonnarotti* (tuna fishermen) sing special songs called *scialome* that have been passed down for generations. At the little harbor of Bonagia, the tuna is unloaded at the old fish market, where it will be sold by the kilogram to local villagers. Sicilian cuisine is all about the sea and the land. Eggplant caponata simmered with figs and olives is the perfect companion for this unique catch. —BERNARD

Sicilian Tuna Pot Roast

Marsala Caponata

SERVES 4

TUNA

¼ **teaspoon** red chile flakes

1 **teaspoon** whole allspice

1 **teaspoon** ground coriander

2 **teaspoons** anise seeds

1 **teaspoon** ground black pepper

1 **teaspoon** sea salt

1½ **pounds** albacore tuna loin, center-cut

Add all ingredients except albacore to small skillet over medium low heat. Cook 1 minute or until fragrant, stirring constantly. Transfer to spice grinder. Pulse to coarse meal. Thoroughly rub mixture onto albacore. Wrap tightly in plastic wrap. Refrigerate at least 2 hours.

POT ROAST AND CAPONATA

¼ **cup** olive oil, divided

as needed canola oil spray

2 **cups** diced, peeled eggplant

1 **cup** chopped red onion

2 **cloves** garlic, finely chopped

3 **tablespoons** balsamic vinegar

2 **cups** chopped ripe tomatoes

1 **tablespoon** oregano leaves

1 **cup** Marsala wine

½ **cup** sliced, pitted green olives

¼ **cup** whole almonds

½ **cup** quartered dried figs

to taste sea salt

to taste ground black pepper

Preheat oven to 350°F. Add 2 tablespoons oil to dutch oven over medium-high heat. Unwrap albacore. Spray all sides with canola oil, leaving spices on albacore. Add to dutch oven. Sear 30 seconds on each side to golden brown. Transfer to side dish. Return dutch oven to medium-high heat. Add remaining oil and eggplant. Cook 1 minute, stirring often. Add onions and garlic. Cook 2 minutes. Add balsamic vinegar, tomatoes, oregano, wine, olives, almonds, and figs. Return albacore to dutch oven. Transfer to oven. Bake 6 minutes for rare, or until desired doneness. Carve tableside.

Trinidad is the southernmost Caribbean island, sitting off the coast of Venezuela and bounded by shallow turquoise waters. Since being named by Columbus in honor of his third voyage, Trini, as the locals call it, has been visited or settled by Indians, Africans, Spanish, Chinese, and French. Each culture added their influence, as if to a mixing bowl, blending with the native island character until a uniquely Trinidadian flavor was formed. Assimilation is a way of life and touches everything from culture to religion to food. In everyday cooking, Trinis always toast their spices to bring out their full character, a technique known as *choonkay.* Seal leftover spices tightly in a resealable container to preserve intensity. Callaloo is a traditional salad of green leaves popular in Trinidad. —RON

Island Spiced Albacore Tuna

Fried Plantain, Mango Callaloo

SERVES 4

CALLALOO

1 mango, peeled, pitted, diced
½ cup thinly sliced red onion
1 teaspoon finely diced red chile pepper
2 tablespoons lime juice
3 tablespoons canola oil
to taste sea salt
to taste ground black pepper
1 cup baby spinach leaves, washed, patted dry, sliced
¼ cup sliced basil leaves
¼ cup toasted unsweetened shaved coconut

Combine mango, onion, chile, lime juice, and oil in mixing bowl. Season with salt and pepper. Add spinach, basil, and coconut. Toss gently to coat leaves.

ISLAND SPICE

1 tablespoon whole allspice
1 teaspoon mustard seeds
2 teaspoons paprika
1 teaspoon onion flakes
1 teaspoon dried lemon peel
1 teaspoon dried red pepper flakes
1 teaspoon black peppercorns
½ teaspoon garlic powder
1-inch piece cinnamon stick, crushed
1 teaspoon sea salt

Add all spices to small skillet over medium-low heat. Toast 2 minutes or until fragrant, stirring often. Transfer to spice grinder. Process to powder. Store in spice jar.

PLANTAINS

2 ripe plantains
¼ cup vegetable oil
to taste sea salt

Peel plantains. Slice ¼-inch thick on the bias. Add oil to skillet over medium heat. Fry plantains 2 minutes on each side or until golden brown and crisp. Transfer to paper towel–lined plate. Sprinkle with sea salt.

TUNA

2 albacore tuna steaks, at least 1 inch thick (10 ounces each)
To taste Island Spice mixture
as needed canola oil spray
2 tablespoons canola oil

Sprinkle tuna generously on all sides with Island Spice mixture. Spray with canola oil to adhere spices. Add oil to skillet over medium-high heat. Sear tuna 30 seconds. Turn fish over. Cook additional 30 seconds for rare, or until desired doneness. Transfer to cutting board. Cut in half on a bias. Arrange plantains in center of warm serving plate. Place mango Callaloo in center. Top with tuna.

Sushi evolved from an ancient Chinese technique of preserving valuable pieces of fish by wrapping in rice, which was allowed to ferment, thereby preserving its enclosed treasure. The rice was discarded before enjoying the naturally pickled fish. Today it is customary to add vinegar and sweet sake to sushi rice, mimicking the sour-sweet flavor once imparted through the process of fermentation. "Vinegared" rice is much more palatable than its fermented predecessor, so now instead of discarding the rice, we embrace it. Like many preserved foods, what was once done out of necessity is now practiced for pleasure. Hand rolls are a fun and easy way to roll sushi at home using your favorite fish and shellfish. —RON

Spicy Tuna Hand Roll

Meyer Lemon Ponzu

MAKES 8

RICE

1½ cups short-grain Japanese sushi rice
1½ cups water
2 tablespoons seasoned rice vinegar
2 teaspoons sugar
⅛ teaspoon sea salt

Wash rice in colander until water runs clear. Place in small saucepan. Gently stir in water. Cover. Place over medium heat. Bring to simmer. Reduce heat as low as possible. Cook 15 minutes. Set aside, covered, 5 minutes. Transfer to plastic wrap–lined baking sheet. Gently fold in remaining ingredients.

TUNA

¾ pound sushi-grade ahi tuna
¾ tablespoon soy sauce
4 teaspoons sesame oil
4 teaspoons mirin
4 teaspoons sriracha chile sauce
1 scallion, finely chopped
1 teaspoon finely chopped pickled ginger

Cut tuna into ¼-inch cubes. Transfer to chilled mixing bowl. Fold in remaining ingredients.

HAND ROLL

4 sheets sushi nori, cut in half across shortest side
½ cup matchstick-cut Asian pear
½ cup matchstick-cut cucumber
½ cup matchstick-cut carrots
1 (2½-ounce) package daikon sprouts

Moisten hand lightly with water. Place half nori sheet on flat surface with long side horizontal. Spread ¼ cup Rice over nori, leaving 1½ inches of right-hand side and ½ inch of bottom side clear. Spread 2 tablespoons Tuna mixture over rice, down the center. Top with matchstick vegetables and daikon sprouts, perpendicular to rice. Roll bottom left corner of rice toward top right corner of rice to form a cone. Moisten the nori overhang with water and adhere to body of cone to seal. Repeat process to form 8 cones.

MEYER LEMON PONZU

¼ cup soy sauce
¼ cup honey
¼ cup Meyer lemon juice
1 teaspoon wasabi paste

Whisk all ingredients together in small mixing bowl. Transfer to serving dishes.

Swordfish

Swordfish are also called broadbill, *emperador, espada,* and *shutome.* Their color is deep blue with bright metallic, smooth skin.

They are one of the most sought-after game fish in the world, with a muscular yet streamlined physique. They are voracious fighters with powerful athletic speed and leaping ability. Swordfish have a beak that they use as a sword to slash their prey. They live a reclusive lifestyle and do not form schools.

In the Wild

Swordfish are found in many oceans around the globe, in both tropical and cold waters. They will migrate to warmer waters in the winter and cooler water in the summer. Notable locations for swordfish are Australia, Trinidad, Japan, Mexico, Ecuador, Costa Rica, and both coasts of the United States.

Swordfish are nocturnal eaters and comb the surface for small fish and squid, but swordfish are not at the top of the food chain. They are hunted by blue marlins, tuna, and killer whales.

Swordfish can reach 15 feet and 1,000 pounds. They live an average of nine years.

In the Kitchen

With a thick, meaty texture and full-bodied flavor, swordfish invites assertive flavors from spice rubs, marinades, and sauces. East Coast swordfish is pinker than Pacific swordfish. Both are high in fat with a good firmness. But beware, swordfish will dry out if overcooked; the best is medium rare. These are our favorite ways to eat swordfish:

- **Cooked like a rare steak** seared on outside, rare in the middle
- **Sushi** like in Japan, where it is called *shutome*
- **Grilled kebabs** with yummy marinade
- **Stewed** flesh stays meaty and doesn't dissolve
- **In *salade niçoise*** replacing the classic tuna

Valuable Nutrients from Swordfish

- Choline: assists in proper cell function, prevents osteoporosis, reduces inflammation
- Iron: vital to the production of energy and a healthy immune system
- Phosphorus: builds healthy bones and strong teeth
- Selenium: antioxidant, prevents arthritis
- Vitamin B_6: for a healthy metabolism and immune system
- Vitamin B_{12}: promotes healthy blood cells, prevents anemia, eases migraines
- Vitamin D: helps the body to absorb calcium and phosphorus, promotes healthy cell function
- Vitamin E: powerful antioxidant that battles free radicals in your body

Warning: Some swordfish may contain high levels of the pollutant methylmercury.

Fun Facts

Swordfish are completely solitary and don't like to come within 30 feet of another swordfish.

Swordfish do not use their spear-like beak to impale their prey; if they did they would have no way to eat it. Instead the beak is used to slice and injure prey, making it easier to capture.

Swordfish are cold-blooded, but they have the unique ability to heat their brains and eyes temporarily, which enhances their vision when hunting for prey.

Swordfish are the gladiators of the sea because of their long, sword-shaped beak and warrior spirit, but orcas and sharks are their fiercest enemies.

This recipe is inspired by a number of Turkish dishes collectively known as *sarma,* meaning "wrapped." A succulent piece of fish is enveloped in grape leaves, adding a briny saltiness while holding in moisture and flavor. The cloaked fish steams gently in the juices sweated from the tomatoes, lemons, oranges, and onions—like a Turkish bath. Yogurt, from a Turkish word meaning "curdled," is ubiquitous to Turkish cuisine. Its creamy, clean flavor balances nicely with the sour, salty, and spicy notes that dominate Turkish dishes. Other fish choices for wrapping are cod, halibut, salmon, and sea bass. —RON

Swordfish Wrapped in Vine Leaves
Zaatar Yogurt Sauce
SERVES 4

SWORDFISH

2 oranges, zested

2 lemons, zested (zest reserved for yogurt)

16 kalamata olives, pitted, quartered

½ cup diced red onions

2 tablespoons capers

¼ cup finely chopped parsley

½ cup diced tomatoes

¼ cup extra-virgin olive oil, divided

to taste sea salt

to taste white pepper

40 grapevine leaves, rinsed, drained

8 swordfish fillets, center-cut, skinless, 1 inch thick
(3 ounces each)

¼ teaspoon paprika

ZAATAR YOGURT

1 tablespoon toasted sesame seeds

1 tablespoon chopped thyme leaves

2 tablespoons chopped, toasted almonds

pinch crushed red pepper flakes

1 cup Greek yogurt

to taste sea salt

1 teaspoon lemon zest (reserved from Swordfish recipe)

Combine all ingredients in small mixing bowl. Transfer to serving dish.

Preheat oven to 350°F. Peel and dice the zested oranges and lemons. Combine orange zest, diced oranges and lemons, olives, onions, capers, parsley, tomatoes, and 1 tablespoon olive oil to mixing bowl. Season with salt and pepper. Lay 5 vine leaves on cutting board, overlapping leaves to create a sheet large enough to wrap swordfish. Place swordfish in center. Top with orange mixture. Tightly wrap leaves over swordfish. Transfer to oiled baking sheet. Brush top with remaining olive oil. Season with paprika. Bake 15 minutes or until slightly underdone.

A century ago on the Turks and Caicos Islands, locals tried to survive from the bounty of the sea and the challenging farming conditions. The main food staple was hominy, also called guinea corn or grits, harvested from local corn and ground into meal to make corn bread. On the island, ginger, sugar, water, Caribbean herbs, spices, yeast, and lemon are brewed into a sparkling, zesty potion named ginger beer. Combining cornmeal with fresh corn kernels and ginger beer, then frying the mixture until light and golden crisp makes a heavenly hush puppy. If swordfish is not available, mahi mahi and wahoo are the best substitutes . . . or simply have the hush puppies with the fragrant red pepper sauce! —BERNARD

Turks and Caicos Barbecued Swordfish

Ginger Beer Hush Puppies

SERVES 4

SWORDFISH

2 tablespoons vegetable oil

¾ cup chopped onions

1 cup chopped red bell peppers

½ scotch bonnet pepper, stemmed, seeded

4 cloves garlic, crushed

¼ teaspoon ground allspice

1 stick cinnamon

2 tablespoons grated ginger

2 cups cored, chopped pineapple

1 cup dark rum

1 tablespoon molasses

1 tablespoon Worcestershire sauce

¼ cup apple cider vinegar

½ teaspoon liquid smoke

½ teaspoon sea salt

½ teaspoon dry mustard

4 swordfish steaks, center-cut, skinless, 1 inch thick (6 ounces each)

as needed canola oil spray

Add oil to heavy-bottomed sauce pot over medium heat. Add onions, peppers, scotch bonnet, garlic, allspice, cinnamon, and ginger. Cook 5 minutes, stirring often. Add pineapple, rum, molasses, Worcestershire, vinegar, liquid smoke, sea salt, and dry mustard. Bring to low simmer. Cook 30 minutes or until liquid is syrupy, stirring often. Remove cinnamon stick. Transfer to blender. Puree until smooth. Brush mixture lightly on swordfish steaks. Set aside. Preheat grill to medium high. Lightly coat grates with canola oil spray. Grill the swordfish steaks 2 minutes on each side or until slightly underdone, brushing lightly with red pepper sauce. Transfer remaining sauce to serving ramekin. Place swordfish on warm serving plate. Serve with hush puppies and red pepper sauce.

HUSH PUPPIES

1 quart canola oil for frying

1 cup cornmeal

½ cup all-purpose flour

1 tablespoon baking powder

1 tablespoon brown sugar

½ teaspoon sea salt

1 large egg

½ cup ginger beer

½ cup minced scallions

1 cup sweet corn kernels

Heat oil in heavy skillet or deep fryer to 325°F, adjusting controls to maintain consistent temperature. If oil gets too hot, batter will pop and splatter. Combine cornmeal, flour, baking powder, sugar, and salt in mixing bowl. Whisk egg and beer in separate bowl. Stir into dry ingredients. Fold in scallions and corn, combining well. Drop 1 tablespoonful of batter into hot oil, deep-frying 7 at a time, 30 seconds on each side, or until golden brown. Transfer to paper towel–lined plate.

The richest fishing grounds in Italy surround the island of Sicily and are made of the Mediterranean, Ionian, and Tyrrhenian Seas. The prime fishing spot for swordfish is in the Strait of Messina, the narrow section of water between the eastern tip of Sicily and the southern tip of Calabria. During Phoenician times, swordfish were captured in fishing nets, cut into fillets, and prepared *mosciame* style—dried in the sun. Nowadays, it is often eaten as steaks or prepared as Messina rolls (swordfish rolled around a filling and baked in tomato sauce). If you are a piccata lover, swordfish is the ultimate impersonator of veal or chicken, as it retains both moisture and tenderness. —BERNARD

Swordfish Piccata
Parmesan Gnocchi, Pancetta, Sage
SERVES 4

SWORDFISH
1½ pounds swordfish loin, center-cut, skinless
½ cup all-purpose flour
1 teaspoon sea salt
¼ teaspoon ground black pepper
½ teaspoon paprika
1 teaspoon dried basil
3 tablespoons olive oil
¾ cup white wine
1 tablespoon lemon juice
¼ teaspoon red chile flakes
¼ cup drained capers
⅓ cup unsalted butter, cut into small pieces
2 tablespoons chopped fresh basil leaves
to taste sea salt and pepper

Cut swordfish loin into eight 3-ounce slices ½ inch thick. Combine flour, salt, pepper, paprika, and dried basil in small bowl. Transfer to large plate. Dredge each swordfish slice in flour mixture, shaking off excess. Add olive oil to large nonstick skillet over medium-high heat. Working in batches, add fish to skillet. Cook 1 minute per side or until slightly underdone. Transfer to serving platter. Return skillet to medium heat. Add wine, lemon juice, chile flakes, and capers. Reduce by three-fourths. Turn off heat. Add butter. Swirl pan vigorously to emulsify. Stir in basil. Return swordfish to pan. Season with salt and pepper. Spoon onto fish.

PARMESAN GNOCCHI
2 pounds whole russet potatoes
1 egg yolk
1 whole egg
2 tablespoons tightly packed parsley leaves
½ cup grated Parmesan cheese
1 teaspoon sea salt
½ teaspoon white pepper
⅛ teaspoon freshly ground nutmeg
1¼ cups all-purpose flour, plus more for rolling out dough
½ cup diced pancetta
1 tablespoon olive oil
6 leaves sage

Add potatoes to large pot of cold water. Place over high heat. Bring to simmer. Cook until fork tender, 30–50 minutes, depending on size. Remove from water. Peel potatoes. Immediately pass through ricer or food mill into large mixing bowl. Refrigerate uncovered 4 hours. Add egg yolk, egg, parsley, cheese, salt, pepper, and nutmeg to blender. Puree 30 seconds. Fold into potatoes. Fold in ¼ cup flour at a time. Turn dough onto floured surface. Knead briefly, adding just enough flour to prevent sticking. Divide dough into 4 equal parts. Let sit uncovered 15 minutes. On floured surface, roll each into ½-inch-diameter logs. Cut logs crosswise into pillow shapes. Freeze half the gnocchi in single layer on cookie sheet for future use. Bring large pot of salted water to boil. Working in two batches, add gnocchi to water, cooking 2 minutes or until they float to the surface. Remove with slotted spoon to oiled cookie sheet. Add pancetta and oil to large skillet over medium-low heat.

Cook until golden brown, stirring often. Raise heat to medium. Add sage and gnocchi. Cook 3 minutes or until golden, tossing often.

We know from archaeological excavations and ancient texts that pomegranates were one of the world's first cultivated fruits. As such, scholars believe that the Eve-bitten apple was actually a pomegranate, though it's hard to imagine biting into a pomegranate—"peeled and nibbled" might be a more accurate description. The popularity of the fruit spread throughout the Mediterranean and to the lands once covered by the Ottoman Empire. With such abundance, it was necessary to preserve the garnet juice by boiling it down to a concentrate. The resulting molasses is used heavily in Lebanese cuisine for its ability to add an assertive tart-sweet flavor and also to tenderize proteins. Pomegranate is a perfect companion to dense-fleshed fish like swordfish, mahi mahi, and salmon. You can make homemade pomegranate molasses by reducing 4 cups pomegranate juice and ½ cup sugar until 1 cup liquid remains. *Mujadara* is an Arabic side dish of lentils and rice. —RON

Pomegranate Infused Swordfish

Green Lentil Mujadara

SERVES 4

SWORDFISH

½ **cup** pomegranate molasses

4 **cloves** garlic, minced

½ **teaspoon** sea salt

¼ **teaspoon** ground black pepper

½ **cup** olive oil

3 **tablespoons** apple juice

4 swordfish steaks, center-cut, skinless,
    1 inch thick (6 ounces each)

to taste sea salt and ground black pepper

1 **cup** thinly sliced carrots

1 **small** red onion, peeled, quartered

12 dried black mission figs

¾ **cup** whole raw almonds

1 **cup** diced skin-on zucchini

¼ **cup** cilantro leaves

12 **sprigs** cilantro

Preheat oven to 375°F. Add pomegranate molasses, garlic, salt, and pepper to mixing bowl. Add olive oil in slow steady stream, whisking vigorously to emulsify. Stir in apple juice. Season swordfish with salt and pepper. Transfer to lidded ovenproof baking dish. Add remaining ingredients (except cilantro sprigs) to pomegranate mixture. Toss to coat. Spoon mixture atop swordfish. Cover with lid. Cook 20 minutes or until swordfish is slightly underdone. Garnish with cilantro sprigs before serving. Serve with Green Lentil Mujadara.

GREEN LENTIL MUJADARA

2 **tablespoons** sesame oil

1 **cup** sliced shallots

½ **teaspoon** cumin seeds

¼ **teaspoon** ground cardamom

6 **sprigs** thyme

¾ **cup** basmati rice

½ **cup** green lentils, rinsed

1 **small** red chile pepper, stemmed, seeded, sliced

½ **cup** white wine

2½ **cups** chicken stock

2 **tablespoons** dried parsley

to taste sea salt and ground black pepper

Add oil to saucepan over medium heat. Add shallots, cumin seeds, cardamom, and thyme. Cook 5 minutes or until shallots are caramelized, stirring often. Fold in rice, lentils, and red chile. Cook 1 minute. Add white wine, chicken stock and dried parsley. Bring to low simmer. Cover. Cook 20 minutes or until liquid is absorbed. Turn off heat. Let sit 5 minutes. Fluff with fork and season with salt and pepper. Transfer to serving dish.

Moroccan local cuisine varies from one region to another, from kebabs to colorful tagines. On the coastal regions, *chermoula* is a pungent, aromatic marinade found in the majority of seafood preparations. The secret to a perfect tagine is preserved lemon, also called *l'hamd marakad,* which literally means "sleeping lemons." Our Moroccan friend Kitty Morse shared with me her ancestor's recipe for preserved lemons. Our favorite lemons are Meyers, but other standard lemons also lend themselves well to this treatment. Preserved lemons keep for one month, and the chermoula for a few days refrigerated in an airtight jar. If you can get your hands on 2-inch thick swordfish steaks, marinate overnight and barbecue them on a hot grill; it will transport you back to the souk. —BERNARD

Swordfish Chermoula Casserole
Preserved Lemons
SERVES 4

SWORDFISH
1 tablespoon chopped garlic
1 teaspoon cumin seeds
1 teaspoon coriander seeds
¼ teaspoon black peppercorns
½ teaspoon sea salt
⅛ teaspoon red chile flakes
1 teaspoon paprika
1 tablespoon chopped fresh mint
1 tablespoon chopped fresh parsley
4 tablespoons extra-virgin olive oil, divided
1 tablespoon chopped Preserved Lemon peel
4 swordfish steaks (6 ounces each), skinless, cut into 1½-inch pieces
12 pearl onions, peeled, halved
1 Anaheim chile pepper, seeded, cut into strips
4 small Roma tomatoes, quartered
to taste sea salt
to taste ground black pepper

Preheat oven to 350°F. Add garlic, cumin, coriander, black peppercorns, sea salt, and chile flakes to mortar. Crush to coarse powder. Add paprika, mint, parsley, 2 tablespoons oil, and Preserved Lemon. Transfer to mixing bowl. Add swordfish. Toss to coat. Cover. Refrigerate at least 1 hour. Add remaining 2 tablespoons oil to large ovenproof skillet over medium-high heat.

Add onions and pepper. Cook 1 minute. Stir in tomatoes. Season with salt and pepper. Cook 1 minute. Turn off heat. Arrange swordfish atop vegetables. Transfer to oven. Bake 10 minutes or until fish is slightly underdone.

PRESERVED LEMONS
12 (or more) unblemished lemons, preferably Meyers, scrubbed
1 cup (or more) sea salt
2 cups fresh lemon juice or more as needed

Cut a thin dime-sized piece from both ends of each lemon. Set lemon on one end and make a vertical cut three-quarters of the way through the fruit from top to bottom. Do not cut in it half. Turn the lemon upside down and make a second vertical cut at a 90-degree angle to the first, three-quarters of the way through fruit. Fill each cut with as much salt as it will hold. Tightly pack lemons in sterilized wide-mouthed quart glass jar. Lemon juice will rise to the top. Seal jar. Place on the kitchen counter. Make sure the lemons are covered with juice at all times, adding fresh lemon juice if necessary. The lemons are ready to use when the rinds are tender, 4–6 weeks. Before using, rinse lemon lightly and discard pulp and seeds. Refrigerate after opening. Preserved lemons will keep for up to 6 months in the refrigerator.

Shark

Mako is the best shark for cooking and is considered to be the best tasting of all the hundreds of shark species.

Also known as sharp-nosed mackerel sharks, blue pointers, and bonito sharks. There are two kinds of mako—shortfin and longfin. The shortfin mako is more common.

Mako sharks are streamlined with slender bodies and pointed snouts, making them hydrodynamic. They have crescent-shaped tails and are a bluish-gray color except for their bellies, which are white.

Makos can be 13 feet long and weigh 1,000 pounds.

Mako sharks are at the top of their food chain, preying on tuna, herring, mackerel, and swordfish, and they even will attack small marine mammals.

In the Wild

The shortfin mako is a highly migratory fish, swimming in tropical and temperate waters throughout the world. In the Pacific it can be found from California to Chile, and in the Atlantic from Newfoundland to Brazil. Makos are also established in the Gulf of Mexico, the Caribbean Sea, Japan, Norway, South Africa, Australia, the Mediterranean Sea, and the Indian Ocean.

The most prolific population of mako sharks is in the waters around Tahiti.

In the Kitchen

Shark has a firm, meaty, lean flesh that resembles swordfish. The two are interchangeable in recipes, but mako is moister than swordfish. Raw mako meat has a very soft texture and pink-tinged color that transforms into a firm ivory-white meat when cooked. Our favorite cooking methods include these:

- **Pan-seared** with onions and sage
- **Marinated and grilled** adds flavor to the lean flesh
- **Fish-and-chips,** wildly popular in Australia

Valuable Nutrients from Shark

- Choline: assists in proper cell function, prevents osteoporosis, reduces inflammation
- Iron: vital to the production of energy and a healthy immune system
- Niacin: increases good cholesterol levels
- Phosphorus: builds healthy bones and strong teeth
- Selenium: antioxidant, prevents arthritis
- Vitamin B_6: for a healthy metabolism and immune system
- Vitamin B_{12}: promotes healthy blood cells, prevents anemia, eases migraines

Warning: Some shark may contain high levels of the pollutant methylmercury.

Fun Facts

Mako sharks are the acrobats of the sea, jumping up to 30 feet above the water's surface.

Makos are the fastest shark in the world, swimming up to 60 miles per hour. They idle at around 35 miles per hour.

A shark's skin feels smooth when rubbed in one direction and like sandpaper when rubbed in the opposite direction.

Sharks do not have bones, only cartilage. That is why it's hard to find fossil remains of sharks. The exception is their teeth.

Sharks have been swimming in the oceans since before dinosaurs existed. Sharks have not evolved much since then.

Cabo San Lucas, aka Cabo, sits at the southern tip of Baja California, where the Sea of Cortez and Pacific Ocean meld into one. This is fish taco territory. Anything brought in from the dayboats is fair game to be battered, fried in lard until golden, then sprawled onto a corn tortilla, like a bronzed tourist in a chaise lounge beneath the Baja sun. A slather of spritzy *crema* and pile of guilt-killing shredded cabbage complete the ritual. Once reserved only for Baja locals and spring-breaking surfers "in the know," the fish taco has now entered the mainstream. When made with shark, one of the common catches in Cabo, marinating is best. If you can't find annatto powder, sub with three parts paprika to one part ground turmeric. —RON

Cabo Shark Tacos

Jicama Orange Salad, Avocado Crema

SERVES 4

SHARK

2 mako shark steaks, skinless, trimmed (8 ounces each)
2 teaspoons ground annatto
1 teaspoon garlic powder
½ cup lime juice
1 teaspoon dried oregano
½ cup tequila
1 cup sliced red onions
1 teaspoon sea salt
¼ cup olive oil
as needed canola oil spray
8 (4-inch) corn tortillas
2 limes, cut into 8 wedges

Cut each shark steak lengthwise into 4 equal-size strips. Combine next eight ingredients (through olive oil) in mixing bowl. Add shark. Toss to coat. Transfer to baking dish. Cover. Refrigerate at least 4 hours. Preheat grill to medium high. Lightly coat grates with canola oil spray. Grill shark on all sides until caramelized and cooked through, basting occasionally with remaining marinade. While shark is grilling, spray tortillas lightly with canola oil. Grill, turning occasionally until hot and pliable, transfering to folded kitchen towel to keep warm. Lay tortillas on warm serving platter. Spoon Avocado Crema onto center. Top with shark and Jicama Orange Salad. Squeeze lime atop.

JICAMA ORANGE SALAD

2 oranges, peeled, cut into segments
½ cup finely diced jicama
¼ cup thinly sliced red onion
3 tablespoons pepitas (hulled pumpkin seeds)
2 tablespoons olive oil
¼ cup cilantro leaves
2 teaspoons finely minced jalapeño pepper
to taste sea salt
to taste ground black pepper

Combine all ingredients, including salt and pepper, in mixing bowl. Refrigerate 1 hour.

AVOCADO CREMA

2 avocados, peeled, seeded
½ cup sour cream
4 teaspoons lemon juice
1 teaspoon sea salt
1 teaspoon Tabasco sauce or hot chile sauce

Add all ingredients to blender. Puree until smooth.

The origin of the word chimichurri is one of mystery. The word may have originated in the Río de la Plata around Buenos Aires in the nineteenth century or in the Basque region of Spain, where there is a sauce called *tximitxurri*. Knowing that Argentina is a country with a strong Italian heritage, perhaps it was brought with immigrants from the island of Sicily centuries ago, as their *salmoriglio* sauce is chimichurri's identical twin. One thing is for sure—chimichurri is the gauchos' (South American cowboys) favorite sauce for their barbecues. Used as a marinade, chimichurri will tenderize and infuse the shark steak before caramelizing on a hot grill. Chimichurri is the pride of all home chefs in Argentina, where everyone has their own secret recipe, handed down for generations. In Argentina, sweet potatoes are called batatas. —BERNARD

Chimichurri Shark Steak

Chorizo Batata

SERVES 4

SHARK

2 tablespoons balsamic vinegar

1 tablespoon lime juice

1 teaspoon sea salt, plus more as needed

¼ teaspoon ground white pepper

1 tablespoon Worcestershire sauce

2 tablespoons minced garlic

1 cup finely chopped cilantro

1 cup finely chopped flat-leaf parsley

2 tablespoons finely chopped fresh oregano

¾ cup extra-virgin olive oil

4 mako shark steaks, center-cut, skinless, 1 inch thick (6 ounces each)

as needed canola oil spray

CHORIZO BATATA

2 tablespoons olive oil

4 links Argentinian chorizo or hot Italian sausage (2 ounces each)

2 cups diced, peeled sweet potatoes

1 large bulb fennel, trimmed, cut into 8 wedges

1 cup peeled pearl onions

4 cloves garlic, peeled, halved

1 teaspoon paprika

¼ teaspoon granulated dried orange peel

1 tablespoon chopped fresh oregano

¾ cup dry white wine

to taste sea salt

to taste ground black pepper

Combine vinegar, lime juice, salt, white pepper, Worcestershire, and garlic in mixing bowl. Let stand 10 minutes. Stir in cilantro, parsley, and oregano. Using a fork, whisk in oil. Remove ¾ cup chimichurri to small bowl. Add more salt if needed. Reserve. Add remaining chimichurri to baking dish. Add shark, turning to coat all sides. Cover. Refrigerate at least 2 hours. Preheat grill to medium high. Lightly coat grates with canola oil spray. Place shark on grill. Cook 2 minutes on each side or until cooked through.

Preheat oven to 375°F. Add oil to large ovenproof skillet over medium heat. Place sausages in skillet. Roast 2 minutes, turning to brown on all sides. Transfer to side dish. Add potatoes, fennel, and onions to skillet. Cook 6 minutes, stirring occasionally. Turn off heat. Fold in garlic, paprika, orange peel, oregano, and white wine. Nestle sausages in skillet. Season with salt and pepper. Transfer to oven. Bake 20 minutes or until sausage is cooked through and potatoes are tender.

The Canary Islands, a Spanish territory off the western coast of Africa, was a springboard to the Atlantic for Spanish conquistadors. The islands gave the adventurers their last and first taste of home as they journeyed to and from the New World. On the return trip, local Canarians were the first to witness the unveiling of strange and wonderful foods carried from across the ocean. Potatoes and peppers were two of the favorite finds, and they were soon prepared in ways very unique to the Canary Islands. Potatoes are cooked in salted water, then drained without rinsing, leaving a dust of powdery white salt on their wrinkled skins. They are dipped in *mojo*, a green or red chile puree thickened with bread crumbs and olive oil. Shark is a common catch in the islands. Frying the shark and then dipping it in the mojo gives it a good bite. —RON

Shark Bites

Wrinkled Potatoes, Mojo Picon

SERVES 4

SHARK

1½ pounds mako shark fillet, boneless, skinless
1 teaspoon dried oregano
1 cup finely chopped pineapple with juice
1 lemon, juiced, zested
2 teaspoons smoked paprika, divided
2 teaspoons sea salt flakes, divided
1 quart canola oil for frying
2 cups semolina flour
2 egg whites, lightly beaten

Cut shark into 1-inch pieces. Combine in mixing bowl with oregano, pineapple, lemon juice, lemon zest, 1 teaspoon paprika, and 1 teaspoon sea salt. Toss to coat. Cover. Refrigerate overnight. Heat oil in deep fryer or large heavy-bottomed pot to 375°F. Combine remaining paprika and semolina flour in casserole dish. Remove shark from marinade. Pat dry with paper towels and transfer to mixing bowl. Add egg whites. Toss to coat thoroughly. Working in batches of 6 pieces, roll in semolina flour to coat. Place in deep fryer. Fry 3 minutes or until cooked through and golden crisp. Transfer to paper towel–lined platter. Sprinkle with remaining sea salt. Transfer to paper cone. Serve with Wrinkled Potatoes and Mojo Picon sauce.

MOJO PICON

¾ cup extra-virgin olive oil, divided
4 cups chopped, seeded red bell peppers
1 teaspoon sea salt
2 red bird's-eye or Thai chiles, stemmed, seeded, chopped
6 cloves garlic
¼ teaspoon ground cumin
2 teaspoons smoked paprika
3 tablespoons sherry vinegar
2 tablespoons toasted bread crumbs
to taste sea salt
to taste ground black pepper

Add ¼ cup oil to skillet over medium heat. Add bell peppers and salt. Cook 10 minutes or until liquid evaporates. Add chiles, garlic, cumin, and paprika. Cook 1 minute. Transfer to food processor. Add vinegar. Process to a paste. With motor running, add remaining oil in slow, steady stream. Add bread crumbs. Adjust seasoning. Pulse to incorporate. Transfer to serving dish.

WRINKLED POTATOES

1 pound small gold potatoes
1 pound small red potatoes
1 pound fingerling potatoes
4 tablespoons sea salt, divided
2 sprigs sage

Place potatoes, 3 tablespoons salt, and sage in large pot. Add just enough cold water to cover potatoes. Place over medium heat. Bring to low simmer. Cook 15 minutes or until potatoes are tender. Turn off heat. Discard all but ¼ inch water from pot. Add remaining salt. Return to low heat. Cook, tossing potatoes occasionally to coat with water and salt, until water evaporates. Turn off heat. Let sit 5 minutes or until powdery layer of salt forms on the potato skins.

Jamaican cuisine started with the Tainos and Carib Indians of South America, who were among the first inhabitants of the island; later it became a fusion of techniques and traditions. Jamaica is a melting pot of culture and foods from around the world. Its kaleidoscope of spices resulted in Jamaican jerk, the backbone of Jamaican cuisine. This blend ranges from mild to spicy to very spicy and even scorching. A spicy meal for Jamaicans means that the meal is well seasoned, but their definition of "well seasoned" could translate to very hot in your kitchen, so practice and measurement are important. Substituting sugarcane skewers for bamboo skewers will impart the flavor of sugary sap while the shark sizzles on the grill! —BERNARD

Jerk Spiced Shark Loin
Red Pepper Papaya Chutney
SERVES 4

SHARK

1½ pounds mako shark loin, center-cut, skinless, trimmed
2 tablespoons vegetable oil
1 lime, zested, juiced
1 tablespoon honey
2 tablespoons Caribbean jerk seasoning
8 (1-inch) cubes peeled pineapple
8 (1-inch) cubes green zucchini
8 cherry tomatoes
8 bamboo skewers, soaked in water overnight
2 tablespoons grapeseed oil for oiling grill
4 sprigs parsley

RED PEPPER PAPAYA CHUTNEY

2 tablespoons coconut oil
½ cup diced red onion
1 tablespoon finely minced ginger
1 teaspoon ground cumin
1 teaspoon ground coriander
6 tablespoons red wine vinegar
2 tablespoons honey
2 large red bell peppers, roasted, peeled, seeded, diced
3 cups diced, peeled, seeded ripe papaya
to taste sea salt
to taste ground black pepper
to taste cayenne pepper

Cut shark loin into 8 rectangular pieces of equal size. Combine vegetable oil, lime zest, lime juice, honey, and jerk spice in large mixing bowl. Add shark. Toss to coat. Refrigerate 1 hour. Thread shark, pineapple, zucchini, and cherry tomatoes onto skewers. Preheat grill to medium-high heat. Coat grates with grapeseed oil. Place skewers on hot grill. Cook 1 minute on each side or until shark is cooked through. Transfer to serving platter atop Red Pepper Papaya Chutney. Garnish with parsley sprigs.

Add coconut oil to saucepan over medium heat. Add onions, ginger, cumin, and coriander. Cook 3 minutes or until lightly brown. Add vinegar, honey, and red peppers. Cook 5 minutes or until peppers are soft. Add papaya. Bring to simmer. Cook 10 minutes or to thick chutney consistency. Season with salt, pepper, and cayenne. Remove from heat. Transfer to serving dish.

Halibut

Halibut is a flatfish, meaning it is a bottom dweller with both eyes on one side. Their top side, which contains the eyes, is dark colored, allowing halibut to blend in with the ocean floor when viewed from above. Their bottom side is white, which blends in with the sky when viewed from below. This sneaky camouflage gives them an advantage over both their predators and their prey. Halibut start their life swimming vertically, like most other fish, but eventually turn on their side with one eye migrating to the top. This allows them to adapt to their bottom-feeding life style.

Halibut is the largest flatfish and among the largest of the saltwater fish, growing up to 8 feet long and easily weighing 600 pounds.

Halibut swim with their body parallel to the ocean floor, like a stingray.

In the Wild

Halibut are caught in Alaska, British Columbia, Russia, and Japan.

Atlantic Halibut

Atlantic halibut is scarce in population and not fished commercially in the United States. They are native to the temperate waters of the northern Atlantic, and found in Greenland, Iceland, and from the Barents Sea (near the Arctic Ocean) all the way down to the Bay of Biscay (north of Spain).

Atlantic halibut can live up to 50 years.

The flesh is white, tender, and lean with big flakes and a more assertive flavor than Pacific halibut. It will dry out if overcooked.

Alaskan Halibut

Also called Pacific halibut, this fish is found in all four bodies of water that surround Alaska: Gulf of Alaska, Bristol Bay, the Bering Sea, and the Chukchi Sea to the northwest of Alaska. Firm, snow-white meat has large flakes and a lean but sweetly delicate flavor. Alaskan halibut cheeks are a delicacy and excellent when braised.

California Halibut

Typically much smaller than Alaskan halibut. Dries very easily when cooked or cured. Highly recommended for raw preparation.

In the Kitchen

Halibut has thick, succulent meat as long as you don't overcook it. It also cooks very quickly. The center of halibut should be translucent not opaque after cooking. These are our favorite preparation methods:

- **Superb for fish-and-chips** can use in any fish-and-chips recipe that calls for a different fish

- **Poached slowly at low heat** succulent flesh

- **Seared and crusted** great synergy with mild flavor of leeks

- **Baked** wrapped in prosciutto

- **Raw as sashimi** tender with a good mouthfeel

Valuable Nutrients from Halibut

- Choline: assists in proper cell function, prevents osteoporosis, reduces inflammation

- Magnesium: maintains healthy blood pressure and strong bones, relaxes nerves

- Niacin: increases good cholesterol levels

- Phosphorus: builds healthy bones and strong teeth

- Potassium: for a healthy heart and kidneys, reduces stress

- Selenium: antioxidant, prevents arthritis

- Vitamin B_6: for a healthy metabolism and immune system

- Vitamin B_{12}: promotes healthy blood cells, prevents anemia, eases migraines

- Vitamin D: helps the body to absorb calcium and phosphorus, promotes healthy cell function

Fun Facts

There is a legend of the Tlingit tribe of the North American Pacific Northwest that involves halibut: One day a fisherman brought a small halibut to his wife. Unimpressed at such a small fish, the snobby wife flung it onto the beach. The fish began to flop about and grow into a giant halibut, smashing the island into pieces. This is how British Columbia's Queen Charlotte Islands were created.

Female halibut lay two to three million eggs a year.

Most halibut have eyes on the right side of their face. But about one in every twenty thousand halibut has its eyes on the left side.

The island of Madeira is an autonomous region located about twenty-five miles from mainland Portugal. Flowers, roses, and bougainvillea cascade down its mountains in festive colors. The capital city of Funchal was named after huge amounts of fennel (*funcho*) that grow wild, rising straight up from the sea. Near the old city you will find the vibrant Mercado dos Lavradores. Vendors in traditional costumes barter vegetables, exotic fruits, and chamomile flowers, and freshly caught fish is sold from stalls. In the early 1800s Funchali fishermen caught their first black scabbard, a very unique fish with huge eyes, razor-sharp teeth and long eel-like body that resides roughly 2,000 to 5,000 feet below sea level. Its white delicate flesh is reminiscent of halibut, which reels in the essence of this beautiful island when cooked in its namesake, Madeira wine. —BERNARD

Aromatic Madeira Scented Halibut

New Potatoes, Kumquats, Dry-Cured Olives

SERVES 4

HALIBUT

8 whole kumquats

4 cups Madeira wine

¼ cup oil-cured olives

½ cup chopped celery

2 bay leaves

1 red onion, peeled, quartered

2 bags chamomile tea

1 tablespoon coriander seeds

½ teaspoon black peppercorns

1 teaspoon sea salt

4 halibut fillets, center-cut, skinless, boneless,
  1 inch thick (6 ounces each)

4 sprigs rosemary

Using tip of paring knife, make 4 small slits in each kumquat. Add kumquats, Madeira, olives, celery, bay leaves, onion, tea, coriander, peppercorns, and salt to large saucepan over medium heat. Bring to simmer. Reduce by half. Add halibut. Turn off heat. Cover. Let stand 5 minutes. Turn fish over. Let stand additional 5 minutes or until slightly underdone. Return briefly to low heat only if necessary. Place halibut atop potato casserole. Spoon poaching liquid over halibut. Garnish with the rosemary, kumquats, and olives from the poaching liquid.

POTATO CASSEROLE

2 teaspoons sweet paprika

20 whole cherry tomatoes

1 cup chopped red onions

1 teaspoon finely chopped fresh rosemary

¼ cup extra-virgin olive oil

8 cloves garlic, crushed

1 pound small red new potatoes, halved

2 teaspoons red hot pepper sauce

1 tablespoon honey

to taste sea salt

to taste ground black pepper

Preheat oven to 350°F. Toss all ingredients in large mixing bowl. Transfer to roasting pan. Bake 45 minutes or until potatoes are tender and lightly browned.

Americans love to grill for the holidays. From Memorial Day to Independence Day to Labor Day, grills are fired up from coast to coast. Friends and neighbors are summoned by the familiar scent of hot coals, turning backyards and parks into budding communities. Whoever tends the grill is the backyard governor—for he who holds the tongs holds the power, at least until the flames dwindle. Seafood lovers can rejoice, knowing that Alaskan halibut season spans all three of the grilling holidays. Halibut's dense, meaty flesh makes it an excellent fish to barbecue, but be sure to undercook slightly for a mouthwatering texture. —RON

Peach Bourbon Basted Halibut Steak
Sweet Potatoes, Romaine, Grapefruit Dressing
SERVES 4

MARINADE
4 Alaskan halibut fillets,
    center-cut, skinless, 1 inch thick
    (6 ounces each)
¼ cup bourbon
2 tablespoons cider vinegar
⅔ cup peach nectar
1 teaspoon onion powder
½ teaspoon red chile flakes
½ teaspoon chopped rosemary leaves
½ teaspoon hickory liquid smoke
to taste sea salt
to taste ground black pepper

Place halibut in non-reactive shallow dish. Whisk remaining ingredients in mixing bowl. Pour mixture over steaks. Turn to coat. Refrigerate 6 hours.

SWEET POTATOES
2 pounds sweet potatoes
¼ cup pure maple syrup
¼ cup unsalted butter, melted
3 tablespoons orange juice
1 orange, zested
1 2-inch stick cinnamon
⅛ teaspoon cayenne pepper
½ teaspoon sea salt
½ cup chopped walnuts

Preheat grill to medium high. Peel and cut potatoes into ½-inch cubes. Combine all ingredients in dutch oven. Cover. Place on grill (or medium-low stovetop). Close lid. Cook 20 minutes or until potatoes are tender, stirring occasionally. Open grill, leaving dutch oven on grill.

PRESENTATION
2 pink grapefruits, peeled, segmented
2 tablespoons walnut oil
to taste sea salt
to taste ground white pepper
as needed canola oil spray
1 tablespoon thyme leaves
1 heart romaine lettuce,
    quartered lengthwise

Add grapefruits, walnut oil, salt, and pepper to mixing bowl. Toss to coat the grapefruit. Refrigerate 30 minutes. Lightly coat grill with canola oil spray. Remove halibut from marinade. Transfer marinade to small saucepan set on grill to heat. Grill halibut 2 minutes on each side for medium rare, or to desired doneness, basting often with marinade. Place potatoes in center of large serving plate. Sprinkle with thyme leaves. Top with halibut. Arrange romaine and grapefruit segments beside potatoes. Drizzle liquid left over from grapefruit segments over lettuce.

Many cities boast about being built on or around seven hills—Istanbul, San Francisco, Rome, and Barcelona are just a few. But Bergen, the seaside city in Norway, takes it a literal step further—for here they are mountains, not just hills. The seven peaks, all accessible by trail or funicular, form a connect-the-dots trail that defines Bergen's geography between slopes and sea. The mountains offer stunning views of the wharf, and vice versa. As in a display of unity, houses of the same shape and size, but different colors, stand side by side looking over the harbor. The fish market is the soul of the city where seafood, vegetables, flowers, and crafts mingle. Norwegian fishermen haul in huge halibut, delicious when coated with another Norwegian favorite: fragrant, sweet leeks. —RON

Leek Parsley Coated Halibut
Oven-Roasted Tomatoes
SERVES 4

OVEN-ROASTED TOMATOES

1 pound Roma tomatoes, cored
3 tablespoons extra-virgin olive oil
8 cloves garlic
6 small leaves sage
1 teaspoon thyme leaves
½ teaspoon sea salt
¼ teaspoon ground black pepper
1 red chile pepper, seeded, sliced
½ cup pitted, quartered large green olives

Preheat oven to 300°F. Cut tomatoes lengthwise in wedges. Gently toss with extra-virgin olive oil, garlic, sage, thyme, salt, pepper, chiles, and olives. Transfer to baking sheet in single layer. Bake 40 minutes, or until tomatoes shrivel and shrink slightly. Remove from oven. Set aside.

HALIBUT

5 tablespoons olive oil, divided
1 cup minced leeks, white part only
½ cup finely chopped parsley
to taste sea salt
to taste ground black pepper
4 Alaskan halibut fillets, center-cut, skinless
  (**6 ounces** each)

Preheat oven to 350°F. Add 4 tablespoons olive oil and leeks to skillet over medium heat. Cook 2 minutes or until leeks are soft, stirring often. Remove from heat. Cool. Stir in parsley. Season with sea salt and pepper. Add remaining tablespoon olive oil to skillet over medium-high heat. Place halibut in skillet. Sear 30 seconds on each side. Transfer halibut to baking sheet of tomatoes. Spread leek and parsley mixture onto halibut. Bake 5 minutes, or until halibut is slightly underdone. Transfer to serving platter.

Savelletri is a seaside hamlet located in the heel of Italy, and every Sunday its evening market awakens those craving the fruits of land and sea. Perched on cliffs, ancient stark-white buildings called *masseries* smile down upon fishermen, as they've done for hundreds of years. Onshore it seems like all of Italy is awaiting the catch with prosciutto, basil, and olive oil in hand. In the orchard, purple and green figs bake on trees in the summer sun, growing fatter and sweeter until their unbridled lusciousness can only be tamed with a splash of balsamic. —RON

Savelletri Baked Halibut
Limoncello Orzo, Roasted Figs, Prosciutto
SERVES 4

LIMONCELLO ORZO
2 tablespoons olive oil
1 cup sliced red onions
1¼ cups orzo
3 cups vegetable stock
1 cup fresh raw green peas
½ cup toasted, sliced almonds
¼ cup mascarpone cheese
3 tablespoons limoncello
1 tablespoon lemon juice
2 tablespoons chopped fresh tarragon
to taste sea salt
to taste ground pepper

Add olive oil to large saucepan over medium heat. Add onions and orzo. Cook 4 minutes without browning, stirring often. Add stock. Bring to simmer. Cover. Reduce heat to low. Cook 8 minutes. Add peas. Cover. Cook 4 minutes. Remove from heat. Fold in remaining ingredients.

HALIBUT
2 tablespoons extra-virgin olive oil
4 halibut fillets, center-cut, skinless, 1 inch thick (6 ounces each)
to taste sea salt and ground pepper
4 slices prosciutto ham, cut paper-thin
8 leaves fresh basil

Preheat oven to 350°F. Add olive oil to large ovenproof skillet over medium-high heat. Season halibut on all sides with salt and pepper. Add to skillet. Cook 30 seconds. Turn halibut over. Cook additional 30 seconds. Remove pan from heat. Transfer halibut to side dish. Cool. Lay 1 slice prosciutto on flat surface. Place 2 basil leaves in center. Top with halibut. Fold prosciutto over to wrap halibut. Transfer to skillet, basil side up and seam side down. Transfer to oven. Bake 5 minutes or until halibut is slightly underdone.

ROASTED FIGS
8 ripe figs, halved
8 small sprigs rosemary
¼ cup honey
2 tablespoons balsamic vinegar
2 tablespoons extra-virgin olive oil
to taste sea salt
to taste ground pepper

Preheat broiler to high. Place figs in baking dish, cut sides up, atop rosemary sprigs. Whisk honey, vinegar, and olive oil in small mixing bowl. Season with salt and pepper. Spoon mixture evenly onto figs. Broil 1 minute or until lightly caramelized. Let cool.

PRESENTATION
Spoon Limoncello Orzo onto center of warm serving plate. Top with halibut. Garnish with Roasted Figs and rosemary. Spoon pan juice from figs onto plate.

CHINA

Hong Kong's markets are windows into a vivid and timeless world of food shopping and the city's cuisine. In addition to stalls filled with fresh meat, live poultry, vegetables, and live frogs, wooden crates loaded with different types of sea creatures stand alongside massive bubbling tanks filled with live fish, just caught that morning. Steaming and braising fish in a clay pot is a popular Cantonese cooking method. This technique helps the fish retain its original taste and succulent texture when served piping hot. Only the freshest fish should be used for steaming. —BERNARD

Hong Kong–Style Steamed Halibut
Shiitake, Bok Choy, Five-Spice
SERVES 4

MARINADE
2 stalks lemongrass,
    tender inner part only, finely minced
4 cloves garlic, finely chopped
2 tablespoons grated ginger
¼ teaspoon Chinese five-spice powder
2 tablespoons honey
1 tablespoon sesame oil
2 tablespoons fermented garlic black bean sauce
2 tablespoons soy sauce
3 tablespoons lime juice
⅓ cup Chinese rice wine or sake
4 halibut fillets, center-cut, skinless,
    1 inch thick (6 ounces each)

Combine all ingredients except halibut in casserole baking dish. Add halibut. Turn to coat all sides. Cover. Refrigerate 30 minutes. Turn fish over. Refrigerate additional 30 minutes.

VEGETABLES
2 cups vegetable stock
1 cup bias-sliced, peeled carrots
4 baby bok choy, halved
½-inch piece ginger, peeled, sliced ⅛ inch crosswise
12 shiitake mushrooms, stemmed
½ cup sliced water chestnuts
¼ teaspoon ground white pepper

Add all ingredients to lidded large, deep skillet over medium heat. Bring to simmer. Cook 2 minutes. Place halibut atop Vegetables. Spoon Marinade atop halibut. Cover. Cook 5 minutes or until fish is slightly underdone. Serve as in Hong Kong—family style.

Sawa, as in *sawa wasabi,* means "mountain stream" in Japanese. Cultivation of wasabi, an Asian herb of the mustard family, started about 1,300 years ago in ancient Japan, and it is now harvested in Shizuoka, Nagano, and Iwate. In Japan, the simplest form of serving raw fish is called sashimi; it consists of thin slices of fresh fish dipped in soy sauce and wasabi paste. The pure and clean pungency of wasabi is the perfect complement to the rich flavor of raw fish and shellfish. Traditional wasabi paste is made by grating fresh wasabi root, which tastes like horseradish, on a grater made from sharkskin, but you can always use a Microplane grater in a bind. You can also buy prepared wasabi paste or powder. Our favorite sashimi are from halibut, tuna, salmon, and scallops. —BERNARD

Halibut Sashimi
Watermelon, Watercress, Wasabi Oil
SERVES 4

WASABI OIL

3 tablespoons wasabi paste
2 tablespoons sake wine
¼ cup grapeseed oil

Combine wasabi and sake in mixing bowl. Whisk in oil in slow stream to emulsify. Transfer to squeeze bottle.

SASHIMI

1 pound halibut fillet, center-cut, skinless, sashimi-quality
¼ cup finely grated white onion
1 tablespoon light sesame oil
⅓ cup mirin
1 tablespoon seasoned rice vinegar
1 tablespoon grated ginger
½ teaspoon hot chile powder

Freeze halibut 1 hour before use to firm up the flesh and facilitate slicing. Combine remaining ingredients in small mixing bowl. Cover. Refrigerate 10 minutes. Strain marinade through fine sieve into baking dish. Place halibut on cutting board. Slice crosswise ⅛ inch thick. Transfer all slices to marinade. Let stand 2 minutes.

PRESENTATION

4 small radishes
1 seedless cucumber
1 small seedless red watermelon
to taste sea salt
to taste hot chile powder
1 cup watercress leaves
2 oranges, peeled, segmented
1 teaspoon toasted sesame seeds
1 tablespoon minced chives

Using mandoline or vegetable slicer, finely slice radishes into rounds and cucumber lengthwise into ribbons. Peel watermelon. Cut into planks 5 x 2 x ¼ inches. Lay on center of chilled serving plate. Sprinkle with sea salt and dust with hot chile powder. Overlap halibut slices across watermelon. Garnish with radishes, cucumber, watercress, orange, sesame seeds, and chives. Spoon halibut marinade atop. Squeeze line of Wasabi Oil onto plate.

CHAPTER 7

One-Pot Meals
SEA TREASURES

SPAIN
Catalonian Paella
pork shoulder, sun-dried
tomatoes, saffron

UNITED STATES
Louisiana Bayou Jambalaya
andouille, blue crab, chicken

FRANCE
Quick and Easy Bouillabaisse
chile garlic rouille

ITALY
Livorno Mercato
Pescheria Ciuppin
anise pepper croutons

PERU
Arequipa Friday Chupe
queso fresco egg salpique

One-pot cooking is considered a catchall for fishermen's catch of the day. Often thought of as the "peasant" or more common way of eating, one-pot cookery is typical in the coastal regions of the world and is an easy cooking method that can make use of a large variety of ingredients. Around the globe, fishermen prepare traditional fish stews or hot pots using their catch surplus. White-fleshed fish, crustaceans, shellfish, leftover fish bones, and the ever-flavorful cheek meat found in the head of the largest fish are coveted ingredients. Each region of the world has its traditional one-pot dish, such as the classic French bouillabaisse, hot pot in China, paella in Spain, and pho in Vietnam, to name a few. The harmony of flavors and textures allows seafood to be the star. One-pot cooking is delicious, therapeutic, and highly nutritious. It will rejuvenate your mind, body, and spirit as each flavor sails onto your palate.

Paella is a rice casserole, traditionally cooked over a wood fire, that originated in the farmhouses of Valencia, although its name is a Catalonian word that means "pan." *Paella* describes both the round, double-handled steel cooking vessel and the dish itself. Originally paella was cooked in the open air of Valencia's countryside using a variety of meats, including duck and snails. As the popularity of the dish expanded to the coast, seafood was used instead. Soon the dish spread across Spain, and many mixed versions were created, influenced by each region's offerings. In the northeast of Spain, along Catalonia's Costa Brava, the paella is filled with shellfish. The most important part of any paella is the *socarrat*—a toasted layer of rice at the bottom of the pan that lends its pleasant smokiness to the broth. —RON

Catalonian Paella

Pork Shoulder, Sun-Dried Tomatoes, Saffron

SERVES 6

2 tablespoons olive oil from sun-dried tomatoes

1½ pounds boneless pork shoulder,
    trimmed, cut in ½-inch cubes

to taste sea salt

to taste ground black pepper

4 ounces Spanish chorizo sausage, finely diced

1 cup diced red onion

1 cup diced, seeded red bell peppers

2 serrano chile peppers, thinly sliced

6 cloves garlic, minced

2 cups paella rice or Arborio rice

½ cup sherry wine

½ teaspoon saffron threads

1 cup sliced sun-dried tomatoes in oil

3 cups vegetable broth

8 shrimp, size U-15, shell on, butterflied

1 pound black mussels, beards removed, scrubbed

1 pound manila clams, scrubbed

½ pound calamari tubes and tentacles, cleaned

½ cup fresh raw green peas

1 lemon, halved

2 tablespoons extra-virgin olive oil

6 sprigs oregano

Heat olive oil in large, deep skillet or paella pan over medium-high heat. Season pork with salt and pepper. Add to skillet. Brown on all sides. Add chorizo, onion, bell peppers, chile peppers, and garlic to skillet. Cook 2 minutes. Fold in rice. Cook 1 minute, stirring continuously. Add sherry, saffron, and sun-dried tomatoes. Bring to boil. Add broth. Bring to simmer. Reduce heat to low. Stir once. Cover. Cook for 10 minutes. Season shrimp with salt and pepper. Add to skillet along with mussels and clams, nestling them into rice mixture. Cover. Cook 5 minutes. Slice calamari tubes into ½-inch rings. Add to skillet along with tentacles and peas. Cover. Cook 5 minutes or until all seafood is cooked. Remove from heat. Squeeze lemon juice atop. Drizzle with extra-virgin olive oil. Garnish with oregano.

Cajun cuisine was born in the deepest southern parts of Louisiana. Influence by provincial French, Africans, and Native Americans, it was adapted by Acadian refugees from Canada in the late eighteenth century. Cajun farmers, fishermen, and villagers were poor and struggled to feed their families. This is where jambalaya was born, in the heart of the bayou, simmering in big black cast-iron pans filled with seafood, andouille sausage, turtle, alligator, rice, and secret family spice blends, all cooking over hardwood fire. It is an all-time favorite one-pot dish to celebrate Mardi Gras. *Laissez les bons temps rouler!* —BERNARD

Louisiana Bayou Jambalaya
Andouille, Blue Crab, Chicken
SERVES 8

¼ **cup** (½ stick) unsalted butter

1½ **pounds** boneless, skinless chicken thighs

3 **tablespoons** Cajun spice blend, divided

2 **tablespoons** olive oil

3 **cups** long-grain white rice

2 **cups** chopped red onions

1 **cup** chopped Anaheim peppers

1 **cup** chopped, peeled carrots

1 **cup** chopped celery

6 **cloves** garlic, chopped

1 **cup** sweet vermouth

6 Roma tomatoes, quartered

2 bay leaves

6 **cups** chicken stock

3 small smoked ham hocks (about 1 pound)

8 **ounces** andouille sausage, sliced ½-inch thick

½ **pound** jumbo lump blue crab meat, shelled

1 **pound** shrimp, size U-15, peeled and deveined

2 **tablespoons** chopped fresh parsley leaves

Melt butter in large skillet or dutch oven over medium-high heat until foamy and lightly brown. Trim excess fat from chicken thighs. Cut into quarters. Season with 2 tablespoons Cajun spices. Add chicken to pot. Cook 3 minutes or until browned. Transfer to side dish. Reserve. Add oil, rice, onions, peppers, carrots, celery, garlic, and remaining Cajun spices to pot. Cook 3 minutes, stirring constantly. Add vermouth, tomatoes, bay leaves, and chicken stock. Add ham hocks, andouille, and reserved chicken thighs. Bring to simmer. Cover. Reduce heat to low. Cook 10 minutes. Fold in crabmeat and shrimp. Cover. Cook additional 15 minutes. Sprinkle with parsley.

The name *bouillabaise* comes from the two Provencal words: *boui* ("bringing the stock to a boil") and *abaisso* ("to lower heat and simmer"). Ask anyone living in Marseille, Provence, or Cote d'Azur who makes the best bouillabaisse and you will get a passionate debate that will have to be sorted out with a few toasts of the anise aperitif called Pernod Ricard! This regional delicacy consists of three types of fish, all firm and flaky, along with local crabs and prawns simmered in fish stock scented with fennel, garlic, saffron, and herbs. Always add a splash of Pernod Ricard before serving, to enhance the fennel's anise flavor. Grilled artisan bread and a generous dollop of aioli complete this fishermen stew. *Délicieux!* —RON

Quick and Easy Bouillabaisse
Chile Garlic Rouille
SERVES 6

SEAFOOD
2 pounds king crab legs

2 pounds littleneck clams

3 lobster tails, cut in half lengthwise, deveined
  (6 ounces each)

6 sea scallops, size 10/20

12 prawns, size U-15, peeled, deveined

1 pound skinless sea bass fillet,
  pin bone removed, cut into 2-inch cubes

1 pound black mussels

¼ cup chopped fresh basil

to taste sea salt

to taste ground black pepper

4 sprigs fresh parsley

¼ cup Pernod or pastis liqueur

1 (1-pound) loaf country bread,
  cut into 1-inch-thick slices, grilled

Add all seafood to simmering vegetable broth in the following order: crab, clams, lobster, scallops, prawns and sea bass. Cover. Return to simmer. Cook 3 minutes. Add mussels and basil. Cover. Cook 5 minutes or until mussels open and seafood is slightly undercooked. Adjust seasoning if needed. Divide seafood and broth between four warm serving bowls. Garnish with parsley. Splash Pernod atop. Serve with Chile Garlic Rouille and grilled country bread.

VEGETABLE BROTH
2 tablespoons olive oil

2 cups diced, peeled celery root

3 cups ¼-inch-thick sliced leeks, white part only

1 large fennel bulb, sliced thinly across grain

6 cloves garlic, crushed

½ cup dry vermouth

1 teaspoon herbes de Provence

½ teaspoon saffron threads

4 cups clam juice

3 cups vegetable stock

2 cups tomato juice

1 teaspoon ground black pepper

Add oil to large dutch oven or stockpot over medium heat. Add celery root, leeks, fennel, and garlic. Cook 3 minutes without browning, stirring often. Add vermouth, herbes de Provence, and saffron. Bring to simmer. Add clam juice, vegetable stock, tomato juice, and black pepper. Bring to simmer. Cook 5 minutes.

CHILE GARLIC ROUILLE

4 cloves garlic, chopped

1 egg yolk

2 tablespoons lemon juice

2 tablespoons white wine

2 mild red chile peppers,
seeded, chopped

1 cup extra-virgin olive oil

1 cup diced sourdough bread
(no crust)

to taste sea salt

to taste ground cayenne pepper

Add garlic, egg yolk, lemon juice, white wine, and chile peppers to food processor. Process 30 seconds. With machine running, add oil in slow, steady stream to emulsify. Add bread. Process to paste. Season with sea salt and cayenne. Transfer to serving dish.

ITALY

In Italy there are more variations of fish soup, *zuppa di pesce,* than there are fish in the sea, and Italians all argue passionately over who makes the best one. Countless variations include the classic *cacciucco, guazzetto, buridda, quadaru, ciuppin,* and *brodetto.* On the eastern part of the Ligurian coast, local fishermen in Livorno sold the best of their catch and used what was left over and unwanted at day's end to make a fish stew called ciuppin. It is usually cooked in an earthenware pot atop the stove. The secret of ciuppin is the variety of fresh fish and aromatic vegetables that go into the pot. The heel of bread is called *scarpetta*—the perfect tool to scoop up the broth from this plate of Italian goodness. —BERNARD

Livorno Mercato Pescheria Ciuppin

Anise Pepper Croutons

SERVES 4

CIUPPIN

2 tablespoons extra-virgin olive oil
1 cup minced red onion
2 tablespoons minced garlic
1 cup matchstick-cut carrots
½ cup thinly sliced celery
¼ teaspoon hot red pepper flakes
2 cups Pinot Grigio wine
1 pound small Roma tomatoes, quartered
3 cups clam juice
¼ cup chopped parsley leaves
¼ cup chopped basil leaves
½ teaspoon dried oregano
2 pounds littleneck clams
½ pound cleaned squid tubes and tentacles
½ pound swordfish, skinless, cut into 1-inch pieces
½ pound tuna, skinless, cut into 1-inch pieces
½ pound red snapper, skin on, boneless,
   cut into 1-inch pieces
to taste sea salt
to taste ground black pepper
½ cup pitted, halved kalamata olives
4 sprigs basil

Add olive oil to large dutch oven over medium-high heat. Add onion, garlic, carrot, celery, and pepper flakes. Cook 5 minutes, stirring often. Add wine. Reduce by half. Add tomatoes. Cover. Cook 2 minutes. Add clam juice. Bring to simmer. Add parsley, basil, and oregano. Fold in clams. Cover. Cook 4 minutes. Cut squid tubes into ½-inch rings. Add to ciuppin along with tentacles and remaining seafood. Cover. Cook 3 minutes or until fish is slightly underdone. Season with salt and pepper. Ladle into warm serving bowls, dividing seafood equally. Garnish with croutons, olives, and basil sprigs.

ANISE PEPPER CROUTONS

3 cups sourdough bread,
   crusts removed, cut into 1-inch cubes
2 tablespoons extra-virgin olive oil
½ teaspoon lemon zest
½ teaspoon sea salt
1 teaspoon anise seeds
¼ teaspoon ground black pepper

Preheat oven to 300°F. Toss bread with olive oil, lemon zest, sea salt, anise seeds, and pepper. Bake 20 minutes or until crispy and golden brown. Set aside.

Arequipa, founded as a faithful Spanish colony in southern Peru, was erected in the emblematic shadow of the double snow-peaked volcano called Picchu Picchu. At the age of forty-two, the city was destroyed by earthquake, then rebuilt with walls of *sillar,* a volcanic stone found at the base of the towering mountain. The stone not only protected the buildings from seismic activity but the pearl-white color was so aesthetically pleasing that it earned Arequipa her nickname, the White City. Arequipa has a unique custom of designating one traditional dish for each day of the week. Every Friday is *chupe de camarones,* or shrimp soup, day. The secret ingredient—evaporated milk—gives the soup its whitish tint, echoing the natural whitewashed color of the sillar stone walls. A sprinkle of colorful ingredients to top a dish is called *Salpique.* —RON

Arequipa Friday Chupe
Queso Fresco Egg Salpique
SERVES 6

2 quarts vegetable broth
1 pound shrimp, size U-15, shell on
½ **pound** gold potatoes, peeled, cut into 1-inch pieces
1 large egg (in shell)
2 ears corn, cut crosswise into 1-inch wheels
½ **cup** evaporated milk
1 tablespoon cornstarch
¼ **cup** olive oil
1 cup chopped onion
2 teaspoons annatto powder or paprika
6 cloves garlic
2 teaspoons dried oregano
1 pound grouper fillet,
    skinless, boneless, cut into 2-inch pieces
2 tablespoons aji amarillo paste or other hot chili paste
1 pound mussels, beards removed, scrubbed
1 pound sea scallops, size 10/20
½ **cup** grated queso fresco
½ **cup** chopped fresh cilantro

Add vegetable broth to large pot over medium-high heat. Bring to simmer. Add shrimp. Cook 2 minutes or until slightly underdone. Transfer shrimp to ice bath, leaving broth on the stove. Peel and devein shrimp. Set aside. Add potatoes, egg, and corn to broth. Cook 10 minutes or until potatoes are tender. Transfer potatoes, egg, and corn to baking sheet to cool. Peel egg. Set aside. Whisk evaporated milk and cornstarch together in small mixing bowl. Whisk into broth. Raise heat. Bring broth to simmer, whisking constantly. Reduce heat to low. Meanwhile, add oil to dutch oven over medium heat. Add onions, annatto, garlic, and oregano. Cook 2 minutes, stirring often. Add grouper and *aji* amarillo paste. Cook 2 minutes. Add broth. Bring to simmer. Add mussels, scallops, and reserved potatoes and corn. Cover. Cook 5 minutes or until mussels open. Chop shrimp. Add to mixing bowl. Grate boiled egg atop. Add queso fresco and cilantro. Toss to combine. Sprinkle mixture atop soup. Serve family style.

Bait and Switch

SUBSTITUTIONS

Missing an ingredient in a recipe? Don't fret! Our recipes are flexible, and we are sure you will be able to create a delicious and exciting meal with what you have on hand. Here are some guidelines to help you at that critical moment—when you are in the middle of preparing a recipe and discover something is missing.

A general rule of thumb is to analyze if the missing ingredient is sweet, sour, bitter, salty, or spicy. Look for a replacement that has similar traits, texture, and flavor, keeping in mind the ethnicity of the recipe. Write your notes in this book so you never lose them. Feel free to experiment and trust your senses—that's what cooking is all about.

Seafood

The key to great results when cooking fish is freshness. If you find a fresher fish than the one listed in our recipe, substitute it. Here is a guide to help you decide:

Arctic char—coho salmon, king salmon, steelhead, sockeye

Salmon—arctic char, cod, halibut, scallops

Sea bass—striped bass, grouper, snapper

Halibut—flounder, fluke, orange roughy

Mahi mahi—ono, yellowtail, swordfish

Mackerel—yellowtail, kampachi, pompano, tuna

Shrimp—lobster, scallops, monkfish, swordfish

Crab—lobster, shrimp

Ono—swordfish, tuna, yellowtail, shark, mahi mahi

Pompano—kampachi, pomfret, John Dory, orange roughy

John Dory—sole, pompano, flounder

Yellowtail—ono, mahi mahi, tuna

Tuna—kampachi, ono, yellowtail

Swordfish—shark, tuna, ono, mahi mahi, yellowtail

Shark—swordfish, ono, mahi mahi

Snapper—sea bass, striped bass, grouper

Sole—flounder, fluke, halibut

Scallops—monkfish, halibut, cod

Monkfish—lobster, scallops, swordfish

Cod—pompano, yellowtail, salmon, scallops

Squid and octopus—interchangeable; stuff squid only

Shells (clams, cockles, mussels)—interchangeable, raw or cooked

Lobster—shrimp, crab, monkfish

Soft-shell crab—no substitute

Oysters—no substitute

From the Butcher

Pork bacon, pancetta, ham hock, guanciale

Sausage andouille, linguiça, Spanish chorizo, smoked hot link

Ham prosciutto, serrano, smoked dried ham, Bayonne ham

Fruits and Vegetables
Here are some favorites we like to play with:

Alliums shallot, leek, cipollini, pearl onions, sweet onions, scallions, ramps, spring onions

Beans green beans, Chinese long beans, haricots verts, yellow wax beans

Shelling beans peas, fava beans, heirloom beans, chickpeas, butter beans

Berries all interchangeable in season

Bitter leaves endive, radicchio, watercress, frisée, arugula, Thai basil, dandelion, mizuna

Citrus essence lemongrass, lemon myrtle, verbena, lemon balm, yuzu, lemon thyme, Kaffir lime leaf

Crunchy jicama, water chestnut, Asian pear, green apple, cucumber, fuyu persimmon

Exotic persimmon, dragon fruit, kiwi, mango, papaya, gooseberry, cherimoya

Crisp and fragrant artichoke, asparagus, sunchokes (Jerusalem artichokes), cardoon, salsify, hearts of palm, celery root, turnips, beets

Mushrooms, exotic chanterelles, morels, king oysters, honshimeji, maitake, porcini, beechwood

Mushrooms, staple cremini, button, portobello, shiitake, oyster

Aromatic roots fennel, celeriac, parsnips, rutabaga, salsify, carrots, sunchokes (Jerusalem arthichokes), parsnips

Stone fruits peach, nectarine, apricot, plum, cherry, pluot

Summer squash chayote, zucchini, Rond de Nice, crook neck, pattypan, sunburst

Winter squash butternut, kabocha, turban, acorn, delicata, sugar pumpkin

Sweet leaves romaine, red leaf, Bibb, mâche, Italian basil, oak leaf

Tart pomegranate, sour cherries, dried cranberry, grapefruit, pomelo

Tuber boniato, yam, sweet potato, Okinawa purple potato, taro root, parsnips

Winter greens bok choy, swiss chard, savoy cabbage, spinach, arugula, collard greens, mustard greens, kale

Herbs
If possible, grow your own herbs and pick just before using for optimum flavor.

Easiest herbs to grow rosemary, mint, parsley, thyme, sage

Delicate herbs parsley, chervil, tarragon, mint, basil, chives, cilantro, lemon balm

Fragrant herbs rosemary, sage, thyme, oregano, lemon balm, bay leaf, lemon verbena, lavender, marjoram

Dried herbs 1 teaspoon dried herb equals 1 tablespoon chopped fresh herb

Cut herbs using a very sharp knife without over chopping so that they don't bruise and lose their potent essential oils.

Oils

We cook with a large variety of oils and use many of them as a seasoning instead of a cooking medium. A drizzle of high-quality oil greatly enhances a dish. Finishing oils are usually interchangeable. Here is a guide of characteristics to help you choose a substitute:

Light nut oils hazelnut, almond, walnut, macadamia, cashew, light sesame

Robust nut oils pistachio, pumpkin seed, roasted sesame seed

Fragrant fruit oils extra-virgin olive, avocado

High heat for searing or wokking grapeseed, rice bran, safflower, peanut, coconut

Multipurpose corn, rice bran, sunflower, pure olive oil, grapeseed

There is no substitute for **truffle oil!**

All oils, especially unrefined oils, should be refrigerated after opening to prevent oxidation and rancidity.

Spices

Always keep spices in small quantities, stored in a sealed container away from direct light. If you have a lot of individual spices on hand, have fun creating your own blends. Be sure to label and date the spices. If you add nuts to your spice mixture, however, it will decrease shelf life.

Woodsy cinnamon, cassia, allspice, clove, nutmeg, star anise, juniper berry

Fragrant cardamom, anise seeds, ginger, fennel seeds, caraway, fenugreek

Accents celery seeds, mustard seeds, caraway, poppy seeds, sumac

Chiles paprika, chile powder, cayenne, togarashi, chile flakes, ancho, Espelette

Earthy turmeric, coriander, annatto, curry powder, cumin, wattleseed

No saffron in the house use turmeric, it will give you the color but not the flavor

There is no substitute for **vanilla bean!**

Vinegars

We use a variety of vinegars in our cooking. Here is a list of vinegars that are compatible:

Fruit-flavored vinegars berry, cider, fig, persimmon, pomegranate, pear

Wood-aged vinegars balsamic, sherry, Banyuls, icewine, *agrodolce*

Blond vinegars Champagne, apple cider, white wine, rice, malt, cane

Red vinegars berry, red wine, plum, cranberry, pomegranate

Asian vinegars seasoned rice, brown rice, black rice, plum, palm

No vinegar in the house use lemon juice, tangerine juice, lime juice, blood orange juice

Wine and Spirits

Always use high-quality wine when cooking so you can enjoy it as well. When substituting a nonalcoholic liquid for an alcohol, keep the volume of liquid the same as called for in the recipe. Use white grape juice for brandy, tangerine juice for Grand Marnier, pomegranate and cranberry juice for red wine. When substituting one alcohol for another, use a similar proof and style.

Dry white wines Chardonnay, Sauvignon Blanc, Chenin Blanc, Champagne, sake, dry vermouth

Light-bodied red wines Pinot Noir, Sangiovese, Beaujolais, plum

Bold red wines old vine Zinfandel, Malbec, Shiraz, Cabernet, Amarone, Petit Syrah

Fortified Marsala, Madeira, sherry, tawny and ruby port, muscat, sweet vermouth

Sweet wines mirin, sweet vermouth, late harvest wines, Viognier

Rock the Boat

COOKING TECHNIQUES

One of the most basic functions in the kitchen is transferring energy from a heat source to food—simply known as "cooking." Throughout the ages many methods have evolved to achieve this, each designed for a specific result. Here are some tips to ensure success when "cooking with fire."

Baking

Baking is a general term that refers to cooking in an oven. Seafood that is coated with toppings such as chopped walnuts or buttered bread crumbs benefits from baking, as all surfaces of the ingredients are exposed to the heat. When placing pans in an oven, they should be staggered to ensure even heat circulation. As a safety net, always set your timer for five minutes less than the recipe calls for. Cooking time can vary according to the type and thickness of the fish. When baking in a convection oven, the air is circulated, which intensifies the heat, cooking the outside of the fish faster. This helps to give a golden brown color to your crusts.

Braising

Braising is the complex and colorful cousin of poaching. Foods are cooked slowly in an enriched liquid in a covered vessel for the purpose of tenderizing. This can be done on the stovetop or in the oven. Always sear fish to golden brown prior to braising. Adding an acidic ingredient to the cooking liquid, such as wine, tomatoes, or pomegranate juice, helps in the tenderizing process and adds flavor. For example, adding root vegetables to the Marsala Braised Monkfish Osso Buco (p. 244) brings an earthy sweetness to the final dish. Our favorite pan for braising is a dutch oven or other sturdy pot with a tight-fitting lid that traps steam and heat inside its chamber.

Deep-Frying

When deep-frying, oil is the medium used to transfer heat to food. Deep-fried foods are fully submerged into the oil. Most seafood should be deep-fried at a temperature between 350°F and 375°F. The best oils for frying have a neutral flavor and a high smoking point, such as grapeseed oil and rice bran oil. When deep-frying, your ingredients should swim freely in the oil for a crispy, golden-brown crust and tender interior. A deep fryer is very convenient, but a thick, heavy-bottomed pot outfitted with a thermometer and filled no more than halfway with oil can be used with equal success—as long as it maintains a steady temperature while frying. After frying, cool, strain, and store oil in a tight container for later use. Oil used to fry seafood should be reused only for seafood.

En Papillote

En papillote, a French term meaning "in parchment," refers to baking fish that is sealed inside a pouch along with aromatic ingredients such as wine, herbs, and vegetables. Although the pouch is baked in the oven, the fish is considered steamed or braised, as it is a moist-heat cooking method. As the papillote cooks, the seafood's own flavorful juices render and become a part of the cooking liquid. Butter and olive oil can be added to the pouch for extra richness. En papillote is an all-in-one meal that is very healthy. Aluminum foil can be substituted for parchment and is ideal for cooking the papillote on the barbecue. In other countries, local plants are used to create papillote—banana leaves in Asia, lotus leaves in China, and corn husks in Mexico.

In the Raw

Raw seafood preparations are prevalent in many cultures. Common techniques that highlight the freshness and delightful texture of just-caught fish are *crudo*, sashimi, tartare, *lomi lomi*, *escabeche*, and ceviche. While sashimi showcases the pure flavor profile of the protein, in lomi lomi other ingredients are added to accentuate the fish. Here is a list of our favorites: halibut, sea bass, snapper, tuna, salmon, clams, scallops, oysters, yellowtail, and ono. For "in the raw" recipes, the freshest, highest-quality seafood should be purchased and properly stored at all times. Consult your local fishmonger or purchase from a reputable fish market.

According to the United States Food and Drug Administration (FDA), seafood should be cooked thoroughly to minimize the risk of foodborne illness. Possible health complications can result from eating raw fish.

On the Grill

The high heat of a grill effectively caramelizes the surface of fish and shellfish while locking in moisture. The best temperature is 550°F. Positioning grates 4 inches above the heat source ensures even cooking. Keep a spray bottle of water handy to extinguish flare-ups. Grilling fish with the skin on prevents it from drying and flaking apart. Use tongs to turn scallops and prawns, and a thin stainless steel spatula to flip delicate fish such as halibut and arctic char. Grilling fish on a cedar plank is a fun way to bring a wonderful, smoky flavor.

Pan Roasting

Pan roasting is a technique in which seafood is first seared and then finished in the oven in the same pan, often coated with spices, nuts, or aromatic vegetables.

In this technique, the searing focuses on attaining a caramelized golden surface, and the roasting finishes the cooking process. Individual portions or small pieces can be pan roasted quickly at high heat. Large cuts such as ahi tuna loin, swordfish, and mako shark may be roasted slowly at moderate heat to achieve a caramelized surface while retaining succulent juices. Using a properly calibrated oven and rotating the food occasionally will help ensure a perfect roast and keep the inside juicy and tender. Basting often during the roasting process adds flavor and prevents drying.

Poaching

Poaching is a delicate cooking method in which heat is transferred slowly to a food's interior, preserving the moisture. The seafood is submerged in a lightly simmering broth or heated olive oil. In both cases, the poaching liquid can be fortified with aromatic herbs and spices, elevating the flavor. Poaching Alaskan halibut in milk will accentuate its snow-white color and delicate flavor. Fish with a high fat content, like salmon, cod, scallops, and lobster, are great candidates to be poached in olive oil. The oil is a great carrier to impart aromatics during the slow-cooking process. When poaching with broth, never bring liquid to a full boil. Boiling is an aggressive cooking method not suitable for the delicate nature of seafood. Leftover poaching broth can be used as a stock.

Preserving the Catch

For thousands of years, the preservation of seafood has been an integral part of every seafaring culture. Coastal communities around the world have perfected the art of curing, smoking, and pickling. These techniques preserved the shelf life of the catch, allowing extended use as food and in trade.

Curing

Curing is an ancient method of preserving fish by slowly drawing the moisture from the flesh, which was especially important during long fishing voyages at sea. This is accomplished by coating the fish in salt. Sugar can also be added to cut the saltiness. Combining the salt with aromatic herbs and spices allows their flavor to penetrate into the flesh. Our favorite fish for curing are salmon, arctic char, cod, tuna, and ono.

Smoking

Smoking is a method that preserves fish by drying the flesh. As smoke coats the surface of the fish, moisture is drawn out while the aroma of the wood infuses the flesh. Before smoking, it is necessary to brine the fish in a salt or salt and sugar solution, which not only initiates the drying process but prepares the flesh to be infused with the smoke flavor.

In the hot smoking method, also called kippering, the fish is exposed to the low, steady heat of the wood fire and becomes fully cooked as it is smoked. This usually is accomplished inside a smoking chamber.

Cold smoking is done at lower temperatures where the fish is not exposed to heat, but is fully cured by the combination of brining and smoking.

Pickling

Pickling is an easy method of preserving seafood in an acidic liquid such as vinegar and citrus juices. The high acidity prevents bacteria growth and adds flavor during the process. Many different pickling liquids can be used, each bringing its own sensation. For best results, use the freshest catch, high-quality sea salt, and water with low mineral content. Our favorite vinegars are apple cider for salmon, rice wine for cod, white wine for octopus, and pomegranate for tuna.

Searing

Searing is a quick and convenient way to cook seafood over very high heat, trapping in juices and flavor for a flaky and tender interior. Dry the surface of seafood, especially scallops, before searing, as moisture inhibits the browning process. A cast-iron skillet is best for searing because of its ability to retain heat. Remember the 1-inch rule: Leave 1 inch of space between each piece when searing, to avoid heat loss in the pan.

Wokking

Cooking in a wok is a way of life in the Asian kitchen. For stir-frying, oil is heated in a deep, bowl-shaped metal pan over high heat and infused with aromatics such as ginger, garlic, and chiles until sizzling. Seafood is then added and tossed around quickly until cooked. Some of our favorites are squid, shrimp, scallops, and clams. Cooking in a wok happens very fast, so be sure to have all ingredients prepared and at hand before you start. A wok is an all-purpose kitchen utensil and can also be used for searing, bamboo steaming, deep-frying, and braising.

Wok hay is a fun Chinese expression to know. It means "hot breath," "energy," or "spirit."

Tackle Box

TOOLS AND UTENSILS

Having spent the majority of our lives cooking in professional and home kitchens around the world, we have grown attached to certain tools and gadgets. Here is a list of our top twenty-six seafood-centric tools for you to collect.

Bamboo Steamer

For centuries, the Chinese have crafted steamers out of bamboo, a material that absorbs excess moisture, which prevents condensation from dripping on the food. Bamboo steamers are also designed to fit snugly inside of a wok, sitting above simmering liquid. Bamboo steamers are made from several interlocking trays that sit on top of one another to create a multilevel cooking chamber. The perforated bottoms allow the steam to move freely between the trays. By putting longer-cooking foods in the bottom tray and faster-cooking ones in the upper trays, you can cook a whole meal at one time. A good tip is to use different steaming liquids such as beer, coconut milk, or aromatic broths to impart their flavor.

Bouillon Strainer

This is the best tool for straining sauces, broths, stocks, and all other types of liquids. Called *chinois* (shin-WAH) in French, a bouillon strainer has a cone shape with a very fine mesh. It is popular in professional kitchens to make sauces with a refined silky texture. Many of the sauce recipes in this book require straining through a fine sieve. We highly recommend you make this a part of your kitchen collection. For easy cleaning, wash your chinois immediately after each use. If possible, hang it when storing to avoid damage to the mesh.

Cast-Iron Skillet

We love cast iron for its durability, versatility, heat retention, and even cooking. It is especially useful for dishes that start on the stovetop and are transferred to the oven. With cast iron you can obtain a beautiful, evenly seared golden surface on fish and scallops. Apply a thin layer of vegetable oil to cast iron cookware after each use to prevent rusting. With a lot of use, cast iron skillets become nonstick.

Coffee Grinder for Spices

Purchasing whole spices and grinding them yourself as needed is the best way to preserve their potency. A coffee grinder is the best tool for this. It is also very effective for grinding woody or hard spices like star anise and peppercorns. Grind spices a little at a time and store them in an airtight container. A good trick is to reuse your empty bottles from store-bought spices. Whirling a tablespoon of rice in your grinder is a great way to clean it.

Digital Scale

This is essential for the quick and precise measurement of ingredients and portioning seafood. Look for a scale that measures in both grams and ounces and has a tare feature for convenient use. Taring a scale means zeroing out the reading so that you can measure the next ingredient without removing the existing one. Get one with an auto shut-off feature to maximize the battery life.

Dutch Oven

A dutch oven is a heavy cooking pot, often made of cast iron, with a tight-fitting lid that traps all the flavors in during cooking. Dutch ovens are multipurpose and excellent for braising, deep-frying, and making soups and casseroles. Because they are entirely heat resistant, dutch ovens are perfect when a recipe calls for starting the dish on the stovetop, then transferring to the oven. In our kitchens, the dutch oven is a workhorse—strong, durable and versatile.

Fish Descaler
A fish descaler is an essential tool for any kitchen where fish is popular. It removes the inedible outer scales from fish without damaging the skin, which is necessary for cooking whole fish or skin-on fillets. A basic handheld fish scaler is perfect for the home kitchen. All you need to do is drag the rasp-like blade firmly down the body of the fish. It's best done outside as the scales tend to fly.

Fish Spatula
Commonly called a "fish slice," this spatula is slotted, allowing liquid or fat to stay behind when food is lifted from a pan. The spatula is also very thin and flexible, making it easy to slide underneath a delicate piece of fish. You can even get a left-handed one. A fish spatula can be used for other proteins as well.

Food Processor
Since their invention in 1946 by a German company, electric food processors have become a staple in kitchens around the world. Their primary tasks are grinding and chopping, but they can also be used for purees. We use the food processor in many recipes. It is easy to use—and a good sous chef. The food processor makes prepping quick and easy, such as grinding salmon into burgers, chopping nuts for fish coating, and pureeing sauces like Mojo Picon (p. 286). It is a must-have in your kitchen.

Grill Skillet (for Grilling Indoors)
When you can't grill outside, stovetop grilling is the next best thing! All you need is a grill skillet. Our favorite is made of cast iron, as the heat distribution is even and the high heat retention gives beautiful grill marks that impart a caramelized flavor. The ribs in the grill's bottom also elevate food, allowing excess fat to drain away. Food slides off effortlessly when cooked in a properly seasoned cast-iron grill skillet. For family style, just bring the skillet to the table and share the bounty of the ocean with family and friends.

Kitchen Shears
Kitchen shears are specially designed scissors for the kitchen. We use them in our home kitchens as the perfect tool to open shrimp and cut through lobster shells and whole chicken. They are also great for clipping fish fins, snipping herbs, and trimming certain vegetables.

Knives
Two essential knives for seafood cookery are a fish fillet knife and a *santoku*, which is a multipurpose knife that looks like a cross between a cleaver and a chef's knife. A knife should feel like an extension of your hand. You should try holding a variety of knives before deciding on one; the shape, weight, and comfort level will determine your personal favorite. Our favorites are Japanese knives, such as Shun brand, forged from one single piece of steel. Bernard's rule: Designate a small serrated knife for tomato and citrus use; high-acid ingredients dull the blade. Ron's rule: A sharp knife is a safe and quick knife.

Large Cutting Board

There's nothing more awkward than a cutting board that is too small for the job. In Bernard's home, his oak butcher block is the soul of the kitchen. Ron is attached to his bamboo board—the wood is sustainable, softer on the knives, and does not stain. Whichever style you choose, a bigger board is better.

Mandoline Vegetable Slicer

The fastest and most effective way to thinly slice or shave ingredients, especially vegetables, is with a mandoline slicer. Instead of moving the blade over the food, as you do with a knife, you move the food over the blade. This creates perfect potato chips, shaved vegetables like fennel, and ¼-inch planks for fine dicing. Mandolines are *very* sharp; to prevent an accident use the safety guard and keep your eyes on the blade, not your fingers.

Measuring Cups and Spoons

We prefer stainless steel measuring cups and spoons for their durability and nonporous surfaces that do not absorb odors and are easy to clean and sanitize. For easy reading of liquid measurements, the OXO angled measuring cups are best. It's also good to have metric cups and spoons, especially nowadays with so many metric recipes available from around the world.

Microplane Grater

With citrus being an essential aromatic ingredient in seafood dishes, zesting is one of the most rewarding activities in the kitchen. It allows you to reap the oils from the pure citrus peel, leaving the pith behind. The Microplane zester is our favorite one for making fluffy shreds very fast. The tool looks like a woodworking rasp, with a large handle and a very long stainless steel zesting blade. It can also be used for shaving Parmesan cheese, truffles, chocolate, ginger, and even ice. If we had to choose one tool that we cannot do without, this is it.

Mortar and Pestle

Working with a mortar and pestle brings spirituality to cooking. Even with all the technology of modern devices, the mortar and pestle remains superior for processing ingredients. The effect of crushing to release essential oils is more effective than the chopping action of a blade. There are many types of mortars and pestles made from different materials. Granite is best for all-purpose use. Durable and nonporous, they are easy to clean and won't develop off aromas or harbor bacteria.

Oyster Knife

Oyster knives are unique in the world of cutlery. They have a short, round-pointed blade designed to pry open oysters without damaging their delicate flesh. The blade isn't sharp, but it can still be dangerous. A good safety measure is to protect your hand with a stainless steel mesh glove or a kitchen towel while holding the oyster. Oyster knives require no maintenance but need to be washed and sanitized thoroughly after each use.

Resealable Glass Jar

Glass jars have been used since the nineteenth century to store and preserve the bounty, for example, for pickling fish from an abundant catch. Originally, the shelf life of jams and preserves was extended by sealing the jars with wax. This was eventually replaced with the Mason jar style that is found in most kitchens today. It is important to follow proper canning procedures and clearly label and date the product. Harvesting ingredients at the peak of the season and processing them in your own kitchen in beautiful glass jars make the best gifts from the heart.

Squeeze Bottles

Squeeze bottles are great fun in the kitchen. They are an easy way to dispense sauces, oils, balsamic syrup, and other condiments. At home, a squeeze bottle can make the difference between home style and elegant presentations. To make fine lines, dots, and drops, use a small nozzle. Buy them at your local kitchen supply store. Be sure to label and date squeeze bottles that contain food.

Swivel Peeler

This is the best and most effective peeler for fruits and vegetables, such as for making the green papaya ribbons for pickling in the Rice Paper Wrapped Pompano recipe (p. 176). They have a slingshot Y shape and a blade that adjusts to the contour of the ingredient. Swivel peelers are fantastic for shaving aged cheeses like Parmesan or Gouda onto your favorite salad, or for creating chocolate shavings for desserts. They can be used left- or right-handed, a plus in the kitchen.

Thermometers

Thermometers are often overlooked, but they should be at the top of your list for food safety and accurate cooking. We recommend that you have the following types:

- **Instant-read thermometer** is essential for roasts, thick cuts of fish, and baked dishes.

- **Deep-frying thermometer** regulates oil temperature for accurate and safe cooking.

- **Oven-safe thermometer** is a must-have for baking.

- **Refrigerator thermometer** is very important for keeping seafood at safe temperatures; don't trust the built-in thermometer, which doesn't stay calibrated.

Tongs

Tongs are like a protective extension of your hand. This versatile grasping tool allows you to pick up, flip, toss, and turn ingredients during prepping, cooking, and serving. A well-stocked kitchen will have at least one pair of kitchen tongs per cook. They come in all sizes, shapes, and colors. Tongs with flat pinchers are best for delicate seafood such as scallops, as they firmly grab and turn food without causing any damage. Tongs are a must-have for the highest-temperature cooking methods such as deep-frying and grilling. Tongs are one of the simplest but most necessary inventions in the history of cooking.

Tweezers

Tweezers were originally intended for cosmetic use, but soon after their invention, cooks started to use them for culinary endeavors. Among their many functions in the kitchen, they are most helpful for removing the thin delicate bones from fish. It is important to find a pair of tweezers that pinch together tightly at the tip. Be sure to have one pair dedicated only for the kitchen and one for the medicine cabinet. Three types of tweezers are available—offset fine tip, straight fine tip, and curved extra-fine tip.

Wok

Two types of woks are available on the market. One has handles on both sides, and the other has a single long handle on one side. Both are multipurpose and can be used for stir-frying, deep-frying, poaching, and bamboo steaming. The best woks are made from carbon steel and can be seasoned in the same way as cast iron. It has pores that absorb oil and seal when heated. The more you use your wok, the more seasoned and nonstick it becomes. Using a wok ring over the stovetop distributes heat up the sides of the wok, simulating the pit cooking of China. Owning a wok means you are ready for a quick and easy dinner.

Wooden Spoons

Bernard has a kitchen fetish—wooden spoons. His collection of different shapes, sizes, and types of wood from around the world is used on a daily basis. Ron likes them for being nonconductive and easy on pots and pans—perfect for risotto. We both agree they make great serving utensils for family-style dishes, bringing a note of earthiness to the table.

Index

Conversion Table

Metric US Approximate Equivalents

LIQUID INGREDIENTS

METRIC	US MEASURES	METRIC	US MEASURES
1.23 ML	¼ TSP.	29.57 ML	2 TBSP.
2.36 ML	½ TSP.	44.36 ML	3 TBSP.
3.70 ML	¾ TSP.	59.15 ML	¼ CUP
4.93 ML	1 TSP.	118.30 ML	½ CUP
6.16 ML	1¼ TSP.	236.59 ML	1 CUP
7.39 ML	1½ TSP.	473.18 ML	2 CUPS OR 1 PT.
8.63 ML	1¾ TSP.	709.77 ML	3 CUPS
9.86 ML	2 TSP.	946.36 ML	4 CUPS OR 1 QT.
14.79 ML	1 TBSP.	3.79 L	4 QTS. OR 1 GAL.

DRY INGREDIENTS

METRIC	US MEASURES	METRIC		US MEASURES
2 (1.8) G	1/16 OZ.	80 G		2⅘ OZ.
3½ (3.5) G	⅛ OZ.	85 (84.9) G		3 OZ.
7 (7.1) G	¼ OZ.	100 G		3½ OZ.
15 (14.2) G	½ OZ.	115 (113.2) G		4 OZ.
21 (21.3) G	¾ OZ.	125 G		4½ OZ.
25 G	⅞ OZ.	150 G		5¼ OZ.
30 (28.3) G	1 OZ.	250 G		8⅞ OZ.
50 G	1¾ OZ.	454 G	1 LB.	16 OZ.
60 (56.6) G	2 OZ.	500 G	1 LIVRE	17⅗ OZ.